YAZOO

LAW AND POLITICS IN
THE NEW REPUBLIC

THE CASE OF
Fletcher v. *Peck*

C. Peter Magrath

The Norton Library
W · W · NORTON & COMPANY · INC ·
NEW YORK

Books That Live
The Norton imprint on a book means that in the publisher's
estimation it is a book not for a single season but for the years.
W. W. Norton & Company, Inc.

ISBN 0 393 00418 X

PRINTED IN THE UNITED STATES OF AMERICA
2 3 4 5 6 7 8 9 0

TO MY MOTHER

Giulia Maria Magrath

WHOSE LOVE AND COUNSEL
I SHALL ALWAYS CHERISH

The Yazoo issue had its roots in a gigantic, fraudulent speculation in western lands that grew into a political and constitutional *cause célèbre* during the formative years of the American republic. For three decades the name "Yazoo" stood for a series of events which scandalized the state of Georgia, troubled Congress and the administrations of Washington, Adams, Jefferson, and Madison, and divided Jefferson's Republican party.

Of intrinsic interest to the historian, the Yazoo issue is no less significant to the student of our political system. For probably the first time a large and well-organized pressure group lobbied a case to the United States Supreme Court. The Yazooists of the New England Mississippi Land Company were very likely the first organized group to see the Supreme Court—then a tribunal of still uncertain powers—as an institution that might be a source of valuable political decisions. The judicial path trod by the Yazooists in the early 1800's has since been followed by many other organized interests: railroad corporations in the late nineteenth century, Liberty Leaguers in the New Deal period, and the legal strategists of the American Civil Liberties Union and the National Association for the Advancement of Colored People in more recent years.

The Supreme Court's decision in *Fletcher* v. *Peck* strengthened the Yazoo lobby, but it had more lasting effects as well. Chief Justice John Marshall's opinion broke new constitutional ground and became a leading precedent for regulating the relationship between government and business during most of the nineteenth century. Yazoo, moreover, provided the occasion for an early demonstration of the Supreme Court at work as a unique yet integral part of the American system of government. Despite all the vast changes that have occurred in more than 175 years of constitutional history, the Court of Earl Warren still functions in ways that are essentially the same as those of the Court of John Marshall.

The story of Yazoo and the Constitution, then, is a story of many things, of land fraud and political strife, of lobbyists and the law, and of courts and constitutional clauses. Above all else, however, it is the story of a colorful and fascinating controversy.

Much of this book deals with the constitutional obligation of contracts. For those who prepare scholarly studies there is also another kind of obligation—the less formal obligation of an author to those who have helped him. One of the pleasures of having a book published is the opportunity it affords to thank those persons and institutions who have aided in its development.

This book had its genesis in a constitutional law seminar paper written for Alan F. Westin, now a professor at Columbia University, in the late 1950's, when I was a graduate student at Cornell University. Professor Westin's suggestion that the case of *Fletcher* v. *Peck* was worthy of investigation in depth awakened me to the fascinating intrigues of Yazoo. My major Cornell obligation, however, is to Clinton Rossiter. His scholarly guidance during my graduate student days and his friendship since then remain a source of great inspiration.

I have incurred obligations at Brown University which are equally pleasurable to acknowledge. Elmer E. Cornwell, Jr., chairman of the Department of Political Science, helped with valuable advice. I am particularly grateful to Forrest McDonald of the Department of History for his detailed critique of the manuscript. As always, I found myself stimulated, intrigued—and disturbed—by his provocative interpretations of the history and politics of the new republic. At my

own peril, though, I have dissented from some of his conclusions.

I am indebted, also, to the following institutions for aid of
various kinds: the Boston Athenaeum; the Boston Public
Library; the Federal Records Center of the General Services
Administration (Boston Army Base); the General Faculty
Research and Reserve Fund of Brown University; the John
Carter Brown Library and the John D. Rockefeller, Jr., Li-
brary of Brown University; and the Social Science Research
Fund of Cornell University. A special word of thanks is
also due to Grant Dugdale, director of the Brown University
Press, and to his capable staff. I especially appreciate the care
bestowed on the manuscript by its copy editor, Mrs. Toni
Beckwith.

Finally, I want to note again a continuing obligation to
my wife, Sandra Hughes Magrath. Her critical eye and her
cheerful common sense were indispensable auxiliaries to my
scholarly speculation in the Yazoo lands.

C.P.M.

Providence, Rhode Island
April 1966

CONTENTS

GEORGIA WESTERN TERRITORY. Under this name is included all that part of the State of Georgia which lies west of the head waters of those rivers which fall into the Atlantic Ocean. This extensive tract of country embraces some of the finest land in the United States, is intersected with a great number of noble rivers, which may be seen by an inspection of the map, and is inhabited (except such parts wherein the Indian title has been extinguished) by three nations of Indians, viz. the Muskogulge or Creek, the Chactaws, and Chicasaws. The Cherokees also have a title to a small portion of the northern part of this territory, on the Tennessee river.

.   .   .   .

The water of the Mississippi, when the river is high, runs up the Yazoo several miles, and empties itself again by a number of channels, which direct their course across the country, and fall in above the Walnut Hills. The Yazoo runs from the N. E. and glides through a healthy, fertile and pleasant country, greatly resembling that about the Natchez, particularly in the luxuriancy and diversity of its soil, variety of timber, temperature of climate, and delightful situation. It is remarkably well watered by springs and brooks; many of the latter afford convenient seats for mills.

—JEDIDIAH MORSE, *The American Gazetteer* (1797)

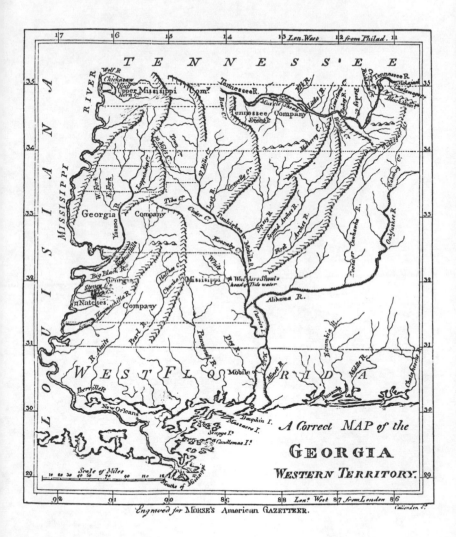

Map of the Yazoo Lands from Morse's *American Gazetteer* (1797)

I

Georgia Lands and Georgia Politics

In the late eighteenth and early nineteenth centuries many Americans speculated in western lands for much the same reason that their descendants today play the stock market: it gave them a chance to turn a small investment into a fortune. "Were I to characterize the United States," an English visitor declared in 1802, "it should be by the appellation of the *land of speculation*." [1] This passion for land speculation was in a sense inevitable. Americans, like the English to whom they were the closest of kin, were a trading people. Their new nation possessed vast unsettled tracts of fertile land west of the Alleghenies, a natural home for a population certain to increase and a ready market for land buyers. As Thomas Jefferson observed in his *Notes on Virginia*, "The present desire of America is to produce rapid population by as great importations of foreigners as possible." [2] And, indeed, in the period between 1790 and 1830 the American population tripled, jumping from four to thirteen million, a figure which had more than doubled by 1860, when it stood at thirty-one million. [3]

Although land speculation was common, it was a dangerous and often dirty business. Many of the deals sponsored by the large land speculators were, at best, semifraudulent. A typical instance was the acquisition by Robert Morris and his North American Land Company of over two million acres of Georgia wasteland called the Pine Barrens. This land, common in southern states, was covered with yellow pines rooted in sandy and essentially sterile soil. But this did not deter Morris and other land dealers from perpetrating what became known as the "Pine Barren Speculation." They prepared literature describing the sandy expanses as a land traversed by streams and clothed with oak, walnut, and hickory trees. Then they sold it to unsuspecting buyers thousands of miles away in the North and in European countries.[4] "A hundred years later," a historian reports, "people were still attempting to locate their lands in Georgia, by looking for streams which did not exist and for walnut, oak, and hickory tree markers in a land where only wiregrass and pine trees have ever grown."[5]

Robert Morris himself, it is worth noting, had a tragic ending. This brilliant man, "the financier of the American Revolution," eventually bought too much land with too little capital and his speculative empire collapsed. In 1798 Morris had to hide from angry creditors by barricading himself inside his Philadelphia house. Soon after, he was committed to a debtors' prison where he served until released in 1801, as "lean, low-spirited and as poor as a commission of bankruptcy can make a man whose effects will, it is said, not pay a shilling on the pound."[6]

Corruption and shaky financing were not the only dangers that beset land speculators. When the speculators acquired land, they almost always had to contend with a tangle of conflicting titles. The western lands were often simultaneously claimed by individual states, which pointed to their colonial titles, and by the United States, which insisted that the lands belonged to the nation as a whole. The claims of the individual states frequently overlapped, while foreign powers, most notably Spain, asserted their own claims. In addition, numerous Indian tribes also had title to many of the lands.

A number of states, such as Connecticut, Massachusetts,

New York, and Virginia, willingly ceded their western lands to the United States during the 1780's; yet other states refused to relinquish their titles. The most prominent of these was Georgia, which laid claim to a gigantic tract that ran west from the Chattahoochee River (the state's present boundary with Alabama) to the Mississippi and south from what is now Tennessee to western Spanish Florida. This territory of some thirty-five million acres, known as the Yazoo lands after one of its major rivers, attracted speculators to Georgia as a magnet attracts metal filings. The very name "Yazoo" suggests mystery and excitement: the Yazoo lands soon provided the new nation with an abundance of both.

Not only did Georgia possess an enormous amount of public land, both east and west of the Chattahoochee, but the state distributed its bounty in a manner that was as corrupt as it was confusing. To encourage immigration, Georgia in the 1780's and 1790's pursued a liberal policy of granting lands to new settlers. Its laws provided that the governor could grant land in the state's organized eastern counties to persons who had cultivated the land for twelve months; no individual was to receive more than one thousand acres. These requirements were simply ignored, as governor after governor distributed huge slices of land, not to migrant settlers, but to greedy speculators. In 1789 Governor George Walton signed land warrants granting up to 50,000 acres per person. His successors progressively outdid each other in their generosity, until in 1794 Governor George Matthews gave away 1,500,000 acres to one person.[7]

So generous in fact were the Georgia authorities that they even distributed nonexistent land. While twenty-four organized counties in 1796 contained 8,717,960 acres, records in the office of the state surveyor general show that three times as much land—29,097,866 acres—had been granted.[8] These bogus titles were then sold to gullible purchasers in the northern states and Europe. One Georgian sarcastically mocked these practices by having this tongue-in-cheek announcement printed:

Halloo, Halloo, Halloo

The subscribers will sell on most moderate terms: Ten millions of acres of valuable *pine barren* land in the province of Utopia, on which there are several very sumptuous air castles, ready furnished, that would make commodious and desirable habitations for the gentleman of the speculative class.

The celebrated island of Atlantis, too well described by the ancient speculator Plato, from whom the subscriber purchased it, to need a description now.

All his water and windmills on the River Lethe and on the Mountains of Parnassus and Olympus.

One hundred millions of acres in the state of Terra Incognita, and elsewhere, too tedious to particularize.

Also that incomparable and most famous riding horse Pegasus. He would be an excellent nag for riding express, and for that purpose he is recommended to the purchaser or purchasers of the foregoing.

HERACLITUS, JUNIOR.[9]

It was in this setting of land giveaways and casual corruption which provoked little public protest that the nation's land speculators made their bid for Georgia's rich western holdings. In 1789 three land companies, the South Carolina Yazoo Company, the Tennessee Yazoo Company, and the Virginia Yazoo Company (whose head was Patrick Henry), were organized for the specific purpose of buying in the Yazoo tract. The Georgia legislature agreed to sell the companies nearly sixteen million acres in return for $200,000 in cash to be paid over a two-year period.[10]

Unhappily for the speculators, however, this first Yazoo sale eventually came apart. The land lay deep in Indian territory controlled by a powerful confederation of Cherokee,

Creek, Choctaw, and Chickasaw tribes. Spain, which claimed the territory south of the Yazoo River, encouraged the Indians to attack the frontier settlements in this vast region. Not surprisingly, the companies found it difficult to promote colonization schemes. They suffered another setback in 1790, when President Washington warned them not to interfere with the treaty rights of the Indian tribes; under the new federal Constitution the power to negotiate treaties with the Indians belonged exclusively to the national government. The final blow came when the Georgia legislature passed a resolution directing the state treasurer to accept only gold and silver in payment for the land, a stipulation the speculators were unable to meet. They defaulted and Georgia reasserted her title. When the state subsequently resold the land, the South Carolina Yazoo Company attempted to sue Georgia in the federal courts for breach of contract. The legal action, however, came to an inconclusive end because of the adoption of the Eleventh Amendment to the Constitution, which exempts states from suits by individuals in the federal courts.[11]

The failure of the first Yazoo adventure merely whetted the speculators' appetites. In the mid-1790's four new and better financed land companies, the Georgia Company, the Georgia Mississippi Company, the Tennessee Company, and the Upper Mississippi Company, which were primarily controlled by speculators from Georgia and Pennsylvania, launched a second campaign for the Yazoo lands.[12] A striking feature of the new Yazoo companies that descended on Augusta, then the state capital, was the political prominence of their leading backers. There were two United States senators, James Gunn, of Georgia, and Robert Morris, of Pennsylvania; two congressmen, Thomas P. Carnes, of Georgia, and Robert Goodloe Harper, of South Carolina; three judges, James Wilson of the United States Supreme Court, Nathaniel Pendleton, the federal district judge in Georgia, and William Stith, a justice on the Superior Court of Georgia; and one territorial governor, William Blount, of Tennessee. Other prominent speculators were Wade Hampton, a South Carolina planter who later served in Congress and was a general in the War of 1812; James Greenleaf, a Philadelphia land dealer; Matthew McAllister, a United States attorney in Georgia; and John Sevier, a controversial Indian fighter who commanded Tennessee's militia and in 1796 became that state's first elected governor.

The largest of these companies was the Georgia Company, and its director, James Gunn, was the chief promoter of the second Yazoo sale. His official position in the Senate was useful to the speculators, for he was very probably aware of the impending Treaty of San Lorenzo signed by Spain and the United States in 1795. Under this treaty Spain abandoned her claims to the Yazoo lands, greatly enhancing their value to prospective buyers. Gunn's re-election to the Senate by the Georgia legislature in 1794 indicated to the Yazoo companies that the time was ripe for the passage of a law selling them the land. In November of that year Gunn and his associates tendered the legislature a bid of $250,000 "to purchase a part of the unlocated territory of the State." [13] The "most obedient humble servants," as they signed their request, did more than send respectful letters to the legislature: they sweetened their bid with personal inducements to the state legislators. Some were given shares in the companies; others settled for cash in the hand. When one representative, Thomas Raburn, was jokingly criticized for selling his vote for a mere $600 while his colleagues were getting $1,000, he blandly replied that "it showed he was easily satisfied and was not greedy." [14] In addition, the Executive Minutes of Governor George Matthews' administration reveal that in 1794 and 1795 a number of the legislators who voted to sell the Yazoo lands received, in flagrant disregard of the state law, large grants of land in the eastern part of Georgia.[15]

According to one legend, and the Yazoo sale has given birth to many tall tales, Senator Gunn speeded the passage of the sale bill by "bullying" the legislators "with a loaded whip." The "virtuous" members, unwilling to sell the western lands, were reportedly "every moment in dread of their lives." [16] Any bullying, however, appears to have been quite unnecessary. When a sale bill passed late in December, 1794, only one of the legislators voting for it had not been bribed in some way by the land companies. The governor, George Matthews, vetoed the bill, claiming that a sale of the western lands was premature and the price insufficient; the sale bill, he further asserted, concentrated too much land in the hands of a few monopolies. Strong as the governor's objections were, he quickly changed his views. A few days later, on January 7, 1795, a revised bill, disarmingly labeled as a bill to appropriate "a part of the unlocated territory of this State" for the purpose of paying its militia and protecting its frontiers, was passed and signed by Governor Matthews. There is no evidence that directly links the governor to the speculators, but he was clearly sympathetic with them. George Matthews was himself a land speculator, and as governor he outdid all of his predecessors in signing illegal land warrants.[17] As for the act of January 7, 1795, it did considerably more than appropriate "a part" of the state's unlocated territory. For $500,000 in specie currency the four companies received thirty-five million acres of land, two-thirds of the Georgia territory west of the Chattahoochee. This was probably, as one writer has called it, "the greatest real estate deal in history." [18]

The events that followed next are a matter of dispute. According to the accounts which appear in many histories of the Yazoo affair,[19] the people of Georgia, realizing that they had been swindled by an unholy alliance of greedy speculators and traitorous legislators, rose in unanimity to undo the evil deed. Throughout the state indignant citizens held meetings of protest, and grand juries made presentments condemning the sale as fraudulent. The anti-Yazooists, as they styled themselves, claimed that it had been rushed through before anyone could protest. In their view the legislature had been bribed into giving away valuable lands for a pittance, and, as further proof of the chicanery, they argued that a much better purchase offer made by a rival group of speculators had been foolishly rejected.

The hero of this popular campaign was James Jackson, a remarkable man and a central figure in the early phases of the Yazoo affair.[20] Born in England in 1757, he migrated to America by himself as a lad of fifteen. He went to Savannah and lived in the home of John Wereat, a family friend from the Old World. Jackson read law but was soon caught up in the Revolutionary War. He became a fierce patriot and, despite his youth, a renowned officer who rose to the rank of lieutenant colonel in the Georgia militia. After the war his activities were varied: he established a lucrative law practice in Savannah, acquired slaves and plantations, served from time to time as a general in the militia, and became prominent in the state's politics.

James Jackson was colorful and combative, a man of "strong passions" and "strong prejudices," in the words of one who admired him.[21] Quick to anger, he was a devotee of the "code duello." His success at dueling began at the age of twenty-three, when he killed the lieutenant governor of Georgia, and it earned Jackson a reputation as the "Prince of Savannah Duellists." [22] Some of the flavor of his flamboyant personality comes through in the conclusion to a "Character of J J Drawn By Himself." Here is how Jackson, writing in the third person, described himself to history:

In publick life he was patriotic and zealous for the preservation of those liberties America had so perseveringly obtained. Strenuous against the least invasion of the peoples rights and totally opposed to any measure of either Titles or otherwise which might endanger true Republicanism. In private life he was affectionate to his Family and kind to his Servants; his Slaves lived & were clothed much better than those of most of his neighbours. The Mechanicks loved him for his punctuality in payment and the poor were never dismissed from his door empty handed. He had however (& where is the Mortal without them) his Foibles. He had a sensibility to extreme & frequently took amiss from even his Friends what was never intended as such, which rendered him frequently unhappy in his disposition and he gave too much way to violent passions which for the moment led him too far. Reason however soon resumed her sway & his natural good temper returned with all but himself; with himself he would be angry for having been so with others. On the whole we may safely conclude that his good qualities far exceeded those of a contrary tendency and that he is a real loss to the community who sincerely lament him.[23]

At the time of the Yazoo sale Jackson was in the temporary national capital at Philadelphia, serving as a United States senator from Georgia. As the chroniclers sympathetic with Jackson describe it, upon hearing of the sale he gallantly resigned his Senate seat and hurried home to take command of the movement to repeal the act.[24] Although the truth concerning Jackson's motives is probably beyond certain proof, his reaction to the Yazoo sale was ambiguous. Jackson was slow to condemn it. Indeed, on January 27, 1795, he laid the Georgia law before the Senate and moved a resolution requesting President Washington to negotiate a treaty with the native Indians in order that their titles might be extinguished and the purchasers could take full possession of the land. The resolution passed, and a treaty was signed in 1796. Jackson made no comment on the fraudulent character of the sale, and he again remained silent on March 2 when Washington sent a message to the Senate calling attention to the dangers of a conflict in the Yazoo tract between the Indians and the white settlers who might soon move into it.[25]

Finally, at the end of March, Jackson began to act, denouncing the sale in a series of articles written under the pen name of "Sicilius" for two Georgia newspapers. To his friends he now spoke of "the rapacious grasping of a few sharks," declaring his intention to leave the Senate and "at the risk of life and fortune go home and break down the speculation." In the late spring he resigned his Senate seat in order to campaign for one in the next Georgia legislature, where he headed the movement to repeal the sale. His anti-Yazooist articles, republished as a pamphlet entitled *The Letters of Sicilius to the Citizens of Georgia,* were widely circulated as a campaign document for the anti-Yazooists running for seats in the 1796 legislature.[26]

From the middle of 1795 until his death in 1806 James Jackson made much of his opposition to what he called "the vile Yazoo Speculation," but it was an issue that he discovered comparatively late in his political career. During the eighties and early nineties, when speculators were already receiving illegal grants of Georgia land, there was no word of protest from Jackson. On the contrary, through grants made to him by Georgia's governors in 1784 and 1796, he obtained 4,594 acres of land, and he held in addition other parcels of land.[27] Nor did Jackson denounce the Yazoo sale of 1789, which occurred under the administration of Governor George Walton, a former law partner with whom he was then politically allied.

Moreover, one may legitimately wonder why Jackson—given his unrelenting attacks on the speculators after mid-1795—waited so long to speak up. It was, after all, no secret that land companies were strenuously lobbying to buy the Yazoo lands for an entire year preceding the sale. A possible explanation may lie in Jackson's friendship with his onetime guardian, John Wereat. In 1794 Wereat was directing the Georgia Union Company, which was also seeking the Yazoo lands. Its offer of $800,000 ($300,000 more than the final sale price) was turned down, a fact loudly trumpeted by the anti-Yazooists. Wereat's security, however, was apparently insufficient, and his offer came when the dealings of the other companies were already at an advanced stage. There is at least the suspicion that the Georgia Union Company was bidding for the sole purpose of forcing the other companies to buy it off.[28] Later, Jackson's enemies charged that he had been connected with the unsuccessful company. Both Jackson and Wereat denied the accusation, and there is nothing to prove it.[29] Nevertheless, it seems evident that Jackson had two standards when it came to land speculation, one for his friends and one for his enemies.

Some of Jackson's private comments do not reveal an ingrained hostility to land speculation. Writing to his close friend John Milledge on November 12, 1794, Jackson declared: "I have really a good mind to ... leave Congress and Congress things, turn speculator and go snacks at home with the best of them. There is a damn sight more to be got by it, depend on it, and I have not got one sixpence ahead, since I undertook [being a congressman]."[30]

An even more revealing statement appears in the same letter: "I shall expect," Jackson wrote, "a long letter with all the politics of Augusta—Speculation, oblivion and so on, I suppose will go together." In the Georgia of the 1790's politics and speculation seemingly went together. They certainly did in Jackson's case. He was elected to the legislature in November, 1795, to lead the movement against the Yazoo sale and from then until his death was the state's undisputed political leader. In those days the legislature elected the state's officers, and Jackson saw to it that his ally, Jared Irwin, was elected for 1796 and 1797. He had himself chosen governor for the next two years, and then in 1800 he returned to the United States Senate. Long after his death in 1806 Jackson's political machine continued to dominate the state under the leadership of two of his protégés, William

H. Crawford (a presidential candidate in 1824) and George M. Troup.

Jackson's political orientation is of interest, too. Nationally, he was a Jeffersonian Republican, but within the state his politics were conservative: he drew his main support from the planters and wealthy citizens of eastern Georgia.[31] Yet Jackson's exploitation of the Yazoo issue appealed to the western frontiersmen, and this appeal was reinforced by his ferocity and his liberal use of the rhetoric of popular democracy. As a consequence, political alignments in Georgia were for a while a topsy-turvy reversal of national ones: the Georgia Republican party was the essentially conservative party of those with wealth, education, and social status; the Federalist party was the party of the poorer and less educated frontiersmen. By the early 1800's the Georgia Federalists, never strong at any time, had disappeared, victims of James Jackson's skills as a political organizer and his attacks on those whom he reviled as "Tories," "Federalists," and "land grabbers."[32]

The actual repeal of the sale law was smoothly executed by the Jackson men. The new legislature of 1796, largely purged of those who had succumbed to the bribes, first appointed a committee to investigate the sale. Its chairman was James Jackson, and one of its members, William Few, had been an organizer of the unsuccessful Georgia Union Company. The committee, finding "fraud," "corruption," "collusion," and "unconstitutionality" in the sale, declared that "the rights of the present generation were violated, and the rights of posterity bartered." A legislative majority of "the utmost depravity," it concluded, had broken down "the bounds of equal rights" and elevated "the principles of aristocracy."[33]

To redeem the state's honor the Jackson committee introduced a bill repealing the 1795 act and nullifying the sale. The repeal act, which became law on February 13,

1796, was accompanied by another law intended to obliterate all official memory of the offensive deed. All documents concerned with the Yazoo sale were ordered excised from the state records. These and the original copy of the act were burned at a ceremony in the public square of Louisville, the site of the legislative session. With the members of the legislature ringing the fire, the Messenger of the House dropped "the usurped act" in the flames, proclaiming, "GOD SAVE THE STATE! AND LONG PRESERVE HER RIGHTS! ! AND MAY EVERY ATTEMPT TO INJURE THEM PERISH AS THESE CORRUPT ACTS NOW DO!!!" [34] The act-burning has passed into Georgia legend embellished with the tale that, just as the public officials were about to burn the act, an old man made his way to the center of the square: "Lifting up his voice, he declared that, feeble as he was, he had come there to see an act of justice performed, but he thought the fire in which the records of corruption were to be destroyed should come from heaven. The people watched him in silence. He drew from his bosom with trembling hands a sun glass, and in this way burned the papers. Then . . . the white-haired old man mounted his horse and rode away, and was never seen again." [35]

The Georgia repeal act, one of the significant documents of the Yazoo affair, needs to be examined more closely. [36] It provides a good illustration of how Jackson, a wealthy planter, put himself forward as the champion of the common man. Three-quarters of the act is devoted to a long preamble which begins with the statement that the sovereignty of the state resides solely in its "free citizens." By selling the western lands to "a few individuals" the previous legislature, it declares, violated the principle of a "democratical . . . government founded on equality of rights, and which is totally opposed to all proprietary grants or monopolies in favor of a few, which tend to build up that destructive aristocracy in the new, which is tumbling in the old world; and which, if permitted must end in the annihilation of democracy and equal rights—those rights and principles of government, which our virtuous forefathers fought for and established with blood."

The preamble then goes on to assert that the sale violated Article 16 of the Georgia constitution, which empowered the general assembly to make all laws "necessary and proper for the good of the State," because it was "opposed to the good of the State." More specifically, the preamble particularly indicts the legislature of 1795 for selling a vast tract of public land to a few companies at a low price and in the face of a better offer from the Georgia Union Company. After making a number of other points the preamble concludes by justifying repeal on the ground that the grants had been fraudulently obtained—"a most grievous injury" to Georgia which called for action by "the representatives of the people." Accordingly, the main provision of the enacting clause declared the "usurped act" to be "null and void; and the grant or grants, right or rights, claim or claims, issuing, deduced, or derived therefrom . . . is hereby also annulled, rendered void, and of no effect . . . and the territory therein mentioned is also hereby declared to be the sole property of the State."

The repeal act, which is a good summary of the anti-Yazooist position, overstated its case against the legislature of 1795. It is true that the land companies had bribed many of its members, but the terms of the sale were not unreasonable. If it was a corrupt bargain, it was not necessarily a bad one. The Georgia treasury was empty, and the state needed cash with which to pay her militia.[37] Was it really such bad trade for Georgia to sell land whose title was in many places clouded by three sets of conflicting claims—those of Spain, the federal government, and the Indian tribes? As a matter of fact, the sale act protected the state of Georgia in case her title should prove defective. It declared that the grantees of the land were to assume all the expenses of extinguishing the Indian claims, and it wisely provided that the state was to be free of suits if any of the competing claims prevailed over those of Georgia. Thirty-five million acres at a penny and a half an acre seems like an astoundingly small price, but it is well to remember that the Yazoo territory was a remote wilderness in the late eighteenth century. "No one could say what was the value of Georgia's title," Henry Adams remarked in his *History of the United States of America,* "but however good the title might be, the State would have been fortunate to make it a free gift to any authority strong enough to deal with the Creeks and Cherokees alone." [38]

Despite the long legal and political controversy which it set off, the repeal act had little effect on James Gunn and the Yazoo land companies.[39] While the law allowed the purchasers to obtain refunds, not all of them applied. Since the acceptance of a refund meant an abandonment of one's claim to the land, many of the purchasers preferred to forego any reimbursement.[40] Much of the Yazoo land was hastily sold throughout the country and especially in the Boston area. The most important of these sales was to the New England Mississippi Land Company, whose prominent organizers—including Connecticut and Massachusetts politicians such as Samuel Dexter, Gideon Granger, Perez Morton, Samuel Sewall, and James Sullivan—came together for the specific purpose of speculating in Georgia lands. On February 13, 1796, the very day that Georgia passed the repeal act, the New England company purchased most of the holdings of the Georgia Mississippi Company. For $1,138,000 it acquired eleven million acres in the southwestern section of the Yazoo tract.[41] The Georgia Mississippi Company, which had paid one and one-half cents an acre, made the kind of profit that explains the beguiling lure of land speculation, nearly 650 per cent on its original investment.

In the years that followed it was this enormous piece of

land that became the focus of the Yazoo affair. And one of the most debated issues was whether or not the organizers of the New England Mississippi Land Company and the many purchasers of modest means who in turn bought land titles from the company were innocent of the original fraud and of Georgia's steps to renounce the sale. The New England purchasers, large and small, steadfastly maintained that they had been ignorant of the circumstances surrounding the sale. As early as March, 1796, "several persons interested in the purchase of [the] lands" declared in Boston's *Columbian Centinel* that they had been duped:

There have been large quantities of these lands sold in this town at various prices, and under very different circumstances— in some instances the purchasers have sought after the holders of the lands; in other instances, industrious people, while engaged in their honest daily occupation have been assailed by artful, interested agents, who, by showing lists of names of respectable citizens, supposed to be selected for the purpose of deception, aided by false and alluring representations, have induced them to become purchasers.[42]

Upon learning of the repeal act, these purchasers went on, they contacted the people whose names had been used by the agents and found that many "on whose judgment and prudence they relied" had "no connexion with the business —but that their names were collected and presented to them as a lure to a ruinous purchase." In their letter to the *Centinel* these buyers announced their intention of legally contesting the validity of the sale by refusing to make payment when the notes they had written fell due.[43]

Years later, in a statement to a congressional committee, George Blake, one of the original subscribers to the New England Mississippi Land Company, swore that the Boston purchasers had been innocent.[44] According to his story, in the summer of 1795 Oliver Phelps, a prominent New York land speculator, introduced him to Walter Williamson, an agent for the Georgia Mississippi Company. Blake agreed to procure subscribers to purchase eleven million acres of Yazoo lands at ten cents an acre, and the New England Mississippi Land Company came into being. Williamson then returned to Georgia to secure the deed of conveyance and reappeared in Boston in January of the next year. On his return Williamson insisted that two modifications be made in the contract. He demanded, first, a one-cent-per-acre increase in the purchase price and, second, the insertion of a clause absolving the Georgia Mississippi Company from liability if the title later proved defective. Williamson argued that this clause was merely intended to exempt his company from any claims based on earlier British grants. It was, he declared, a matter of complete indifference to him whether or not the sale was made; indeed, he declared his willingness to rescind the contract and cheerfully pay the penalty that had been provided. These statements, Blake testified, so disarmed the subscribers, who were "utterly ignorant" of the alleged fraud, that they accepted Williamson's terms on February 13, 1796. The first rumors that Georgia had rescinded the sale had an "astonishing effect . . . on the minds of the purchasers." Once the passage of the repeal act was confirmed, the lands, which were now being resold for as much as sixteen cents an acre, could not be sold at any price. "Almost irreparable injury," a Boston editor wrote, was visited upon "very many worthy and respectable citizens of this and other States in the Union." [45]

Anti-Yazooists in Georgia and elsewhere just as steadfastly denied that there were any innocent purchasers, even among the second- and third-hand buyers.[46] The repeal act ordered the governor, "in order to prevent future frauds on individuals," to promulgate it as soon as possible throughout the United States. James Jackson and other opponents of the sale argued that its repeal was widely forecast and that the act of 1796 was in fact promptly publicized. The facts in the

Yazoo dispute are complicated, and at this distance in time it is impossible to decide whether or not the New England purchasers, the primary objects of contention after 1796, were innocent or guilty purchasers. It is, for example, true that the spectacular circumstances of the sale were soon known outside Georgia. Within three months of the passage of the Yazoo act, the Philadelphia *Aurora,* the leading Republican newspaper in the nation, commented on it as "melancholy proof of the depravity of human nature." The *Aurora* alluded to the possibility that "the base deed" might be repealed or somehow undone "by an extraordinary exertion" of the people's power.[47] It is, moreover, difficult to believe that the worldly-wise politicians and speculators of the New England Mississippi Land Company had not by February, 1796, thirteen months after the original sale, heard a single word about the fraud and the threat of repeal.[48]

On the other hand, communication was slow then, and a conjecture that the act might be repealed was not the same as hard news that it had been. In fact, no matter what Jackson said publicly, he was privately concerned at the time because the repeal act had not even been officially publicized within Georgia. On April 7, 1796, nearly two months after its passage we find him writing to Governor Irwin, "Is there no procl[amatio]n yet about the Yazoo Act? has it never been published in the Augusta papers. The Act at least should be published or it cannot be said to be promulgated."[49] Since so many of the land speculation schemes of the period were semifraudulent and rooted in what we today call "influence peddling," the early charges that the Yazoo sale was tainted by corruption may well have seemed unexceptional. The notion of "innocence" is, after all, a relative thing. To many Americans in the late eighteenth century the purchase of land that had initially been sold because of bribery caused them no moral discomfort, no more than an illegal wager on a horse or a numbers game disturbs most

Americans in the twentieth century. But all those Yazoo purchasers who bought without definite knowledge that the repeal act had passed, and there were probably a good number of them, undoubtedly considered themselves wronged.

Regardless of their guilt or innocence, the holders of shares in the New England Mississippi Land Company were determined to make good on their investments. Their determination made the Yazoo question an irritating national issue for the next twenty years, and it led to a major interpretation of the American Constitution.

II

Georgia Lands and
National Politics

The passage in 1796 of the Georgia repeal act transferred the
Yazoo question to the national scene. Before it was settled,
the dispute was to reveal much about the nature of politics
in the new republic. Less than a year after the sale, pamphlets began appearing throughout the country. The South
Carolina Federalist, Representative Robert Goodloe Harper,
a shareholder and lawyer for the land companies, was among
the first in print with *The Case of the Georgia Sales on the
Mississippi Considered.*[1] Much of his pamphlet consisted of
an exhaustive survey intended to prove that Georgia's title
to the land was good and that the sale had been "completely
valid and binding in law." Having made this point, Harper
then argued that a legislature could not declare its past actions void; only the courts could examine the validity of the
sale. "The judicial power," he wrote, "is to declare what the
law is; the legislative what it *shall be.*"

But Harper denied that there was any justification for
judicial nullification of the Yazoo act. Even if there had
been fraud, "a legislative act could not be invalidated because
of the legislator's motives." His argument went even further:

These sales moreover were contracts, made with the utmost solemnity, for a valuable consideration, and carried deliberately into
complete execution. It is an invariable maxim of law, and of
natural justice, that one of the parties to a contract, cannot by
his own act, exempt himself, from its obligation. A contrary

principle would break down all the ramparts of right, dissolve the bonds of property, and render good faith, to enforce the observance of which, is the great object of civil institutions, subservient to the partiality, the selfishness, and the unjust caprices of every individual. There is no reason why governments, more than private persons, should be exempt from the operation of this maxim; nor are they considered as exempt by our constitution or our laws.

Harper's pamphlet is of particular interest because its appendix included a legal opinion by Alexander Hamilton, who was then practicing law in New York City. Whether in active service as the highly controversial Secretary of the Treasury or in political retirement (when he was not very retiring), the Federalist leader found ways to express his unusually creative mind. He was also, it needs to be remembered, one of the ablest lawyers in America.[2] Hamilton's opinion, which assumed the validity of Georgia's title to the land, made two basic points. First, like Harper, he argued in a general way that the Georgia legislature could not undo the consequences of the sale act and take away the property that it had granted:

Without pretending to judge of the original merits or demerits of the purchasers, it may be safely said to be a contravention of the first principles of natural justice and social policy, without any judicial decision . . . to revoke a grant of property regularly made for valuable consideration, under legislative authority, to the prejudice even of third persons, on every supposition, innocent of the alledged fraud or corruption; and it may be added, that the precedent is new, of revoking a grant on the suggestion of corruption of a legislative body. Nor do I perceive sufficient ground for the suggestion of unconstitutionality in the first act.

Second, Hamilton sharpened up Harper's suggestion that Georgia's nullification of the sale was contrary to the "maxims" of our "constitution." He argued that the repeal act violated a specific provision of the new federal Constitution:

In addition to these general considerations, placing the revocation in a very unfavourable light, the constitution of the United States, article first, section tenth, declares that no state shall pass a law impairing the obligations of contract. This must be equivalent to saying, no state shall pass a law revoking, invalidating, or altering a contract. Every grant from one to another, whether the grantor be a state or an individual, is virtually a contract that the grantee shall hold and enjoy the thing granted against the grantor, and his representatives. It, therefore, appears to me, that taking the terms of the constitution in their large sense, and giving them effect according to the general spirit and policy of the provisions, the revocation of the grant by the act of the legislature of Georgia, may justly be considered as contrary to the constitution of the United States, and, therefore null; and that the courts of the United States, in cases within their jurisdiction, will be likely to pronounce it so.

This opinion is almost certainly the first statement of what eventually became a major constitutional doctrine: an act of a state legislature may have the quality of a legal contract, and it cannot be broken without violating the contract clause of the Constitution.[3]

Other pamphlets written on behalf of the land companies echoed Harper's. Sometimes the arguments went from the sublime to the ridiculous. A pamphlet put out by the Georgia Mississippi Company argued that the validity of the original purchase was upheld by "the eternal principles of justice, founded on the laws of nature and the institutions of society." Then, to refute the argument that the legislature had acted corruptly, the pamphlet asserted, "The majority [in the Georgia House of Representatives] being 17 to 8 is a refutation of this calumny—men who pay for a majority will be satisfied with a smaller one."[4]

Wide publicity was given to the Harper-Hamilton view of the Yazoo sales in Jedidiah Morse's *American Gazetteer,* a popular geography of North America by a Congregational minister from Massachusetts who is best remembered as the "father of American Geography." [5] Under a long entry entitled "Georgia Western Territory," Morse described the Yazoo region in glowing terms as a potential land of milk and honey. He then gave a pro-Yazooist interpretation of the original sale and condemned the repeal act for its "tumultuary effects" on "a numerous and respectable body" of intermediate purchasers. The Reverend Jedidiah Morse was theologically conservative, and he was equally orthodox in his politics, which were staunchly Federalist. This was reflected in a "STATEMENT of the CLAIMS upon the GEORGIA WESTERN TERRITORY" which Morse added as an appendix to the 1797 edition of *The American Gazetteer*. Although it claimed to present both sides "with impartiality," Morse's description drew heavily upon Harper's pamphlet and "Mr. Hamilton's opinion." It was unmistakably Federalist and pro-Yazooist. The validity of the sale act was "a judiciary question, triable only in a judiciary court," the geographer insisted:

The legislature, therefore, having no authority in this case, this examination [by the repeal legislature of 1796] can be considered no otherwise than as mere usurpation, and void.

. . . .

In short, it seems to be generally agreed among the informed part of the community, that, whether Georgia had cause of complaint on account of unfairness in the sales, or not, the repealing law must be considered as a "contravention of the first principles of natural justice and social policy," and void.[6]

Opponents of the sale were not silent either. In 1797 Abraham Bishop, a Connecticut lawyer and an ardent Republican, published a two-part booklet, which he entitled *Georgia Speculation Unveiled*.[7] Bishop had many unkind words for land speculators: ". . . aiming with feathers [pens] to cut throats, and on parchments to seal destruction,—these are the robbers of modern days.—They bring desolation among our farmers—they spread distress in towns—they scorn the paltry plunder of pocket-books, and watches—they aim at houses and lands—strike at the foundation of many generations,—and would destroy families, root and branch." Bishop devoted much of his broadside to a states' rights defense of "the sovereign independent state of Georgia," which had a "wholly uncontrollable" right to make or repeal its own laws "at pleasure." Georgia, the pamphleteer insisted, could exercise her sovereign power irresponsibly, though she had not done so in this case: "The high approbation with which the rescinding act is now received by an impartial public establishes its conformity to the laws of morality and of nature."

Interesting in themselves, the pamphlets are also suggestive of the partisan cleavage that the Yazoo issue provoked. It was no coincidence that Harper and Hamilton, who defended the sale and denied the validity of the repeal act, were Federalists, and that Abraham Bishop, who wrote an anti-Yazooist tract, was a Jeffersonian.[8] For Federalists were inherently likely to be pro-Yazooist in their sympathies, just as Jeffersonian Republicans were naturally likely to be defenders of the repeal act. At the surface level, perhaps, this was because the principal Georgia antagonists, James Gunn and James Jackson, were leaders of the two opposing parties. But the ultimate reasons are deeper, and to understand them it is necessary to recall the political climate in the late 1790's.

Although they were only dimly aware of it, the politicians of the nineties—Adams, Hamilton, Jefferson, and Madison—were constructing the world's first system of democratic political parties. In retrospect, the emergence of parties seems inevitable. The young republic was amply stocked with the ingredients for a party system, and it confronted difficult and unavoidably divisive decisions in economic and foreign affairs. Its constitutional practices, moreover, encouraged the free expression of political ideas and the ultimate control of the governors by the governed.[9] Nor did the republic lack talented men who saw in the profession of politics an outlet for their ambitions and energies. By the time of the Adams-Jefferson presidential election of 1796, recognizable, if structurally immature, political parties were operating in America.[10]

On one side stood the Federalists, organizers of the new government and advocates of a strong central authority. Believing in the mercantilist idea of an alliance of government and wealth, they were anxious both to protect established property rights and to further the influence of business and finance. The Federalists were suspicious too of agrarian radicalism, and, remembering the troubled 1780's, they feared particularly legislatively sponsored attempts to benefit debtor groups at the expense of their creditors. The guiding genius of the Federalist party was Alexander Hamilton, who as President Washington's Secretary of the Treasury and his unofficial prime minister, put through a program of funding the state and national debts and creating a national bank. Less successfully, Hamilton also sought to promote America's fledgling manufacturing industries through subsidies and protective tariffs.

In foreign policy the Federalist administrations of Washington and Adams faced difficult decisions. Trade with Europe, England, and the West Indies, the lifeline of the American economy, was seriously threatened by the economic and military rivalry between France and Great Britain. The warring nations were determined to cripple each other's trade, and both, as a consequence, treated American shipping in a high-handed manner, frequently searching and seizing merchantmen that flew the United States flag. While American policy officially aimed at preserving neutrality, thereby keeping all the channels of trade open, it was virtually impossible to avoid aggravating one side at the expense of the other. The Federalist administrations of the nineties were "neutral" in favor of England, while following a "hard line" toward France.[11] Their policy, no less than that of the rival Republicans, who favored friendly relations with the old Revolutionary ally, reflected their ideological predilections. The Federalists recoiled, horrified, from the radicalism of the French Revolution. They were shocked by its disdain for tradition and the established order and by its ultrademocratic deification of the common man. Not without justification, Federalists pointed out that this deification had led to the Terror of Robespierre and the chaos of the Directory; only with the military dictatorship of Napoleon Bonaparte did the turmoil temporarily end.

The culmination of the pro-British policy of the Federalists came with the Jay Treaty of 1795; in return for Britain's promise to evacuate her forts in the Northwest Territory and to arbitrate the question of compensating Americans whose vessels had been seized, the United States dropped her demand for the restitution of slaves taken during the Revolutionary War and agreed to an arbitration of the claims that British creditors had against Americans for debts incurred prior to independence. The treaty provided for mixed American-British commissions to settle the disputed boundary with Canada, but it ignored the galling issue of British impressment of American seamen. However justified—the United States was then a weak nation greatly dependent on trade with the former mother country—the Jay Treaty was an unpopular and one-sided bargain. It antagonized the southern planters, and, skillfully exploited by the Republicans, it almost cost the Federalists the election of 1796.

Despite the conclusions of earlier generations of historians, who located the hard core of Federalist support in the commercial, financial, and shipping interests clustered in the larger towns and cities, it now seems clear that the party's demographic make-up was an extremely complicated matter.

Few generalizations, and particularly those which seek to distinguish sharply the bases of Federalist and Republican electoral strength, can withstand empirical scrutiny.[12] In so far as approximate descriptions are possible, the Federalists at the turn of the century were likely to be the socially and politically *established* elites and those who, either through a habit of deference to their betters or through force of economic circumstances, followed their lead. North of the Potomac the Federalists had a strong constituency among merchants, manufacturers, and financiers, but so did their Republican opponents. South of the Potomac Federalists and Republicans alike drew support from both the well-to-do planters and the less affluent farmers. The only pattern which seems to emerge from a confusing demographic picture is that the Federalist leaders were representatives of the older and more established wealth and of the traditional social and political aristocracy; Federalism appealed to those Americans who for one reason or another believed in government by a hereditary establishment.

It is equally difficult to locate precisely the geographic centers of Federalist support, but an important recent study demonstrates that Federalism was strongest in the nation's more static regions, such as the Connecticut River Valley, or the Delmarva Peninsula (lower Delaware, Maryland's southeastern shore, and Virginia's Accomack and Northampton Counties), where the rate of population growth was lowest.[13] This evidence conforms to the hypothesis that Federalism drew its greatest strength from among those who viewed society as properly governed by a more or less traditional aristocracy. Such views were inherently more likely to have currency in static and socially stratified regions. Republicanism, by contrast, which loudly proclaimed the equality of man and the virtues of popular government, flourished best in the dynamic and fast-growing sections of the country.

The Republicans, in fact, were in many ways the exact opposite of the Federalists. Led by the aristocratic democrat, Thomas Jefferson, and originally motivated by a desire to oppose the policies of Alexander Hamilton, they organized the first structurally mature modern political party. As in the case of the Federalists, only perhaps more so, their support was diversified. The Jeffersonian Republicans were fundamentally the party of freehold farmers, and in a nation then overwhelmingly agricultural the support of small farmers was an invaluable asset. But the Republicans also had a following among slaveholding planters and among socially insecure merchants and manufacturers whose new wealth marked them as parvenus in the eyes of the traditional elites. Other Republican support came from the "meaner sort" of the cities—the craftsmen, manual laborers, and small shopkeepers whose occupations, while often profitable, were not socially respectable.[14]

Jeffersonian Republicans conceded the necessity of an effective central government but were profoundly anxious that it not overshadow the states. In Jefferson's view the federal government should be "a very simple organization and a very inexpensive one" with "a few plain duties to be performed by a few servants." Jefferson contrasted his objectives with those of the Federalists, who, he said rather unfairly, aimed to "sink the state governments, consolidate them into one, and to monarchize that."[15] Suspicious of concentrated power, the Republicans opposed the nationalist economic policies adopted by the Federalist administrations. They saw the Federalist laws subsidizing commerce as special interest legislation that violated their cherished principle of "equal rights for all, special privileges for none."[16] Agriculture and commerce both, they believed, would prosper best if allowed to develop on their own, unhindered by governmental interference. The Republican preference, in short, was for states' rights and a general economic policy of laissez faire.

In foreign affairs the Republican party was as pro-French as the Federalist was pro-British. Britain was pictured as a monarchy, saddled with an aristocracy; France had joined the march of freedom by banishing kings and establishing a republic. At times, of course, the French behaved in a way that was terribly embarrassing to their American friends. Citizen Genet, the tactless French ambassador to the United States, promoted military activities against the English in 1793 and went so far as to challenge publicly Washington's policy of neutrality. Four years later in the XYZ Affair, the Directory behaved with incredible arrogance in demanding that the American envoys pay a bribe as a precondition to the beginning of negotiations. These incidents, however, did not lead the Republicans to change their basic posture. They wanted a peaceful settlement of American differences with France, and they favored stern reprisals against the English for their attacks on American shipping. After 1795 "the Frenchified zealots," as John Adams called them,[17] used the Jay Treaty as their primary vehicle for attacking Federalist foreign policy.

This, then, was the political context into which the Yazoo issue was injected. The Federalists were predictably pro-Yazooist, for four different reasons. First, as Harper's pamphlet suggested, they perceived the repeal act as an interference with vested property rights. Second, they balked at Georgia's suggestion that *legislatures* could declare previous laws unconstitutional. Instead, echoing Alexander Hamilton's magisterial argument in the seventy-eighth *Federalist* paper, they contended that a proper separation of powers made it the exclusive province of the courts to void unconstitutional legislation. Third, the Federalists were unconcerned with Georgia's status as a sovereign state; as the avowed centralizing party, they had no qualms about trying to overrule with federal power the state's anti-Yazoo policy. Their fourth reason was less lofty. The Yazoo claimants, men of economic and social stature,[18] were concentrated in New England; so were the Federalists. Since the Federalist party in Congress drew most of its strength from New England, support for the Yazooists was rooted in that most basic instinct of democratic political parties, concern for the interests of its influential constituents. Theoretically and practically the Federalists had good reason to favor the Yazoo cause, as they did with virtual unanimity.

Unfortunately for the Yazoo claimants, Federalist support was not enough, for after 1796 the Federalist party began a rapid national decline, and the principles of the rising Republican party made it far less hospitable to the Yazooist position. Unlike that of the Federalists, the Jeffersonian Republican ideology emphasized states' rights, viewing the legislature as the popular branch of government and, therefore, the rightfully dominant one. Thus, as the Republican pamphleteer, Abraham Bishop, urged in *Georgia Speculation Unveiled,* the repeal act was a legitimate expression of the popular will by a "sovereign independent state."[19] Nor were Republicans well disposed to Hamilton's suggestion that the federal Supreme Court would void the repeal act. Bishop strongly rejected it; the Court, he wrote, "cannot judge what laws ought to exist."[20]

Consistent with these attitudes, the Jeffersonian resistance to the Alien and Sedition Acts implied that legislatures might properly void unjust laws.[21] In addition, because the Republican party's political center of gravity lay south of the Mason-Dixon Line, it had far less interest in the plight of the northern claimants than did its electoral competitor. Yet here a paradox soon developed: as Federalist strength in New England declined and that of the Republicans grew, the Jeffersonians inherited the region's pro-Yazooist interest along with their new constituents. And this in turn led to a severe tension between the party's northern and southern wings, compelling its national leadership to concern itself with at least partially satisfying the demands of the Yazoo claimants.

The specific intrusion of the Georgia lands issue into congressional party politics began in 1795, even before the repeal act, when President Washington called the attention of the Senate to the Yazoo sale. Washington's concern was with its impact on United States relations with Spain and the Indian tribes in the territory; he strongly implied that the Senate should investigate the legality of the sale. But the Federalist senator, James Gunn, architect of the Yazoo deal, wanted to block any federal action which might hinder the resale of the Georgia lands. Gunn found his opportunity in the Jay Treaty, which was so bitterly opposed that for a time it seemed as if the Washington administration would be unable to muster the two-thirds majority required by the Constitution for Senate approval of treaties. A few months after the treaty had cleared the Senate by the rock-bottom majority of 20 to 10, the Philadelphia *Aurora* cited "good authority" for this allegation: "It *is said* the Treaty was carried in the Senate *on this ground,* one member it is said, in the first instance was opposed to it but being assured that no Congressional investigation [of Georgia's sale] should take place, he readily gave his consent to the ratification." [22]

William Duane's *Aurora,* a sometimes venomous Republican paper, is a naturally suspect authority, but there is independent confirmation of its allegations. Some years later Senator William Branch Giles, a leading Virginia Republican, identified Gunn as the senator in question. Gunn, Giles informed William Plumer, had voted for the treaty, not because of "the conviction of his own mind," but because a Federalist politician (Rufus King, of New York) had assured him "that if he would vote for the treaty—their party would ratify and confirm the *Yazoo claim.*" [23] This account has a ring of authenticity to it. Not only is Plumer a generally reliable source, but the Federalists were in fact desperate for votes. Gunn would have been expected to join his Georgia colleague, James Jackson, in opposing the treaty, which was highly unpopular in the Deep South.[24] Gunn may not have obtained a federal blessing of the Yazoo sale, but there was no investigation and no congressional condemnation.

The federal government, nevertheless, hesitantly began to involve itself in the Yazoo issue. On March 2, 1795, the House of Representatives passed a resolution authorizing the President to negotiate with Georgia for the acquisition of its western lands, a reflection of the long-standing United States interest in persuading the states to cede their unorganized territories. On that same day the Senate passed a resolution directing the Attorney General to report on the validity of Georgia's title to the lands "claimed by certain companies under a law of the State of Georgia."[25] The report of Attorney General Charles Lee, which he submitted to the Senate in April, 1796, did not take a position. It was simply a collection of thirty-four documents, many of them relating to grants of land made by the British Crown in the early eighteenth century.[26] Lee's report added nothing that was new and it had no perceptible impact.

Two years later Congress enacted legislation specifically providing that there be negotiations with Georgia for her western lands. In the course of considering this bill in the House there occurred the first congressional test directly involving the effect of the Georgia repeal act on the land titles held by the second- and third-hand purchasers under the original sale law. This came about when John Milledge, a Georgia Republican, made a motion to strike from the Senate version of the bill certain words that implied the existence of legitimate claims to the Yazoo lands. The controversial language authorized the United States to negotiate for land claimed by "or under" Georgia's title. Milledge denied the existence of any valid claims except for those officially put forward by his state, and he threatened that the failure of his amendment would compel Georgia to hold on to its lands.[27] The amendment carried.[28] Once the Senate agreed to it, President Adams signed the legislation providing for the appointment of three federal commissioners to negotiate with Georgia. At the same time the state made clear its willingness to cede its western lands to the United States. The Georgia constitution of 1798, which had again affirmed the invalidity of the Yazoo sale, also declared that the state legislature might sell to the United States the lands west of the Chattahoochee River "on such terms as may be beneficial to both parties." [29]

Congressman Robert Goodloe Harper, who told the House that he had "given up" his personal Georgia claims, unsuccessfully opposed the Milledge amendment. His remarks reveal the changing nature of the Yazoo interest: "[The claimants] have no hope while Georgia possesses this territory; but if the United States hold out in this act the idea of an amicable settlement with them, would they not be enlisted in behalf of the cession, and this by two words in the bill before the committee [of the whole House]?" [30] The old Yazooists, such as Gunn and his confederates, who engineered the sale had accomplished their objectives by dealing with the Georgia state government. Up until 1795 the transfer of the Georgia lands to the United States was opposed by those interested in their acquisition; presumably it would have been more difficult for the land companies to bribe the federal Congress than it was for them to reach the Georgia legislature. But the new Yazooists—those who had in turn purchased the land acquired by the companies—eagerly sought cession of the lands after Georgia repealed the sale. These Yazooists realized that their titles were worthless as long as Georgia, whose government was dominated by the political machine of James Jackson, held on to the territory. The federal government was another matter, and so the new, or second-generation, Yazooists supported cession, hoping that Congress and President would view their claims with sympathy.

President Adams appointed the three commissioners, but there were no serious negotiations. In Congress, however, the Yazoo lands issue continued to show its potential divisiveness. The House in 1800 passed an amendment to the act of 1798, directing the federal commissioners to *investigate* all claims against any lands ceded by Georgia and to propose a compromise settlement. This amendment then went to the Senate, where it was referred to a committee headed by James Gunn, ever loyal to the welfare of speculators. Gunn's committee amended the House bill by having the key clause direct the commissioners to *"settle* . . . any claims which are or shall be made by settlers, *or any other persons whatsoever."* [31] The Senate, which was still under Federalist control, accepted this change by a vote of 19 to 8. Most of the senators can be identified by party, and the tally indicates that 15 Federalists and only 2 Republicans supported Gunn's amendment, while 7 Republicans and 1 Federalist opposed it.[32] When the revised bill returned to the House, it encountered strong opposition and heated debate. Samuel Sewall, of Massachusetts, a Federalist and prominent Yazoo claimant whose impartiality was challenged, finally refrained from voting.[33] By a vote of 46 to 34 the Republican House rejected the Gunn amendment. It is possible to identify 26 Federalists and 1 Republican who voted in favor of the Yazoo claimants; 29 Republicans and 10 Federalists (of whom 8 were from the South) voted against Gunn's amendment.[34]

Among those voting to compensate the claimants was a young Federalist from Virginia, John Marshall, who two days earlier had also spoken in support of the amendment.[35] In view of the great formal pronouncement that Chief Justice Marshall would one day make on the subject of the

Yazoo lands, it would be fascinating to read Congressman Marshall's earlier and more informal statement, but, unfortunately, his remarks went unrecorded. Because of the refusal of the House to accept Gunn's proposal that the Yazoo claims be settled, the final version of the act of 1800 simply charged the commissioners with the responsibility of investigating all claims on the Georgia lands.

When Jefferson became President in 1801, he appointed three of the nation's most prominent Republicans, Secretary of State James Madison, Secretary of the Treasury Albert Gallatin, and Attorney General Levi Lincoln, to be the United States commissioners. Serious negotiations then began with the Georgia commissioners, James Jackson, Abraham Baldwin, and John Milledge. On April 24, 1802, the two governments signed "Articles of Agreement and Cession." The core of the agreement was Georgia's transfer of her western lands to the federal government in return for $1,250,000. In addition, the Georgia commissioners, whose leader of course was Jackson, agreed that one-tenth of the Yazoo lands could be reserved "for the purpose of satisfying, quieting, or compensating . . . any claims . . . which may be made to the said lands, or to any part thereof." [36] Jackson's acceptance of this provision directly contradicted the loudly proclaimed principles underlying his opinion of the Yazoo sale, for he had made petty, sometimes fanatical, opposition to every manifestation of any legality or justice in the Yazoo claims the cornerstone of his political career. His sympathetic biographer writes that "those who knew best his bitterness on this subject were astonished" but offers no explanation for it. [37] If one assumes that Jackson's anti-Yazoo stance was at least in part based on political calculation— and there is much evidence that it was—his behavior as Georgia commissioner is not surprising. [38] Jefferson's administration, as will be seen, was anxious to settle the Yazoo claims issue; James Jackson's action is readily understandable as an accommodation for his fellow Republican politicians.

On February 16, 1803, as a sequel to the agreement between Georgia and the United States, Commissioners Madison, Gallatin, and Lincoln reported to Congress their conclusions on the validity of the Yazoo claims. "Under all the circumstances which may affect the case," they declared, "the title of the claimants cannot be supported." Nevertheless, they concluded that "the interest of the United States, the tranquility of those who thereafter may inhabit that territory, and various equitable considerations . . . render it expedient to enter into a compromise on reasonable terms." [39] Madison and his two colleagues proposed the following terms: that five million acres of the former Georgia lands be set aside to satisfy all legitimate claims which were a consequence of the repeal act, and that the claimants be allowed to choose compensation either in the form of land or in money, not exceeding five million dollars, to be derived from the sale of land in the Mississippi Territory. Congress moved a step in this direction by enacting on March 3, 1803, a law that set aside five million acres to settle claims "derived from any act or pretended act of the state of Georgia, which Congress may hereafter think fit to provide for." [40] In other words, while not really settling anything, the law now held out the hope that compensation might eventually be forthcoming.

III

The New Yazooists

As a result of the act of 1803 the New England Mississippi Land Company was in a position to pursue a specific objective: a federal law indemnifying its shareholders. The company's title on paper amounted to eleven million acres of Georgia lands, and its shareholders, who had paid seven times more for their titles than had the original purchasers, held on to their investment. Instead of obtaining the small refund offered by the state of Georgia, they gambled that, in spite of the repeal act, they would be able to make a profit from their investment. In presenting their case in 1802 to the federal commissioners, Gallatin, Lincoln, and Madison, the company had vainly argued that its shareholders ought to receive two dollars per acre for the entire eleven million acres. When this proposal was rejected, it then put its weight behind the compromise proposal, which reserved for it a share of the five-million-acre tract.[1] A gamble for even this smaller potential compensation was one well worth taking. Because of Eli Whitney's invention of the cotton gin in 1792, the South's cotton exports were growing at a fantastic rate. As they grew, the value of the Yazoo claims grew with them. In 1795 the South exported six million pounds of cotton; in 1800, eighteen million pounds; and in 1810, ninety-three million pounds.[2]

The speculators of the New England Mississippi Land Company were the new Yazooists, and they formed an almost classic illustration of a political interest group.[3] Although there were sizable Yazoo claims from New York and smaller ones from Georgia, Pennsylvania (Philadelphia),

37

and South Carolina, approximately three-fifths of the claimants were concentrated in New England.[4] The New England Yazooists were united by their common land claims, and they were agreed on a specific public objective: federal compensation.

As an interest group, the dominant characteristics of the New England Mississippi Land Company were its sectionalism, its bipartisan composition, and the prominence, in business and politics, of its directors and largest shareholders. The best illustration of these characteristics is a list of the company's leading claimants. They included George Blake, a Republican politician who served as President Jefferson's United States attorney for Massachusetts in 1808 (250,000 acres in Yazoo lands); Elias H. Derby, Jr., shipowner and prosperous Boston merchant (320,000 acres); Samuel Dexter, a Federalist congressman from 1792 to 1797 and Secretary of War in the Adams administration, who was one of the company's organizers and major directors (over 1,000,000 acres); Gideon Granger, a Connecticut Republican and Postmaster General in the Jefferson administration (160,000 acres); James Lloyd, a wealthy Massachusetts merchant who served as a Federalist senator from 1808 to 1813 and again from 1822 to 1826 (188,000 acres); Perez Morton, a prominent Massachusetts Republican politician, who was a director and lobbyist for the company (acreage unknown); Oliver Phelps, a Massachusetts merchant and land promoter (1,575,000 acres); Samuel Sewall, a Federalist who served in Congress from 1797 to 1800, when he accepted a judgeship on the Supreme Judicial Court of Massachusetts (113,000 acres); and James Sullivan, a leader of the Massachusetts Republicans who was state attorney general and later, in 1807 and 1808, governor (80,000 acres).[5]

The New England Mississippi Land Company was ably equipped to lobby its cause in the national legislature. At times its shareholders or agents sat in Congress, but, more important, almost all New England congressmen, whether Federalist or Republican, were responsive to the company's demand for a compensation law. The company, moreover, shrewdly recognized the shift from Federalist to Republican rule in 1801. No longer were such Federalists as Harper and Sewall active as its primary representatives, nor, in this time of Jeffersonian triumph, did the company cite the views of Alexander Hamilton on the validity of the Georgia repeal act. Instead, the leadership of the Yazoo cause was put into the hands of Gideon Granger and Perez Morton, both prominent Republicans. In the House of Representatives Ezekiel Bacon, a Republican from western Massachusetts, operated as the chief Yazooist agent until Joseph Story, the talented Salem attorney who combined Republican politics with Hamiltonian constitutional principles, took his seat as a representative in 1808. Story had already spent a long time in Washington as a paid agent for the New England Mississippi Land Company, and upon his election to the House Bacon wrote him that "I shall with much pleasure resign into your hands next winter the sole management of *Yazooism* in the national councils." [6] In the Senate John Quincy Adams, who until 1807 still regarded himself as a Federalist, deliberately stayed in the background. The son of the former President believed that the claimants were "suffering injustice," but he was convinced "that the most effectual aid I can give to the Georgia Land Bill is by remaining silent, at least until the members of the majority [the Republicans] have come forward in its favor." [7]

When in 1804 the lobbyists of the New England Mississippi Land Company began to concentrate on getting a compensation law passed, they encountered an absolutely unmovable obstacle, John Randolph of Roanoke. In a sense John Randolph was to the New England Yazooists what James Jackson had been to the Georgia Yazooists, for he made a frenzied and doctrinaire opposition to the claims a central feature of his political career. Like Jackson, Randolph was an extraordinary person, and it is no exaggeration to say that he shared much of the responsibility for Congress' refusal, session after session, to pass a compensation law. Randolph, a Virginia Republican, entered the House of Representatives in 1799, at the age of twenty-five. He quickly made his mark: by the time the Jeffersonians assumed power in 1801 he was the acknowledged Republican leader in the House. That year he became the first permanent chairman of the important Ways and Means Committee, a position from which he exercised a dominating influence until 1806, when, in large part because of the Yazoo dispute, he came into conflict with Jefferson.

John Randolph's forte was oratorical brilliance, which he used to convey an uncompromising insistence on the doctrines of pure Republicanism. More Jeffersonian than Jefferson, he worshiped the agrarian way of life, believed intensely in states' rights, and favored a caretaker federal government. Above all else, he believed in the prerogative of the landed aristocrat. As Randolph put it in an epigram: "I am an aristocrat; I love liberty, I hate equality." [8] Impetuous and arrogant, he had a talent for using words as bullets. "He is a man of splendid abilities," Randolph said in attacking an opponent, "but utterly corrupt. He shines and stinks like a rotten mackerel by moonlight." [9] A description of Randolph by William Plumer gives an interesting glimpse into how this strangely talented man appeared to his colleagues: "Mr. Randolph goes to the House booted and spurred, with his whip in his hand, in imitation it is said, of members of the British Parliament. . . . The Federalists ridicule and affect to despise him; but a despised foe often proves a dangerous enemy. . . . I admire his ingenuity and his address, but I dislike his politics." [10]

According to his most recent biographer, Randolph's opposition to the Yazoo claims went back to his experiences as

a young man: on a visit to Georgia in 1795 he learned of
~~the fraud~~ and developed a life-long animosity toward the
Yazoo interest.[11] This is too pat an explanation, and there
are much more plausible reasons for the fiery Virginian's
behavior. The Yazoo claims issue aroused his political principles on a number of points. As an agrarian of the Virginia
plantation aristocracy, Randolph saw the land speculators
as a species of the financial capitalists whom he despised.
Federal recognition of the claims would mean a repudiation
of the validity of the Georgia repeal act, and this ran counter
to his conviction that federal powers under the Constitution
should be strictly construed so as not to trespass on the more
important rights of the states.[12] In addition, Randolph dis-
liked Secretary of State James Madison, who in Jefferson's
administration was the leading advocate of compromise with
the Yazoo claimants. Madison possessed considerable influence himself in the House, and he posed a threat to Randolph's leadership. Since Madison drew much of his support
from the northern Republicans, whose political purity Randolph strongly questioned, this made him doubly suspect in
Randolph's eyes.

Finally, John Randolph opposed the administration-
backed compensation bill because he was a natural oppositionist. He was at his best as a critic, and in his few years as
an administration leader he was really out of character.
"Ours is not a government of confidence," he once asserted,
"it is a government of diffidence and suspicion, and it is only
by being suspicious that it can remain a free government."[13]
The role of oppositionist was very likely in part a response
to his emotional needs.

Tall and thin, with a small head and a boyish face, Randolph spoke with a shrill, piercing voice, particularly when
excited. "You would think from his voice," a senator's wife
once remarked, "that he belonged to the feminine gender,"
a comment made by many who knew him.[14] There is some

evidence that Randolph, whose courtship ended in failure, was sexually impotent, although his latest biographer strongly questions this. In any event, it is clear that throughout his life Randolph was tormented by a succession of physical maladies and that he experienced periods of insanity. "His mind," William C. Bruce has written, "was at certain periods of his life positively deranged; and at others so nearly so that it was hard to say whether his mental condition was normal or not; for rarely has any human being ever furnished a more striking illustration of the saying that great wits to madness are near allied." [15]

Whatever the explanation, there is no doubting the depth of John Randolph's hatred of the Yazoo speculation. "This is one of the cases," he announced in 1804, "which . . . I can never desert or relinquish, till I shall have experienced every energy of mind, and faculty of body I possess, in refuting so nefarious a project." [16] On one occasion, after debating in Congress with a pro-Yazooist representative, Randolph met him at a dinner party and resumed the attack. Randolph's language became so violent that the ladies fled the room; he smashed a wine glass on his opponent's head and threw the bottle at him. Subsequently, he apologized to all at the party, with the exception of "that dammed puppy." [17]

When the New England Mississippi Land Company had its supporters introduce a House bill in 1804 providing that the claimants be compensated, Randolph responded by introducing a set of eight proposed resolutions. Covering every aspect of the Yazoo dispute, they were intended to rally the Republican majority under the banner of classic Jeffersonian dogma. The Randolph resolutions declared that the Georgia legislature had been empowered to sell its western lands only "in a rightful manner and for the public good" and that the sale of 1795 was both immoral and unconstitutional. In contrast, the resolutions declared, the repeal act restored Georgia's honor and was constitutional because "it is the inalienable right of a people, so circumstanced, to revoke the authority thus abused, to resume the rights thus attempted to be bartered, and to abrogate the act thus endeavoring to betray them." If Congress passed a compensation law, it would in effect be validating the Yazoo claims and interfering in the internal affairs of the sovereign state of Georgia.[18] As Henry Adams pointed out, "These resolutions covered the whole ground; they swept statements of fact, principles of law, theories of the Constitution, considerations of equity, like a flock of sheep into one fold to be sheared."[19]

A significant test of the strength of the Yazooist and anti-Yazooist forces began on March 7, 1804: both the Randolph resolutions and the compensation bill came before the House. After an attempt to add four crippling amendments to the compensation bill failed, a lengthy debate began on the resolutions. To Caesar Rodney, of Delaware, they were "like axioms in mathematics; they only require to be stated to be self-evident." James Elliot, a Vermont Federalist, tried to throw the states' rights argument back at Randolph by claiming that it would be "an act of usurpation" for Congress to adopt resolutions which passed judgment on the actions of the Georgia legislature. Randolph took the floor in defense of his resolutions, saying in part that to pass the compensation bill would be to "do an act which whole ages of political penance will never atone." "I have during the whole course of this discussion listened with profound attention," he continued, "and the words expediency and policy alone have reached my ears. But I cannot comprehend that expediency which would countenance fraud, nor the policy which would foster corruption."[20] Randolph's resolutions failed to carry. They were postponed by narrow margins of from 2 to 5 votes, but the compensation bill was similarly postponed by a vote of 59 to 49.

Early the next year, 1805, the Yazoo dispute burst out
again in Congress even more violently. In the House of
Representatives the Committee on Claims recommended a
resolution calling for the appointment of three commissioners to make a final settlement of all Yazoo claims. This
provoked a bitter tirade by Randolph. In a speech made on
January 29 he contemptuously rejected the assertion that
the New England claimants had been innocent purchasers.
He called them "guilty of gross and willful prevarication,"
and, paraphrasing La Rochefoucauld, bitingly added, "They
offer indeed to virtue the only homage which she is ever
likely to receive at their hands—the homage of their hypoc-
risy." As he was speaking, Randolph observed that Postmaster General Gideon Granger, one of the leading figures
in the New England Mississippi Land Company, had entered the House chamber. All congressional supporters of
the claims, whom Randolph called "the Yazoo Squad," had
been bribed, he insinuated, and Granger had come to the
House to "buy and sell corruption in the gross." The alleged
bribes were mail-carrying contracts, and he suggested that
Matthew Lyon, a well-known Republican from Kentucky,
was one of the recipients.[21]

John G. Jackson, of Virginia, a brother-in-law of James
Madison, answered Randolph with a sharp but well-rea-
soned speech supporting a compromise with the claimants.
Representative Jackson was widely regarded as having spoken on Madison's behalf, and this infuriated Randolph
anew.[22] Two days later he again charged that "the Yazoo
estate" was buying congressional votes, and he renewed his
allegations against Granger and Lyon. (While Randolph
was publicly impugning the Postmaster General, Senator
William Branch Giles was privately telling John Quincy
Adams that Granger had bribed Lyon "to the amount of
several thousand dollars.")[23] Lyon, who could be as combative as Randolph, dismissed the attack as "the braying of

a jackall" and "the fulminations of a madman." And he concluded with a stinging retort: "These charges have been brought against me by a person nursed in the bosom of opulence, inheriting the life services of a numerous train of the human species; and extensive fields, the original proprietors of which property, in all probability, came no honester by it than the purchasers of the Georgia lands . . ."[24]

Although the Yazooist resolution recommending a settlement passed by a vote of 63 to 58, the House took no action to pass a law actually indemnifying the claimants. In 1806 the Senate passed a compensation bill, but the House again refused. By this time it was becoming increasingly evident that the emotion-laden Yazoo issue was having a destructive impact on the Republican party and, consequently, on relations between Jefferson and Congress. One of John Randolph's speeches provides an excellent illustration of its divisive effect:

What is the spirit against which we now struggle, and which we have vainly endeavored to stifle? A monster generated by fraud, nursed in corruption, that in grim silence awaits his prey. It is the spirit of Federalism! That spirit which considers the many as made only for the few, which sees in Government nothing but a job, which is never so true to itself as when false to the nation! When I behold a certain party [the Federalists] supporting and clinging to such a measure, almost to a man, I see only men faithful to their own principles; pursuing, with steady step and untired zeal, the uniform tenor of their political life. But when I see associated with them, in firm compact, others [Republicans] who once rallied under the standard of opposite principles, I am filled with apprehension and concern. Of what consequence is it that a man smiles in your face, holds out his hand and declares himself the advocate of those political principles to which you are also attached, when you see him acting with your adversaries upon other principles, which the voice of the nation has put down, which I did hope were buried, never to rise again in this section of the globe? I speak of the plunder of the public property. Say what we will, the marrow and pith of this business will be found in the character of the great majority of its friends, who stand, as they have before stood on this floor, the unblushing advocates of unblushing corruption.[25]

An analysis of party voting on the Yazoo issue confirms the accuracy of Randolph's assertion that almost to a man the Federalists supported the claimants while the Republicans were badly divided. One of the key votes in the House of Representatives occurred on March 12, 1804, when 59 representatives voted to postpone (and thus kill) a compensation bill, and 49 voted against postponement. In so far as party affiliations can be identified, the vote of March 12 shows that 44 Republicans and only 2 Federalists took an anti-Yazoo position; but 18 Republicans and 20 Federalists voted for the Yazoo claims.[26] On March 28, 1806, when the Senate passed a compensation bill, 13 Republicans and 6 Federalists supported the Yazooist position; 8 Republicans and 2 Federalists (one of whom was William Plumer, then in the process of switching his party allegiance) voted against it.[27] The House vote of 62 to 54 on March 29, 1806, rejecting the Senate compensation bill, revealed 47 Republicans and 2 Federalists against the Yazoo claims, while 23 Republicans and 20 Federalists supported them.[28]

Even more striking, perhaps, is the sectional pull evident in the Yazoo voting. Thus, in the Senate vote on the pro-Yazooist Gunn amendment on April 16, 1800, 9 New England senators voted for and none against it, while only 4 southern and border state senators voted for and 8 voted against it.[29] In the House 20 New Englanders voted for the Gunn amendment and only 2 against it; 30 southern and border state representatives were opposed to it, and only 8 supported the amendment.[30] Six years later the sectional patterns in the Senate and House votes remained unchanged. On March 28, 1806, New England senators voted 8 to 1 in favor of compensation, while southern and border state senators split 6 to 5 in favor of the claims.[31] The House vote on March 29 was even more sharply divided: New England representatives voted to compensate the claimants by a margin of 28 to 2; southern representatives (border states excluded) voted 32 to 2 against the claims.

If there was, then, as Randolph of Roanoke charged, a "Yazoo Squad," it united New England Federalists and Republicans across party lines. The pull of section was more important than the pull of party, and this was made easier by the fact that the parties were not sharply split along economic and ideological lines. In Massachusetts, the hub of the Yazoo interest, the Federalist and Republican parties were complex coalitions of diverse population groups. Contrary to a once common stereotype, the Bay State Republicans of the early nineteenth century cannot be accurately characterized as a radical party of debtors, farmers, and the poor any more than the state's Federalists can be described as a conservative party of creditors, merchants, and the well-to-do.[32] Equally important, the Jefferson administration very clearly favored a settlement of the rancorous Yazoo issue without regard to party considerations. Madison, Gallatin, and Lincoln, each one a major figure in the Republican administration, had officially endorsed a compromise with the claimants, and the President's Postmaster General, Granger, was an open lobbyist for the New England Mississippi Land Company. On the other hand, it is also evident that Jefferson was reluctant to antagonize Randolph, who, after all, had been a valued floor leader during the first Republican administration.[33]

Eventually, and probably inevitably, Jefferson and Randolph came to a parting of the ways. The break came in 1806, when Randolph resisted the President's plan to purchase West Florida from Spain and, as chairman of the Ways and Means Committee, was able to block an appropriation for that purpose. At the same time he also denounced

Jefferson's Nonimportation Policy, which was intended to apply commercial pressure on England and France in retaliation for their continuing depredations on American shipping. Then, on March 28, he lashed out at Yazooists in the administration, charging that "the whole weight of the Executive Government has had a bias to the Yazoo interest ever since I had a seat here." [34] Randolph, moreover, challenged the President on another front by opposing the presidential aspirations of James Madison, whom Jefferson wanted as his successor. According to Randolph, Madison would be a "Yazoo President," and he tried to thwart the President and his Secretary of State by pushing a not unwilling James Monroe as the Republican candidate in 1808.[35]

Thomas Jefferson, for all his love of theoretical speculation and his seeming remoteness from the day-to-day political infighting, knew a threat when it confronted him; he also knew what to do about it. Jefferson as President was preeminently a party leader, and he governed, in a rather subterranean manner, through his congressional majorities. He worked closely with floor leaders, who were regarded as his personal agents (men like William Branch Giles, Wilson Cary Nicholas, Caesar Rodney, and, until 1806, Randolph himself), and he frequently relied on caucus meetings with his cabinet and key congressmen before taking important political steps.[36] In 1807 Jefferson had Randolph ousted from his position on the Ways and Means Committee. Taking with him a small band of supporters who fancied themselves as "the old republicans," the Virginia congressman went into permanent and uncompromising opposition. Randolph of Roanoke had come into his true calling.[37]

Despite John Randolph's fall from Jeffersonian grace, the Yazoo claimants came no closer to victory. Randolph still retained negative influence, and, particularly in the House, the Georgia congressional delegation kept anti-Yazooism alive. And within Georgia, politicians continued to exploit the issue. In 1807, after a compensation bill had been beaten back, the state legislature passed a resolution bitterly denouncing the Yazoo speculators and thanking John Randolph "and the late majority of the ninth Congress, for their virtuous and manly opposition to a compromise which . . . would compromise the dignity of the United States, and the sovereignty of this State." [38]

It seems evident, too, that the demand for compensation pressed by the New England Mississippi Land Company, coming as it did from an organization based in Massachusetts and composed principally of financiers and speculators, grated on the barely latent sensibilities of the agrarian South, which viewed with suspicion the more commercial and industrial North. By 1807 the Yazooist campaign to secure federal compensation had failed in four consecutive congressional sessions. But the claimants were persistent, and by this time they were also directing their efforts to another branch of the federal government.

IV

The Yazooists
Go to Court

From the very beginning, the Yazooists indicated their willingness, indeed their eagerness, to have the federal judiciary adjudicate their dispute. As early as 1798, during one of the first congressional debates over the legality of the Georgia sale, Robert Goodloe Harper argued that "whether the claims were well or ill-founded . . . their validity must be determined in a Court of Justice." [1] Gideon Granger and Perez Morton, agents of the New England Mississippi Land Company, went even further. They asked Congress to pass legislation directing the United States Supreme Court to adjudicate the dispute, saying they would "cheerfully submit" to its decision. [2] The constitutionality of such an act would have been most questionable, and Congress failed to pick up the suggestion. [3]

The Yazooists had good reasons for wanting to take their dispute to the Supreme Court. If the Court handed down a decision supporting their claims, they would then have stronger legal and moral arguments to press in the campaign for a congressional compensation law. Harper, a learned lawyer, had written a strong legal brief upholding the legality of the original sale and declaring the repeal act unconstitutional; Alexander Hamilton had unequivocally endorsed his views. [4] Then, too, there was a very practical reason why the lobbyists of the New England Mississippi Land Company felt that they would be welcome in the courtroom. It was simply that the American judiciary, and especially the federal judiciary, was staffed by well-to-do men who were naturally sympathetic to the nation's commercial, financial, and manufacturing interests. The framers of the Constitution had in fact candidly proclaimed the judiciary to be "an essential safeguard against the effects of occasional ill humors in the society," which would mitigate the severity of "unjust and partial laws" injurious to "the private rights of particular classes of citizens." [5] Freely translated, this meant that the framers hoped that federal judges would protect creditors and those with established property interests against the effect of laws disrupting the stability of contractual and business relations. And was not Georgia's repeal act precisely such a law?

On the other side, the anti-Yazooists, both in Georgia and on the national scene, made plain their desire to keep the issue out of the courts. The repeal act of 1796 declared that it was beneath Georgia's sovereign dignity to contest the validity of the sale in any court, and it specifically provided that neither the "usurped law" nor any grant or contract issued under it could be received in evidence in the state's courts. In the congressional debate of 1804 Thomas Mann Randolph, President Jefferson's son-in-law and a Virginia representative, addressed himself to the possibility that the Yazoo claimants might "venture into the courts of justice of the Union with their fictitious title paper in their hands." Although he believed that "every judge on the bench of the Union" would declare the claims to be void, Thomas Randolph added a threat: "If I thought otherwise I would readily acquiesce in any, however strong, remediable measures. I would vote for a law forbidding the admission of such evidence into our courts. If nothing else would do, I would even give my voice in this House for imposing a heavy penalty on the man who should dare assert such a detestable claim to the indisputable property of the nation . . ." [6]

This was no idle warning, for at that very moment the Jeffersonian Republicans were unveiling their plans for the federal judiciary. Almost all of the judges were holdovers from the Washington and Adams administrations. The Republicans decided to oust as many of them as possible in impeachment proceedings because they held "subversive"—that is, Federalist—political views. Senator Giles had openly boasted to John Quincy Adams that "we want your offices, for the purpose of giving them to men who will fill them better." [7] Already one district judge, the half-insane John Pickering, of New Hampshire, had been removed by the Republican Congress. Two days after Thomas Randolph's speech the House voted to impeach Supreme Court Justice Samuel Chase. [8]

In addition to these general considerations which underlay the willingness of the Yazooists to go to court, they already had tangible evidence that their claims would be favorably received in the judicial arena. In 1799 two of the largest speculators in the New England Mississippi Land Company, George Blake and Elias H. Derby, Jr., contrived to get a case into the Massachusetts courts which tested the legality of the Georgia repeal act. (The facts are somewhat complicated, but in essence Derby sued Blake for failing to pay a note which he had given to Derby in return for some of the Yazoo lands; Blake's defense was that the agreement was invalid because the repeal act had removed Derby's title to the land.) The Supreme Judicial Court of Massachusetts ruled for Derby that the repeal act was "a mere nullity" and "a flagrant, outrageous violation of the first and fundamental principles of social compacts."

Derby v. Blake is the earliest recorded decision by a state court holding that a state law violates the federal constitution, and it reveals its indebtedness to the Harper and Hamilton opinions of 1796. A sketch of the judges' reasoning was made by the editor of the Boston *Columbian Centinel* and published on its front page:

The idea of a Legislature reclaiming property they had once sold, and been paid for, was said by the Court to be not less preposterous than for an individual to repeal his own note of hand, or to render void by his own act and determination, any contract, however sacred or solemn. The vociferations of the Georgia Legislature, who were the very granters of the property in question, about fraud and circumvention, could not be admitted in a Judiciary of *Massachusetts,* as evidence of the real existence of such facts—Whether the original grant of the Georgia Legislature were valid or not, was considered by the Court a cause of judicial, and not of legislative cognizance. The Repealing Act of *Georgia* was moreover declared void, because it was considered directly repugnant to Article 1st. Sec. 10, of the United States Constitution, which provides that "no State shall pass any *ex post facto Law,* or Law impairing the obligation of contracts." [9]

While it had no effect, if *Derby* v. *Blake* were a sample of what the Yazoo claimants might expect, their desire to take their case to the federal courts was readily understandable. The problem was to get a case raising all the relevant questions before the federal judges in order that it might be carried to the Supreme Court. Two obstacles had to be bypassed: first, the repeal act foreclosed a test of the claims in the Georgia courts, and, second, the Eleventh Amendment to the Constitution, adopted in 1798, protected Georgia from being sued in the federal courts. There were a number of Yazoo cases pending in the United States Circuit Court for Connecticut between 1797 and 1805, but they did not involve the New England Mississippi Land Company and were eventually dismissed without a decision on the basic questions.[10] In 1803, however, the Yazoo claimants were able to enter the federal courts under a provision of the Constitution giving United States courts jurisdiction over controversies between citizens of different states (technically known as diversity of citizenship suits). On June 1, 1803, Robert Fletcher, of Amherst, New Hampshire, sued John Peck, of Newton, Massachusetts, for a "covenant broken" because he had sold him that which he did not rightfully possess: 15,000 acres of land derived from the Georgia sale of 1795.

Beyond any doubt the case of Fletcher against Peck was a collusive suit, an arranged case between friendly "adversaries" acting on behalf of the New England Mississippi Land Company. Those who arrange collusive suits—less politely called faked cases—do not normally leave records, but in this instance explicit documentation would provide little more than a useful footnote to the impressive circumstantial and internal evidence showing that *Fletcher* v. *Peck* was a rigged case. John Peck, who claimed 600,000 acres of Yazoo lands, was a director of the New England Mississippi Land Company; Robert Fletcher, although not clearly linked to the Yazoo interest, was also a seasoned speculator who had once been associated with William Plumer in land ventures in New Hampshire.[11] In a letter written in 1810, Joseph Story, who served as one of Peck's attorneys in the later stages of the case, noted that Peck's expense in the case was "a concern of the whole [New England Mississippi Land] Company, and they are taking measures to collect from all parties interested the money necessary to discharge a variety of incidental expenses."[12] Besides Story, Peck's attorneys included Robert Goodloe Harper, who had been prominent in the Yazoo speculation from its beginning, and William Sullivan, a Massachusetts politician and himself a claimant to 20,000 acres of Yazoo lands.[13]

The actual contract by which Peck sold Fletcher 15,000 acres was constructed in such a way as to test every single question of interest to the New England Yazooists. In his sale to Fletcher, Peck made these stipulations:

1) At the time of the passage of the act of 1795 Georgia was legally seized of the lands in question.
2) The Georgia Legislature had good right to sell and dispose of the land.
3) The Georgia Government had lawful authority to issue the grant by virtue of the act.

4) All the title which Georgia had in the land had been legally conveyed to John Peck.

5) . . . [T]he title to the premises so conveyed by the State of Georgia . . . had been in no way constitutionally or legally impaired by virtue of any subsequent legislation of the State of Georgia.[14]

Not only was the suit of *Fletcher* v. *Peck* collusive, but it lacked the inherent quality of an adversary proceeding. Fletcher and Peck, after all, shared a common interest in having the validity of the land title upheld. If the federal courts ruled in Peck's favor, both parties stood to gain: Peck would have made a legal sale, and Fletcher would have acquired a potentially valuable title. A ruling that the title was good would also serve the long-run interest of both, since a favorable judicial decision might induce Congress to recognize the Yazoo claims and to vote financial compensation for all titleholders.

Fletcher's suit was filed on June 1, 1803, in the United States Circuit Court for Massachusetts, which in those days served as a trial court of first instance. By the consent of both parties it was continued without disposition for three judicial terms. Then, in October, 1806, the case was tried before a jury which returned a special verdict on one of the underlying legal issues, whether Georgia or the United States had title to the lands as of January 7, 1795, the date of the original sale. The jury's verdict provided the court with little assistance: in over 5,000 words it traced the history of the Georgia lands from the time of the reign of Charles II (1660–1685) to 1795 and helplessly concluded that "whether . . . the state of Georgia, at the time of passing the act . . . was seized in fee-simple . . . the jury are ignorant and pray the advisement of the court . . ." It requested the two judges who sat as the circuit court, Supreme Court Justice William Cushing and District Judge John Davis, to pass on Fletcher's charges against Peck. This they did in October, 1807, upholding John Peck on every disputed point: Georgia's title was good; the sale of 1795 was valid; and the repeal act had not impaired it.[15]

In a review of these developments one question immediately comes to mind: Why was *Fletcher* v. *Peck* allowed to repose quietly from 1803 to 1807? The question cannot be answered with certainty, for there are no sources to provide specific documentation. A speculative answer, however, can be supplied that is in harmony with all that is known about the Yazoo dispute. If one assumes that Fletcher's suit against Peck was in reality a collusive case arranged by the New England Mississippi Land Company—and the circumstantial and internal evidence on this point are overwhelming—several conclusions emerge. The first is that a solitary circuit court ruling would have been of little value to the claimants. They were after what the agents of the company had explicitly requested, a ruling from the nation's highest judicial tribunal, the United States Supreme Court. For the claimants the circuit court was only a way station, not the final destination. Any decision by it would be no more than a prelude to a Supreme Court ruling, and there are two reasons why the Yazooists may have preferred to bide their time.

In the first place, a circuit court ruling on *Fletcher* v. *Peck* in 1803 or 1804 would have led to an appeal and a decision by the Supreme Court sometime between 1804 and 1806. A decision favorable to the claimants (which they confidently expected) during this period would have been a decision by a Court that was being rocked by political pressure. The Republicans came to power in 1801, convinced, as Jefferson put it, that "the Federalists have retired into the Judiciary as a stronghold . . . and from that battery all the works of republicanism are to be beaten and erased."[16] They were reinforced in this view by indisputable evidence. In twelve years of power the administrations of Washington and Adams had appointed none but Federalists to the bench, and many of these judges later enforced the Sedition Act with great severity against Republican politicians and editors. The lameduck Federalist Congress and administration of early 1801 aroused anew all the old Republican suspicions by making the expansion of the federal judiciary one of their last official acts. The Judiciary Act of 1801 vastly enlarged the civil jurisdiction of the federal courts at the expense of the state courts. A primary motive was the desire to create a broad jurisdictional avenue that would funnel disputes over land titles, such as the one over the Yazoo lands, directly into the federal courts. Under the assumption that federal judges would be more sympathetic than state judges to land speculators whose interests collided with those of state governments, the Federalist Congress endowed the federal courts with jurisdiction over all disputes over land titles between citizens of different states without regard to the monetary value of the land (previously, all of the diversity jurisdiction of the federal courts had been limited to cases where the amount in dispute was no less than $500).[17] In addition, the Judiciary Act of 1801 created sixteen new district and circuit positions, and the names of the judges that John Adams appointed to fill them read like an honor roll of Federalism: Richard Bassett,[18] John Davis,[19] Jared Ingersoll,[20] Philip Barton Key,[21] Charles Lee,[22] Jacob Read,[23] John Sitgreaves,[24] Jeremiah Smith,[25] William Tilghman,[26] Oliver Wolcott.[27] Republican fears were further confirmed in *Marbury* v. *Madison* (1803). In that historic case, the Federalist Chief Justice, John Marshall, delivered a stinging personal rebuke to Jefferson's administration and strongly implied that the judiciary could restrain executive actions that violated its notion of legality.[28]

As a consequence of these events, which were nourished by its own worst suspicions of all Federalist motives, the new Republican administration gave high priority to curbing the federal—or, in its view, the Federalist—courts. In addition to verbal attacks on the courts, which included many specific threats of legislative retribution, the Republicans repealed the Judiciary Act of 1801, thereby eliminating the newly created circuit judgeships. In 1804–1805 they set out to purge the Supreme Court by removing its Federalist judges through the impeachment process. The failure of the attempt to oust Samuel Chase ended this attack, but it so scared Chief Justice Marshall that he acted timorously in his appearances before the Senate during the impeachment trial, and he actually proposed that Congress be allowed to override the decisions of the Supreme Court. This was, his biographer writes, "the most radical method for correcting judicial decisions ever advanced, before or since, by any man of the first class."[29] Since the Court was on the defensive, the New England Yazooists had little to gain from a decision voiding the Georgia repeal act. It would anger southern Republicans, who were largely anti-Yazooist in their sentiments, and perhaps make the prospects for a compensation bill even bleaker. In short, a Supreme Court decision on the legality of the claims in the years between 1804 and 1806 was not in the best interest of the Yazooists.

In the second place, the New England Mississippi Land Company may well have been reluctant to press *Fletcher* v. *Peck* because of its belief that Congress was on the verge of passing a compensation bill. At all times the claimants had the covert support of the Jefferson administration and strong support within Congress. They made a nearly successful push in 1806, when a compensation bill passed in the Senate but lost in the House by only 8 votes out of 116 cast. Nevertheless, as the year 1806 ended, the Yazooists had failed in three major attempts (1804, 1805, and 1806) to get a bill through, and there were soon other indications that their financial crusade was stuck on dead center. In 1807 not only did Congress again refuse to enact a compensation law, but it passed instead a law that prohibited the claim-

ants, under penalty of forfeiting their claims, from settling
on the lands ceded to the United States until authorized by
law. Its effect was to prevent the claimants from forcing a
court test of their titles by taking possession of the disputed
land. An amendment proposed by the Massachusetts Federalist, Josiah Quincy, which would have reversed the purpose of the act by providing that "nothing in this act shall
prevent any person claiming title to any such lands, under
or by virtue of an act or grant of any State, from peaceably
entering thereon, for the purpose of . . . bring[ing] a judicial decision at law or in equity on the validity of the
title," was soundly defeated by a House vote of 60 to 34.[30]

These discouraging developments left the circuit court
case of *Fletcher* v. *Peck* as the last vehicle for a fresh attempt
to secure compensation of the Yazoo claims. When Judges
Cushing and Davis gave their decision upholding the claimants in the fall of 1807, the path was cleared for a legal test
before the Supreme Court. Robert Fletcher, citing errors in
the decision, asked the Supreme Court to examine it by
issuing a writ of error to the lower tribunal. Judicial review
under such circumstances was automatic in the nineteenth
century, and the Court issued the writ; the case was set for
argument early in 1809. Nearly fifteen years after Georgia
had made its controversial sale of thirty-five million acres
for $500,000, the Yazooists stood at the bar of the United
States Supreme Court.

The tribunal before which the Yazoo claimants appeared
bore little resemblance to the Supreme Court which today
sits in a splendid marble palace. So insignificant was the
early Court that when the federal government moved from
Philadelphia to Washington in 1800, no building had been
provided for the justices. A mere two weeks before its 1801
term was to open the third branch of government was assigned cramped quarters on the first floor over the east en-
trance hall of the still uncompleted Capitol.[31] There were

other reminders of the Court's low prestige. John Jay had found the chief-justiceship unworthy of his talents and resigned it to be governor of New York. When President Adams gave him a second opportunity to be chief justice in 1800, Jay declined, writing the President that he was convinced the Supreme Court "would not obtain the energy, weight and dignity which are essential to its affording due support to the National Government, nor acquire the public confidence and respect which . . . it should possess." [32]

Jay of course was mistaken. In America concern with legality was great, as the Yazoo issue itself demonstrates, and the complementary ideas of inalienable natural rights and of government limited by written constitutions were accepted by both the people and the politicians. The gradual development of the Supreme Court into an institutional guarantor of constitutional limitations, passing on the constitutionality of state and federal legislation, was in short a natural outgrowth of the American experience and its dominant political thinking. But ideas and values must be expressed through men, and only in its potentiality was the Supreme Court of 1800 an institution capable of playing a significant role within the American political system. The man who took the position that Jay had refused, John Marshall, saw its potentialities and, by the force of his convictions and the skill of his leadership, gave the Supreme Court "energy, weight and dignity." Indeed, the very fact that the Jeffersonians attacked it so insistently between 1802 and 1806 was a backhanded tribute to the Court's potential power and to Marshall's great abilities.

John Marshall served as chief justice from 1801 to 1835, and although he did not always control its decisions, he dominated the Court. Marshall was a Virginia conservative, an Adams Federalist; and the anchor of his legal and political philosophy was a belief in the sanctity of acquired property and a conviction that the United States could survive as a nation only with a strong government. Unlike his distant cousin, Thomas Jefferson, Marshall feared that too many states' rights—in other words, too much state power— would have a corrosive effect on the all-important federal government. He saw judicial review as a mechanism for asserting the rightful authority of the new government, especially when confronted with the claim of the states' rights school that the Constitution strictly limited federal powers. Marshall held to these ideas with a powerful tenacity, and because he knew precisely what he believed in and why, the Chief Justice could be a forceful advocate.

His political and intellectual commitment was made even more effective by a captivating personality and a physical environment which encouraged its expression. The Court then sat for about eight weeks a year, and the judges did not bother to move their families to Washington. Instead they roomed together in a boardinghouse and ate their meals in common. Since there was little formal entertainment in the new capital, the judges and the small band of Supreme Court lawyers with whom they were closely associated spent much of their leisure time at informal dinner parties and small social gatherings. Such a setting was ideally suited to Marshall's personality. If Jefferson was an aristocratic democrat, Marshall was a democratic aristocrat. Simple and unassuming in manners and dress, almost to the point of casualness, he had a genuine liking for all kinds of people, the humble as well as the well-born. Neither stiff nor overbearing, John Marshall was a gregarious man who loved to talk and joke with friends; political differences never interfered with personal relations. "I love his laugh," a thoroughly entranced Joseph Story once wrote, "it is too hearty for an intriguer,— and his good temper and unwearied patience are equally agreeable on the bench and in the study." [33]

The strength of Marshall's convictions and the force of his personality were reinforced by his political astuteness.

The Chief Justice acted cautiously during the intense political attack of the first Jefferson administration, and it is clear that Marshall often modified his own judicial position in order to conciliate the Court and thereby prevent the expression of opinions and decisions which he regarded as constitutionally dangerous.[34] One of his first steps upon assuming the chief-justiceship was to put an end to the practice by which justices announced their opinions seriatim, each delivering his own separate opinion when decisions were announced. In its place Marshall persuaded his colleagues to express their decisions through a collective Opinion of the Court, which he very often delivered himself. By unifying the Court behind a single opinion and by concurrently discouraging the filing of dissenting opinions by judges whose views were overruled in conference, Marshall gave the Court both the fact and the public appearance of institutional solidarity. Its effect was not lost on Jefferson, who repeatedly criticized the Marshall Court's practice of delivering as an order of the entire Court "an opinion . . . huddled up in conclave, perhaps by a majority of one, delivered as if unanimous, and with the silent acquiescence of lazy or timid associates, by a crafty chief judge, who sophisticates the law to his mind, by the turn of his own reasoning."[35]

Jefferson's ire was motivated more by his dislike of the Court's decisions expanding national powers at the expense of the states than by an abstract concern with its internal procedures. It is hard to believe that he would have taken offense at judicial decisions announced through single Opinions of the Court, if he believed the opinions stood for strict construction of the Constitution. But Jefferson was correct in sensing Marshall's enormous influence: during his long tenure the Chief Justice gave the Court's opinion in 519 out of 1,106 decisions, and he spoke for it in 36 of the approximately 60 cases involving major constitutional questions.[36]

In addition to the chief justice, the Supreme Court in 1809 had six associate justices. Three were Jefferson's appointees, but they rarely deserted Marshall. The most prominent was William Johnson, of South Carolina, the only judge to challenge the Chief Justice's opinions with some frequency. But even Johnson, who has acquired a reputation as the Court's "first dissenter," did not begin to dissent until the 1820's and then only after Jefferson's insistent prodding.[37] As a matter of fact, there were broad areas of agreement between the South Carolina Republican and his Federalist chief. Johnson was a firm, almost extreme, believer in natural law, and he never questioned the Court's right to review the constitutionality of legislation. Like Marshall, he valued private property and on at least one memorable occasion expressed a nationalistic interpretation of the Constitution that went far beyond Marshall's opinion for the Court.[38] And when Johnson, sitting in circuit court in 1808, ruled that certain directives issued by President Jefferson under the Embargo Laws of 1807 and 1808 were illegal, the Republicans were infuriated. Their newspapers assailed him, and Jefferson's Attorney General, Caesar Rodney, denounced Johnson as "the champion of all the high-church doctrines so fashionable on the Bench." "You can scarcely elevate a man to a seat in a Court of Justice," Rodney sputtered, "before he catches the leprosy of the Bench." [39]

Less distinguished and even more docile were Johnson's two Republican colleagues, Justices Henry Brockholst Livingston and Thomas Todd. Appointed in 1806, Livingston sat on the Court for seventeen years and wrote the majority opinion in only thirty-eight cases, none of which dealt with constitutional issues; he dissented but eight times.[40] Todd, a lawyer and politician from Kentucky, served from 1807 to 1826. He contributed but twelve opinions to the Court and differed from Marshall only once.[41]

Three Federalist judges sat with Marshall in 1809. Perhaps

the most distinguished was Bushrod Washington, a nephew of the first President. Washington was an able lawyer, but he was so closely identified with the Chief Justice that his own judicial personality has been obscured. As their colleague Justice Johnson observed, Marshall and Washington "are commonly estimated as one judge." [42] The other two judges were aging men near the end of their lives. Samuel Chase, a signer of the Declaration of Independence and once a prominent Maryland politician, had been discredited by impeachment charges against him that had grown out of his partisanship and his vindictive enforcement of the Sedition Act. Chase's best days lay behind him. Much the same thing can be said of William Cushing, who had passed on *Fletcher* v. *Peck* in circuit court. A high-toned Federalist, he had had a long political career in Massachusetts and had served for many years as the state's chief justice. But by 1809 Cushing, who is remembered as the last American judge to wear the full English wig, had been half-senile for a number of years.[43]

The Yazoo claimants saw to it that they were represented by able counsel in the proceedings before the Supreme Court. John Peck's side of the case, which argued for the validity of the Georgia sale of 1795 and the invalidity of the repeal act, was handled by John Quincy Adams and Robert Goodloe Harper. Harper, one of the original Yazooists, stood in the front rank of the lawyers of his day. Adams, a senator from Massachusetts, would soon attain even greater distinction as ambassador to czarist Russia, Secretary of State, and between 1825 and 1829 President of the United States. Robert Fletcher's side of the case, which challenged the validity of the sale and upheld the repeal act, was put in the hands of Luther Martin, of Maryland, one of the most prominent of the men who appeared regularly before the Supreme Court. Martin, whose career embraced law and politics, had once been a militant anti-Federalist. He was one of the few delegates to the Constitutional Convention of 1787 who fought the ratification of the Constitution; but he later had a complete change of political heart and embraced Federalism. Martin successfully defended Samuel Chase in the impeachment trial and, as one of the lawyers representing Aaron Burr in the famous Burr treason trial, made a sharp attack on the Jefferson administration. In a fit of anger Jefferson referred to him as an "unprincipled and impudent federal bull-dog," and the appellation stuck.[44]

Fletcher v. *Peck* was argued in the winter of 1809, but the Court refrained from deciding the basic issues. At the inaugural ball for President James Madison, Justice Livingston commented to John Quincy Adams on "the reluctance of the Court to decide the case at all, as it appeared manifestly made up for the purpose of getting the Court's judgment upon all the points"; Chief Justice Marshall made a similar comment to William Cranch, the Supreme Court reporter.[45] On March 11, 1809, the Supreme Court reversed the circuit court decision because it found a technical defect in the pleadings made by Peck's attorneys in the proceedings before the lower court. One of Fletcher's charges was that Peck had committed a breach of contract because he purported to convey land which the Georgia legislature lacked authority to sell. Peck's attorneys answered the charge by arguing that the Governor had been authorized to make the conveyance of land to the four Yazoo companies. In a brief opinion, Marshall declared that Peck's answer was legally insufficient: "The breach alleged is that the legislature had not authority to sell. The bar set up is, that the governor had authority to convey. Certainly an allegation, that the principal [the Georgia legislature] has no right to give a power, is not denied by alleging that he has given a proper power to the agent [the Governor]."[46]

According to the Adams diary, Marshall added an oral statement to his written opinion. On the question of Georgia's title to the lands and on the right of the legislature to sell, he announced that "if the opinion of the court had been against the defendant they would have given it." [47] In other words, Marshall let it be known that on two of the main questions the Supreme Court agreed with the Yazooists; but Peck's failure to argue the question properly forced the Court to rule against him. The Chief Justice also announced that "from the complexion of the pleadings they [the Court] could not but see that at the time when the covenants were made the parties had notice of the acts covenanted against." [48] Marshall's statement comes close to recognizing officially the collusive nature of *Fletcher* v. *Peck*. If the parties to the covenant knew of the acts they had so precisely covenanted against—if, that is, Fletcher and Peck were aware of the events in Georgia and their effect on the land titles—the contractual agreement in which Peck stipulated to Fletcher that no circumstances had invalidated the titles was a fictitious one arranged for the sole purpose of eliciting a judicial opinion.

John Marshall was never one to let legal technicalities stand in the way of reaching a decision, when he wanted to reach a decision, and it is hard to believe that Peck's defective pleading stopped the Chief Justice from deciding the case. Marshall himself hinted at another explanation. His oral remarks from the bench cited the "difficulties" caused by the presence of only five judges during the 1808 term, for Justices Chase and Cushing were ailing and absent.[49] If the Court intended to uphold the Yazooist position—Marshall's remarks, not to mention his deepest judicial and political values, clearly pointed in this direction—the decision would attract criticism. A ruling endorsed by all seven Justices might provide a somewhat greater protection against the kind of political attack which the Court had experienced earlier in the decade.[50]

Marshall, in fact, wanted to adjudicate *Fletcher* v. *Peck*.

Upon hearing his opinion of March 11 the attorneys for
Fletcher and Peck immediately agreed to amend the technical pleas, and the Court, instead of returning *Fletcher* v.
Peck to the circuit court, continued the case on its docket for
the next term. The speed with which the attorneys agreed
to change their pleas in the interest of obtaining a complete
decision provides still further evidence that the case was a
collusive suit engineered by the New England Mississippi
Land Company. On March 15 the two "sides" to the case
filed an "Agreement of Counsel" signed by Luther Martin
for Fletcher and by John Quincy Adams for Peck. One cannot read this document, reproduced here for the first time,
without acquiring a strong impression that the case lacked
any adversary quality and that it was put together in order
to get an advisory opinion from the Supreme Court:

In this case it is agreed between the parties, that all exceptions to
the pleadings shall be waived and the case submitted to the
Court, upon the Covenants contained in the plaintiff's [Fletch-
er's] declaration, and on the facts stated in the Special verdict—
And if the Court should be of opinion that on the 7th day of January 1795 the State of Georgia was not entitled to the lands
mentioned in the declaration—or that the Legislature of the said
State had no authority to sell and dispose of the lands—or that the
act of 7-January, 1795, and the grant issued under it, by the Governor of Georgia, as stated upon the record, were originally null
and void, or that the title conveyed by them, if any, has been legally and constitutionally impaired and rendered null and void, by
the rescinding act of 13. February 1796. recited upon the record,
then that the Judgment of the Circuit Court in favour of Peck
shall be reversed—But if the Court shall be of the opinion that
the title to the lands on the 7th of January 1795 was in the State
of Georgia; and that the Legislature of the said State had good
right to sell and dispose of the land; and that the act of that
date, and the grant under it were not originally null and void
and conv[eyed] the title of Georgia; and that the title conveyed
by them has not been legally and constitutionally impaired and

rendered null and void by the rescinding act of 13. February. 1796, then the Judgment of the Circuit Court in favour of Peck shall be affirmed.[51]

The case was re-argued in 1810 with an important change in counsel. John Quincy Adams, whom President Madison had appointed ambassador to Russia, was replaced by Joseph Story. Story's connections with the Yazooists were deep-rooted. His second wife, Sarah Waldo Wetmore, was a daughter of Judge William Wetmore of the Boston Court of Common Pleas; Judge Wetmore was one of the original investors in the New England Mississippi Land Company.[52] Story, in addition, had been a paid Washington lobbyist for the company since 1807. While he had directed his attention to Congress, he had also cultivated the Supreme Court. "The scene of my greatest amusement, as well as instruction, is the Supreme Court," Story wrote in 1808. "I daily spend several hours there, and generally, when disengaged, dine and sup with the judges."[53] Marshall and Story quickly formed a mutual admiration society, for their tastes in law, poetry, politics, and religion were remarkably congenial; a recent student of Story's early career is convinced that the two men discussed the Georgia claims.[54]

In their argument before the Court, Harper and Story defended Peck by asserting that Georgia possessed the lands in 1795 and that the legislature was authorized to sell them. Any improper influence used to secure passage of the act was no ground for questioning its validity. Moreover, they echoed the argument made by Harper in his Yazoo pamphlet of 1796 by contending that the legislature was powerless to revoke a grant: "It had no right to declare the law void; that is the exercise of a judicial, not a legislative function." Finally, Harper and Story claimed that the repeal act violated the federal Constitution because it impaired the obligation of a contract.[55]

Luther Martin's argument for Fletcher was half-hearted

and uninspired. The "federal bull-dog" was a toothless advocate in *Fletcher* v. *Peck,* and his mediocre performance fitted in with the requirements of a collusive case. So far as the records disclose, Martin's argument consisted of some brief remarks on the invalidity of Georgia's title to the land, the insufficiency of one of Peck's pleadings (the subject of Marshall's 1809 opinion), and the inadequacy of Peck's assertion that he was innocent of any flaw in the titles he conveyed to Fletcher. Martin, it is important to remember, was theoretically on the "Georgia side" of the case, the side which asserted the invalidity of the original land sale and defended the legitimacy of the repeal act. Yet he wholly ignored two of the most critical questions, whether the bribery made the Georgia law of 1795 a nullity and whether the repeal act violated the contract clause of the Constitution. In one way only was Luther Martin's argument notable: he was so drunk during its presentation that Marshall had the Court adjourn until the counsel regained his sobriety—the only recorded incident of its kind in Supreme Court history.[56]

V

John Marshall
Delivers an Opinion

On March 16, 1810, in one of the leading decisions of American constitutional law, Chief Justice John Marshall announced the decision of the Supreme Court in *Fletcher* v. *Peck* with an opinion that upheld the Yazooists on every disputed point. He ruled that Georgia in 1795 possessed the Yazoo lands and that, despite the alleged corruption of the legislature, the sale was valid and forever binding. As for the repeal act, the Marshall Court declared it to be in violation of the federal Constitution, primarily on the ground that it broke a contract between Georgia and the land companies and therefore overstepped the restriction of Article I, section 10, which prohibits state laws impairing the obligation of contracts. There were no dissents, though two justices, Chase and Cushing, did not participate; Justice Johnson supported the Yazoo claimants in a special concurring opinion.

The Chief Justice was irresistibly drawn to the Yazooist position both because of his principled convictions and, less consciously, because of his own personal interest. Ten years earlier, as a congressman from Virginia, Marshall had supported James Gunn's amendment to compensate the Yazoo claimants. His desire that government promote, and not disrupt, the stability of established interests in property was unmistakable. He was, his admiring biographer writes, "profoundly interested in the stability of contractual obligations. . . . No man in America could have followed with deeper anxiety the Yazoo controversy than did John Marshall." [1]

During the 1780's, as a legislator in the Virginia House of Delegates, he unsuccessfully opposed the policy of the state's Republican government, which encouraged its citizens to ignore the debts they owed to English creditors. Virginia refused to heed the Treaty of Peace (1783) between England and the United States by failing to repeal its wartime laws relieving Virginians of their English debts. This refusal, Beveridge writes, made a deep impression on Marshall: "The popular readiness to escape, if not repudiate contracted obligations, together with the whimsical capriciousness of the General Assembly, created grave misgivings in his mind." [2]

Marshall was especially disturbed by the casual manner in which the state legislatures of the Confederation period interfered with business and financial arrangements by passing laws that aided debtors. Some of the states, responding to economic fluctuations that had brought hardship to many farmers and small merchants, tried to ease the money shortage by printing a great volume of cheap paper currency and declaring that it was acceptable tender for the payment of debts contracted earlier in harder currency. They also used more direct methods to aid debtors at the expense of their creditors by passing stay laws that extended the time for discharging debts and by interfering in other ways with the contracts between creditors and debtors. [3]

In Marshall's view, as he wrote in 1807, all such efforts to meliorate the plight of debtors were "wild projects" whose only effect was an "instability in principles" that further depressed business conditions. These comments are from his *Life of George Washington*, and they may appropriately be taken as the historical underpinning of Marshall's opinion in *Fletcher* v. *Peck*. At one point, describing the history of the Confederation period, he wrote:

> At length, two great parties were formed in every state, which were distinctly marked, and which pursued distinct objects, with systematic arrangement.

The one struggled with unabated zeal for the exact observance of public and private engagements. By those belonging to it, the faith of a nation, or of a private man was deemed a sacred pledge, the violation of which was equally forbidden by the principles of moral justice, and of sound policy. The distresses of individuals were, they thought, to be alleviated by industry and frugality, not by a relaxation of the laws, or by a sacrifice of the rights of others. According to the stern principles laid down for their government, the imprudent and idle could not be protected by the legislature from the consequences of their own indiscretion, but should be restrained from involving themselves in difficulties, by the conviction that a rigid compliance with contracts would be enforced. They were consequently the uniform friends of a regular administration of justice, and of a vigorous course of taxation which would enable the state to comply with its engagements. By a natural association of ideas, they were also, with a very few exceptions, in favor of enlarging the powers of the federal government, and of enabling it to protect the dignity and character of the nation abroad, and its interests at home. The other party marked out for itself a more indulgent course. Viewing with extreme tenderness the case of the debtor, their efforts were unceasingly directed to his relief. To exact a faithful compliance with contracts was, in their opinion, a measure too harsh to be insisted on, and was one which the people would not bear. They were uniformly in favor of relaxing the administration of justice, of affording facilities for the payment of debts, or of suspending their collection, and of remitting taxes. . . . In many of the states, the party last mentioned constituted a decided majority of the people; and in all of them, it was very powerful. The emission of paper money, the delay of legal proceedings, and the suspension of the collection of taxes, were the fruits of their rule wherever they were completely dominant.

.   .   .   .

The restlessness produced by the uneasy situation of individuals, connected with lax notions concerning public and private faith, and erroneous opinions which confound liberty with an exemption from legal control, produced a state of things which alarmed all reflecting men, and demonstrated to many the indispensable necessity of clothing government with powers sufficiently ample for the protection of the rights of the peaceable and quiet, from the invasions of the licentious and turbulent part of the community.[4]

Marshall's partisan interpretation of the political forces active in the 1780's, with the nascent Federalists cast as the party of frugality, industry, and personal and public honor, and with the nascent Republicans cast as the party of indulgence, license, and repudiation of personal and public commitments, cannot withstand scholarly scrutiny.[5] But it is significant as a statement of how Marshall perceived the needs of established business and property interests. He was, moreover, convinced that the federal Constitution provided a defense against the kind of threat which he so vividly described. The new Constitution, he wrote, "was understood to prohibit all laws impairing the obligation of contracts," and this "had in a great measure restored that confidence which is essential to the internal prosperity of nations." [6]

John Marshall's innermost conviction that "public and private engagements" were "a sacred pledge" was reinforced by his personal problems as a land speculator. During the 1790's Marshall and his brother James bought 160,000 acres in Virginia known as the Fairfax lands after the British baron who had once owned them. The problem arose because the state of Virginia, claiming that its Revolutionary War confiscation acts nullified Fairfax's title, had sold the land to its citizens. But Fairfax's descendant challenged the legality of Virginia's confiscation and sold the land to speculators like the Marshall brothers. They contended that the Treaty of Peace, as well as the Jay Treaty of 1795, contained guarantees which protected the Fairfax lands from the effect of state confiscation laws. The question of which set of titles was valid, those recognized by Virginia or those under the Fairfax name, became urgent to the two brothers when the ubiquitous financier, Robert Morris, went bankrupt in

1798. Morris had underwritten their venture, and his bankruptcy put the full responsibility for completing the payments on the 160,000 acres on the shoulders of James and John Marshall. If the Fairfax title proved invalid, their own titles, acquired at a great financial sacrifice and risk, would be worthless.[7]

The Chief Justice, then, had good reasons for opposing state actions that disturbed original titles to property, whether expressed in the form of a Virginia law confiscating the lands of a British baron or in the form of a Georgia law rescinding grants of land sold to four companies of speculators. To say this is not to imply conscious dishonesty on his part, for even if Marshall had never heard of the Fairfax dispute, he almost certainly would have voted to uphold the Yazooists. While still a youth living in the half-wilderness of eighteenth-century Virginia, he had been weaned on the first American publication of Blackstone's *Commentaries,* the monumental legal treatise which extolled the virtues of vested rights in property. In common with an entire generation of lawyers, Marshall learned in Blackstone that "the free use, enjoyment, and disposal" of property is an "absolute right" inherent in every Englishman. "So great," Blackstone lectured, "is the regard of the law for private property, that it will not authorize the least violation of it; no, not even for the general good of the whole community." [8] All of Marshall's personal and political sympathies and close associations were with those who represented the interests of commercial and financial enterprises and who sought stability for vested property and business relationships. His own interest in the Fairfax lands dispute does not explain his reaction to the Yazoo controversy; it was simply one more event reinforcing his belief that the states needed a constitutional guardian—the Supreme Court—to prevent them from ceaselessly tampering with private property.

The opinion in *Fletcher v. Peck,* in short, was a statement of some of John Marshall's deepest convictions. While many of his judicial opinions reflect at least partial adjustment to the divergent views of the other justices, *Fletcher* v. *Peck* is vintage Marshall on the subject of the rights of property and the power of courts to review legislation. It is also an almost perfect example of Marshall at work as a constitutional logician who could brilliantly combine dogmatic assertion of first principles with ingenious and, as Jefferson charged, sometimes sophistical reasoning, all with an air of artlessness.

There are three main parts of lasting constitutional interest to the *Fletcher* v. *Peck* opinion, if one excludes a section in which Marshall concluded that in 1795 Georgia had title to the Yazoo lands. In the first part, he examined the validity of the Georgia sale act and found that nothing in the state constitution then in force prohibited the legislature from selling the western lands. Indeed, in upholding the law of 1795, the Chief Justice used self-effacing language:

The question, whether a law be void for its repugnancy to the constitution, is, at all times, a question of much delicacy, which ought seldom, if ever, to be decided in the affirmative, in a doubtful case. The court, when impelled by duty to render such a judgment, would be unworthy of its station, could it be unmindful of the solemn obligations which that station imposes. But it is not on slight implication and vague conjecture that the legislature is to be pronounced to have transcended its powers, and its acts to be considered as void. The opposition between the constitution and the law should be such that the judge feels a clear and strong conviction of their incompatibility with each other.[9]

Marshall's diffidence toward and respect for the Georgia legislature continue in the second part of the opinion, where he answers the contention that the sale act is inherently null because the legislators who voted for it had been bribed. That "corruption should find its way into the governments of our infant republics" and that "impure motives should contribute to the passage of a law," he wrote, "are circumstances most deeply to be deplored." But though deplorable, the principle that state acts could be overturned by courts because of the bad motives of their framers was unworkable. How does one evaluate the motives of legislators, and how much corruption would it take to nullify a law? "Must it be direct corruption, or would interest or undue influence of any kind be sufficient? Must the vitiating cause operate on a majority, or on what number of members?" Such probing of legislative motives, Marshall commented, would constitute "judicial interference." In any event, the case of Fletcher against Peck was a suit between two private parties, not an action instituted by Georgia herself to vacate the act of 1795. It would, therefore, be "indecent, in the extreme . . . to enter into an inquiry respecting the corruption of the sovereign power of a State."

Up to this point, Marshall had in effect upheld the Yazooist position—the sale, despite the corruption, was valid—but in a way that placed his Court in the best possible light. Marshall's words on the sovereignty of Georgia and the indelicacy of examining the motives of her legislators leave an impression of disingenuousness, but they provided the Court with a verbal shield against charges that it casually interfered in the affairs of the states. Whatever his own reasons, there was constitutional wisdom in the argument that courts lack the tools to probe the inner motives of legislatures; with only occasional exceptions, the modern Supreme Court, in passing on the constitutionality of legislation, does not attempt to do so.[10] The opening sections of the *Fletcher v. Peck* opinion also include a favorite Marshall device, his protest that the Court was reluctant to invalidate legislation. When the Chief Justice used language explaining how painful was the solemn obligation to void unconstitutional legislation, the opinion in which it appeared was sure to contain a declaration that a legislature had acted unconstitutionally. "It hurts us more than you," Marshall would seem to say and then proceed to administer the constitutional *coup de grâce*.[11]

In *Fletcher* v. *Peck* the blow came in the third main part of the opinion, where Marshall took up the subject of the Georgia repeal act. He began by accepting the point long urged by the Yazoo claimants, that the repeal act made them innocent victims. "If the original transaction was infected with fraud, these purchasers did not participate in it, and had no notice of it." As Marshall saw the events, the legislature had "annihilated" the property rights of innocent purchasers by repudiating the sale after its completion. If the legislature was to sit as judge in a case affecting its own interest, and thereby make a mockery of the separation of powers, at least "its decision should be regulated by those rules which would have regulated the decision of a judicial tribunal." And any court, Marshall argued, regardless of its conclusions about the alleged fraud practiced by James Gunn and the original speculators, would have been bound "by the clearest principles of equity, to leave unmolested those who were purchasers, without notice, for a valuable consideration."

How then could the Georgia legislature justify its refusal to heed "those rules of property which are common to all the citizens of the United States" and "those principles of equity which are acknowledged in all our courts"? Only, Marshall answered, by asserting the principle of unrestrained legislative power, "that a legislature may, by its own act, devest the vested estate of any man whatever, for reasons which shall, by itself, be deemed sufficient." The Chief Justice conceded that legislatures possessed great powers and that in general a legislature was free to repeal laws passed by a previous legislature. "But," he went on, "if an act be done under a law, a succeeding legislature cannot undo it." Georgia had made a conveyance of land; it had vested "absolute rights"; and if these could be recalled, so too could any right of any individual. John Marshall could accept no such principle of legislative omnipotence: "It may well be doubted whether the nature of society and of government does not prescribe some limits to the legislative power; and if any be prescribed, where are they to be found, if the property of an individual, fairly and honestly acquired, may be seized without compensation." Even if Georgia were a completely sovereign and independent state, the validity of its rescinding act would be in doubt because it broke down the separation of powers. An act taking the property of individuals and transferring it to the state was not, he suggested, "in the nature of the legislative power."

Georgia, of course, was not a sovereign and independent state. She was "a member of the American Union," and her actions were limited by the superior federal Constitution. Here Marshall introduces the most innovative part of his opinion, developing the idea that the original sale of lands to the Yazoo companies was a "contract," and that the repeal act, by attempting to undo it, violated the contract clause of the Constitution. A contract between two parties implies mutual obligations to perform certain actions, but in the case of Georgia and the land companies all actions had been completed by the time of the repeal act. The state, that is, had conveyed its lands and the speculators had made their payment. The contract clause of the Constitution forbids state laws "impairing the obligation of contracts," and Marshall argued that contracts were of two kinds, executory and executed. In an executed contract, such as the Georgia grant of land, there is a continuing obligation not to undo that which has been done. Just as a state was forbidden to release an individual from his obligation to repay a man who had lent him money, so too was a state forbidden to repeal a grant, to undo an "executed contract," that it had made.

In reaching this conclusion Marshall slid over the fact that those who framed and ratified the Constitution never gave even the slightest indication that the word "contract" in Article I, section 10, applied to anything but agreements made between private individuals to buy and sell goods or to borrow and repay money. Nor, with the possible exception of James Wilson, did anyone hint that a public grant had the character of a contract, much less that a state was subject to judicial restraint if it violated its own contracts.[12]

Yet, if these interpretations of the contract clause had not been affirmed in the proceedings of 1787–89, neither had they been denied. The contract clause, in fact, had attracted little attention, either in or out of the Convention. This gave Marshall his opening. Since, he wrote, "a fair construction of the constitution" required that grants be treated as a form of contracts, why should state grants be exempted from the prohibition of the clause? The clause itself, after all, drew no distinction between private and public contracts. Indeed, Marshall insisted, Article I, section 10, with its clauses prohibiting the states from passing bills of attainder, *ex post facto* laws, and laws impairing the obligation of contracts, had grown out of a fear of "violent" state acts. In adopting the Constitution, the people of the United States "manifested a determination to shield themselves and their property from the effects of those sudden and strong passions to which men are exposed." "What motive, then," he asked, "for implying in words which import a general prohibition to impair the obligation of contracts, an exception in favor of the right to impair the obligation of those contracts into which the State may enter?"

Marshall's answer, of course, was None, and he concluded that the Georgia repeal act was unconstitutional because it violated the contract clause. Less clearly, he also implied that the act was unconstitutional as a bill of attainder and an *ex post facto* law. The clauses against bills of attainder, legislative acts imposing punishments without benefit of a judicial trial, and *ex post facto* laws, legislative acts imposing punishments for actions that were legal when committed, were generally thought to apply only to criminal matters.[13] One scholar has made the apt comment that Marshall's vague references to these clauses are "principally indicative that he was uncertain as to precisely why the repeal act was invalid, although he was very sure it was invalid."[14] The Chief Justice summarized his case against the repeal act in these words: "It is, then, the unanimous opinion of the court, that, in this case, the estate having passed into the hands of a purchaser for a valuable consideration, the State of Georgia was restrained, either by general principles which are common to our free institutions, or by the particular provisions of the Constitution of the United States, from passing a law whereby the estate of the plaintiff in the premises so purchased could be constitutionally and legally impaired and rendered null and void."[15]

Although there were no dissents to the decision, Justice William Johnson gave a concurring opinion that rejected some parts of Marshall's reasoning.[16] "I do not hesitate to declare," the Court's leading Republican wrote, "that a state does not possess the power of revoking its own grants." But where Marshall had invalidated the repeal act on the twin grounds that it was contrary to general principles "common to our free institutions" and that it violated specific provisions of the Constitution, Johnson relied exclusively on natural law principles. "I do it," he declared, "on a general principle, on the reason and nature of things: a principle which will impose laws even on the Deity." So commanding were the laws of nature that even God, the ultimate creative force in the universe, was restrained by them. In Johnson's view the Georgia legislature, having conveyed the property, lost all control over it. The property was now vested in each purchaser and "intimately blended with his existence, as essentially so as the blood that circulates through his system."[17]

Johnson, however, sharply challenged Marshall's conclusion that the contract clause forbade Georgia's attempted repeal of the grant. He did not believe that the state's "obligation" continued once the grant had been made, and he feared that a broad interpretation of the clause would unduly restrict legitimate state powers. The states, Johnson argued, are continually passing beneficial laws that affect contracts by prescribing how they shall be authenticated, when suits may be instituted for noncompliance, and the conditions under which they lose their effect. There were, in addition, rare occasions when a state might have to seize individual property. As a consequence, it was unwise to restrict constitutionally, "in favor of property rights," the ultimate right of the states to act for a great public end. By this line of reasoning Johnson managed to have the best of both constitutional worlds: his opinion supported the claimants' argument that they had been victimized and thus added the endorsement of a prominent Republican judge to the pro-compensation policies of the Madison administration; at the same time he adhered to Jeffersonian orthodoxy regarding the importance of states' rights.

The suspicion that Johnson's opinion was a political document is reinforced by its concluding paragraph. He had been, he wrote, "very unwilling" to decide the case at all, because "it appears to me to bear strong evidence, upon the face of it, of being a mere feigned case." Nevertheless, "my confidence . . . in the respectable gentlemen who have been engaged for the parties, has induced me to abandon my principles, in the belief that they would never consent to impose a mere feigned case upon this court." Johnson's easy "confidence" is, at the very least, an expression of profound judicial naïveté. John Quincy Adams, Robert Harper, and Joseph Story, to be sure, were all "respectable gentlemen," but they were also men long identified with the Yazooists and deeply interested in getting a decision from the Supreme Court. Adams had consistently supported the claimants while in the Senate; Harper was himself an original Yazooist; and Story was a paid agent of the New England Mississippi Land Company. As for Fletcher's nominal attorney, Luther Martin, a Federalist whose sympathies probably lay with the claimants, his weak defense of Georgia's position is but another indication that the case was indeed collusive.[18]

Had Johnson wished, he could have made the question of collusiveness the focus of a damaging dissent and thereby further blackened the claimants' reputation, already under the heavy cloud of corruption. Johnson, no doubt, was sincerely disturbed by the fictitious nature of the case; otherwise he would not have mentioned it. But, as a judge very conscious of his Republicanism, he was also reluctant to write an opinion that might upset the quiet efforts of two Republican administrations, those of Jefferson and Madison, to settle the festering Yazoo controversy. Johnson's opinion, while preserving Republican (and his own) integrity, reflected the competing values within his mind.[19]

John Marshall's opinion in *Fletcher* v. *Peck* is a landmark in the constitutional history of the young republic; within its contours are to be found the essential doctrines which made the contract clause the leading bulwark of private property for over half a century.[20] It is also the first major decision striking down a state law for violating the federal Constitution, making the case a sort of "state" equivalent to the "federal" case of *Marbury* v. *Madison,* which seven years earlier had led the Court to assert its power to void congressional laws for unconstitutionality.[21] Yet, in spite of the great significance of *Fletcher* v. *Peck* as an innovating decision in American constitutional law, there was little that was original with Marshall in the opinion. The Chief Justice's strength lay in his knowing exactly what he wanted to accomplish in a decision and in being able to execute his objectives with an ingenious, if not always ingenuous, line of argument. Although it is obvious that Marshall's opinion was fed from a number of sources, such as Harper's *The Case of the Georgia Sales,* the heart of *Fletcher* v. *Peck* belonged to Alexander Hamilton. In Hamilton's brief opinion of 1796 are to be found the key elements of Marshall's opinion: the assertion that the repeal act violated "the first principles of natural justice and social policy" to the detriment of "innocent" purchasers, the contention that the Georgia grant was a legal contract, and the finding that the repeal act violated the contract clause.[22]

Marshall's interpretation of the contract clause had even been foreshadowed, though not spelled out, in earlier judicial decisions. In a 1795 circuit court case, *Van Horne's Lessee* v. *Dorrance,* Justice William Paterson ruled that a Pennsylvania law repealing an earlier state law that had confirmed the land title of certain settlers was unconstitutional. Paterson treated the first Pennsylvania law as a "contract" and claimed that its repeal defrauded the claimants of "rights ascertained, protected, and secured by the constitution and known laws of the land." "It impairs the obligation of a contract," he concluded, "and is therefore void."[23] The parallel with *Fletcher* v. *Peck* is evident. And Marshall himself, in an 1805 case that required the Court to construe a state law providing for the sale of land, spoke of the law as a "contract." Although, he wrote, "a state is a party, it ought to be construed according to those well established principles, which regulate contracts generally."[24]

The opinion which Chief Justice Marshall delivered on March 16, 1810, was, then, a constitutional landmark, but it was neither a revolutionary legal statement, nor, from the Yazooist point of view, an unexpected ruling. On the contrary, the New England Mississippi Land Company had correctly calculated the response of the federal courts. Not a single judicial vote, Federalist or Republican, was ever cast against its basic position. A miscalculation, of course, would probably have ended all hope of getting a compensation law through Congress. For the Yazooists had made the charge that the repeal act was illegal one of their central contentions, and they had thoroughly committed themselves to submitting the dispute to the Supreme Court. As it was, the decision in *Fletcher* v. *Peck* provided them with fresh ammunition, but it did not automatically end the long fight over the Yazoo claims.

VI

The "Arch-Fiend" Triumphs

John Peck proved to be a somewhat ungrateful litigant. He owed Robert Goodloe Harper $250 for his work on the case but delayed paying it for over two years. On June 9, 1810, Joseph Story informed his co-attorney that, while the legal expenses were "a concern of the whole Company, and they are taking measures to collect from all parties interested the money necessary to discharge a variety of incidental expenses," Peck had "very cheerfully" accepted his draft for $250. More than a year later, however, an embarrassed Story reported to Harper, "I have applied to him again & again & I regret to say that though he has promised fairly, he has never fulfilled." Finally, under the threat of a suit Peck paid his bill, including $14.37 in interest charges.[1]

If Harper had trouble collecting his legal fee, so did the Yazoo claimants have trouble in obtaining indemnification from Congress. *Fletcher* v. *Peck* was a major victory, but it did not provide them the dollars and cents they had been seeking for more than a decade.[2] Reaction to the Supreme Court's decision was subdued. The news columns in the public prints had largely been pre-empted by the "late foreign intelligence" on the Napoleonic Wars, which continually disrupted American trade, and by the accounts of America's deteriorating relations with Great Britain. The New York *Evening Post,* a Federalist newspaper, carried only a brief announcement of the Court's decision "in favor of the New England Land Company." [3] The *Columbian Centinel* of Boston carried a report by its Washington correspondent which expressed great satisfaction with the decision. Its editor commented, "We trust this judgment will have the effect to restore to a number of our distressed fellow citizens, the benefits of claims which they have for years been most unjustly debarred." Another Boston newspaper carried a notice of "a numerous Meeting of Citizens" holding Georgia claims which appointed "a committee of Five Gentlemen of the first respectability . . . to devise some system of arrangement, whereby the Proprietors might the most effectually avail themselves of the important decision of the *Supreme Judicial Court* of the *United States* upon the Question of these Claims." [4] William Duane's Philadelphia *Aurora,* which in past years had filled its columns with eloquent denunciations of the "Yazoo league," did not comment on *Fletcher* v. *Peck.*[5] Such leading southern newspapers as the *Richmond Enquirer* and the *Savannah Republican* reprinted the full text of Marshall's opinion but without editorial comment.[6]

In Congress John Randolph of Roanoke asked his colleagues to take note of "a judicial decision of no small importance" concerning the Yazoo claims. He feared that "an abandonment on the part of the House of an examination of [the ruling] . . . would wear the appearance abroad of acquiescence in that judicial decision on their part." [7] For the normally vitriolic Randolph these remarks were a model of restraint and can probably be explained by Randolph's friendship with John Marshall. The two Virginians, both landed aristocrats, never clashed over the Yazoo sale, though one made opposition to it the *cause célèbre* of his life and the other defended it with the best legal rhetoric at his command.[8] George M. Troup, of Georgia, a young firebrand who had been a protégé of James Jackson, was much sharper than Randolph in his comments. Marshall's opinion,

Troup declared, was one "which the mind of every man attached to Republican principles must revolt at."[9] A year later, Troup helped defeat a Senate bill that would have permitted as few as three Supreme Court justices, instead of the legally required four, to hear cases. Asserting, in reference to *Fletcher* v. *Peck,* that five judges had given away eighty million dollars of public property, Troup argued that he was unwilling to confide such power on an even smaller number of judges. Although it had easily passed the Senate (23 to 2), the judiciary bill was postponed in the House by a vote of 89 to 22. With the exception of two Virginians, every southern representative voted, in effect, to kill the bill; the anti-Yazooist undertones were obvious.[10] Its rejection forced the Court, whose membership was depleted because of illness and an unfilled vacancy, to adjourn its 1811 term.[11]

From Monticello came the rumblings of Thomas Jefferson. Writing to President Madison two months after the decision, he criticized Marshall's "twistifications" in "the late Yazoo case" as an example of "how dexterously he can reconcile law to his personal biases" and of "the cunning and sophistry within which he is able to enshroud himself." [12] But the displeasure expressed by the Sage of Monticello was more a general criticism of John Marshall than part of any major political attack on the Court because of its decision in *Fletcher* v. *Peck*. Jefferson himself as President favored an indemnification of the claimants, and so did James Madison.

While southern opposition made it exceedingly difficult to get Congress to enact positive legislation compensating the claimants, the extent and intensity of anti-Yazooist feeling should not be exaggerated. There is, for instance, no evidence that, as some writers suggest, the Yazoo issue and Marshall's opinion profoundly stirred public opinion.[13] After all, 1810 was fifteen years removed from the original Georgia sale. The nation was preoccupied, not with the claims of a New England land company, but with Napoleon's Berlin and

Milan Decrees, making the British Isles off limits to neutral shipping and making violators subject to French seizure, and with the British Orders in Council. In the background was a growing clamor from the War Hawks, who demanded that Madison abandon his peace policy, join the issue with England, and seize Canada, which they fancied a ripe and easily plucked plum. Finally, the decision in *Fletcher* v. *Peck* enjoyed the support of a well-organized group of land speculators backed up by virtually all of New England's politicians. Not surprisingly, they soon renewed the campaign for a federal compensation law.

The Yazooist drive got off to a good start early in 1813, when the Senate, by a majority of nearly 2 to 1, passed a bill allocating five million dollars to the claimants. The money was to come from the sale of five million acres which the Georgia–United States agreement of 1802 had reserved in case Congress should consent to an indemnification.[14] But a real obstacle to the bill's passage lay in the House, where George M. Troup, of Georgia, replaced John Randolph as the leading opponent of the New England Mississippi Land Company.[15] Along with William H. Crawford, senator and presidential candidate in 1824, Troup controlled the powerful political machine built by their sponsor, James Jackson. Anti-Yazooism was still good politics in Georgia, and it blended imperceptibly with the attachment that many Southerners had to the doctrine of states' rights. George Troup, it might be added, was a conscientious, indeed, fanatical, states' righter. As governor (1823–27) he successfully defied the federal government and illegally seized Creek Indian lands within the state. At other times he opposed rechartering the Bank of the United States and in 1830 upheld South Carolina's attempted nullification of the "Tariff of Abominations"; Troup went so far as to advocate secession because of the federal "aggression." He later opposed the Compromise of 1850 and advocated the development of arsenals, munitions plants, and military schools to safeguard southern rights.[16]

As soon as the Senate bill reached the House in the winter of 1813, Troup moved its rejection, arguing that it contained "a principle destructive of republican government," because it rewarded those who had corrupted the legislature and defrauded the people.[17] "We say, no!" Troup exclaimed. "Let ruin overtake the corrupters of the Representatives of the people and all claiming under them." But Troup directed most of his fire against the Supreme Court. Congress, he urged, had repeatedly turned the claimants back by taking the simple and just position that, since the Yazoo act was a fraudulent contract, it conferred no rights upon the original purchasers and none therefore on the later purchasers.[18] "Seeing you firm and inflexible," the Georgia Congressman charged, "they turned about and addressed themselves to the Judiciary." The speculators, he continued, arranged a fictitious case and procured a decision identical to the one they themselves would have given had they sat on the Supreme Court:

. . . it is proclaimed by the Judges, and is now to be sanctioned by the Legislature, that the Representatives of the people may corruptly betray the people, may corruptly barter their rights and those of their posterity, and the people are wholly without any kind of remedy whatsoever. . . . If, Mr. Speaker, the arch-fiend had in the bitterness of his hatred to mankind resolved the destruction of republican government on earth, he would have issued a decree like that of the judges; he would have said, in the spirit and language of this bill, let the claimants under the corrupters of the Representatives of the people be rewarded.

The principal reply to Troup was given by Representative John A. Harper, of New Hampshire, a Republican who had been elected to the Twelfth Congress as a "War Hawk."[19] Harper argued that the Senate bill was predicated on the wise legal principles that a fraudulent contract could not be set aside to the injury of innocent persons and that the New England claimants, in purchasing land under the Georgia act of 1795, had done no more than extend "full faith and credit" to the acts of a state government, as the Constitution bade them do. He invoked the Supreme Court's decision, cleverly emphasizing that, if states' righters objected to the ruling, they would do well to remember that it was the product of a Jeffersonian Court:

> It was upon these principles that, in the important case of Fletcher vs. Peck, (VI Cranch's Reports, 87,) before the Supreme Court of the United States, that final tribunal decided, and unanimously, (where a majority of the judges on the bench were Republicans, appointed by Jefferson, "the Father of Democracy,") that the title to all these lands was, by law, in the innocent purchasers, who now offer to receive one-eighth of the value in stock, bottomed on the lands alone, without in the least interfering with or entangling any other fund of the nation.[20]

He also played on the widows-and-orphans theme, insisting that many of the claimants were now those "who, in consequence of these contracts, innocently entered into on the part of their deceased husbands and parents, have been driven from a state of ease and affluence to that of wretchedness and misery."

But the most important parts of his address were the introduction of two new considerations in favor of a settlement. The first was the desire of the Mississippi Territory to organize itself as a state and be admitted to the Union. Nearly 40,000 settlers (who had purchased their title from the federal government) lived in the territory carved out of the Yazoo lands, and they were represented in Congress by a nonvoting delegate who constantly lobbied for statehood. Yet statehood and the immediate personal interests of the territory's inhabitants required a settlement of the Yazoo claims. For so long as the claimants asserted their titles, whose legitimacy was now confirmed by the Supreme Court, immigration into the territory would be discouraged and the people already there would live under a pall of uncertainty over their right to the land they were tilling. The law passed by Congress in 1807 prevented the Yazoo claimants from trying to eject resident settlers through legal proceedings in the territorial courts.[21] Once Mississippi became a state, however, she would acquire federal courts with full jurisdiction to hear ejectment actions. The question of the Mississippi titles, Harper warned, would again come before the Supreme Court, "and the whole country will be in dispute."

Second, the New Hampshire congressman obliquely, but nonetheless unmistakably, suggested that settlement of the Yazoo claims was necessary to appease New England, which had long suffered because of the embargo and non-importation policies directed against the warring British and French nations. With the coming of the War of 1812 and the further disruption of commerce the grievances of the region's merchants intensified. Hard-shell old Federalists spoke of states' rights in language worthy of Thomas Jefferson at the time of the Virginia and Kentucky Resolutions, and there was even loose talk in some quarters about secession. Against this background Representative Harper insisted that the ruling in *Fletcher* v. *Peck* gave the claimants a constitutional right to compensation. If Congress, he argued, failed to pass a compensation law, it would in effect annul the Supreme Court's decision, threaten the integrity of the Constitution, and strike another blow at New England interests. The consequences would be serious:

... when a section considers any portion of its citizens oppressed or treated with severity, that section will lose a part of its confidence. From this want of confidence will arise actual distrust and jealousy, and from these feelings an indisposition to the public service, with some chances of eventual resistance. These natural operations of the mind furnish, in some part, an explanation of the causes of irritation, which exist in the North.

Remove the cause, by allowing to injured and virtuous citizens those rights to which they are entitled, as well by the rule of morality and equity as by your laws, and you lay a foundation for the restoration of confidence, and a consequent unity of action. To be sure, there are other causes of irritation, in their opinion; and, by this measure, full confidence might not be regained, but certainly one of the great obstacles to national harmony would be destroyed.

Later in his speech Harper again made the same point, citing the social contract theory so familiar to Americans of the Revolutionary generation. "You cannot be ignorant," he declared, "that when the rights of a portion of people, belonging to any section, are withheld, they are absolved from the obligations resulting from the social compact." The lesson was clear: appease the Yazooists and mute New England's disaffection with the federal policies; ignore their just constitutional rights and contribute to the possible breakup of the Union.

The new strength in the Yazooist position showed in the House vote, even though the Twelfth Congress failed to enact a compensation law. Troup's motion to defeat the Senate bill was defeated by a vote of 59 to 55. While 38 representatives from southern and border states joined Troup, 15 from this region voted against it, including 7 representatives from Virginia and the Carolinas. By contrast, 27 New Englanders opposed the Troup motion; only 2 defected.[22] Despite the Yazooist gains, the House voted 63 to 48 in favor of a motion by Speaker Henry Clay to table the bill until the next session because "there was not time to discuss the subject fully during the present limited session, without neglecting business of immediate and pressing importance."[23]

Encouraged by their strong showing, the Yazooists continued their campaign in the Thirteenth Congress. The New England Mississippi Land Company submitted a new petition, pushing hard on the theme that they were "innocent victims." They also picked up the argument made by Representative Harper in the previous session. In purchasing the Georgia lands, the claimants had "only performed the duty enjoined by the Constitution to give full faith and credit to public acts of other States." Nor did the company's agents neglect the ruling in *Fletcher* v. *Peck*, contending that the repeal act violated the contract clause of the Constitution, "the supreme law of the land." [24] The Yazooist prospects, already strengthened by New England's unrest over the War of 1812 and the unsettling effect of *Fletcher* v. *Peck* on land titles in the Mississippi Territory, were further improved when John Randolph lost his congressional seat in the fall election of 1812 to John W. Eppes, one of Jefferson's sons-in-law. Eppes had deliberately moved into Randolph's district in order to capitalize on the loss of popularity suffered by Randolph for his bitter attacks on Madison's decision to use armed force against Great Britain. [25]

On February 28, 1814, the Senate again passed a five-million-dollar compensation bill, this time by the largest margin ever: 24 to 8. Eleven senators from southern and border states voted in favor of compensation, including Virginia's William Branch Giles. In fact, Giles, a doctrinaire Jeffersonian of the states' rights school, had once been vehemently opposed to the claims. No man from Virginia, he told John Quincy Adams in 1805, "who should give any countenance to the proposed compromise, could obtain an election after it." [26] When the Senate bill reached the House, it was referred to a select committee. The proposed compromise required the claimants to waive their titles to the Yazoo lands; in return they became eligible for United States stock certificates (not bearing interest) in amounts proportionate to their claimed holdings. Up to five million dollars was made available for the compensation. Agents for the New England

Mississippi Land Company assured the committee that the claimants would accept this compromise, and the House committee recommended passage of the bill. Although, it reported, the "strict legality" of the claimants' title was in doubt, "the committee cannot forbear remarking that that title appears to have all the sanction which can be derived from a solemn decision of the highest judicial tribunal known to our laws." In the committee's view the compromise was desirable for two basic reasons: the claimants were innocent purchasers who deserved some compensation; and it would help clear up the confused claims in the Mississippi Territory, thereby encouraging its "quiet and speedy settlement." [27]

While Congress considered the Yazoo bill the press debated its merits. One newspaper fervently opposed to the compromise referred its readers to the arguments of George M. Troup, "vigorous and manly champion of virtue and honesty from Georgia." His speeches, the *Baltimore Whig* declared, would convince all honest men that "the Yazoo men . . . have no claim, either in equity or in justice, to an acre of the land in question." It attacked Congressman Robert Wright, a former Republican governor of Maryland who warmly supported compensation in the debates of 1813 and 1814, for asserting principles that "are not the principles of a republican." [28] On the other hand, to that old Federalist Boston newspaper, the *Columbian Centinel,* "the justice of the measure must be apparent to everyone not willfully blind." [29] But other Federalist journals saw the compensation bill as a crude attempt to "bribe" those interested in Yazoo lands "into an acquiescence in and support of the measures of the present [Madison] administration." "Is there," the *Repertory* of Boston asked, "to be no end to corruption? Men of Massachusetts, reflect—justice was evaded or denied until it could be used as an instrument for the destruction of your liberties." [30]

Equally interesting in revealing the subtle changes in sentiment on the Yazoo question are the views of two leading Republican newspapers, the Philadelphia *Aurora* and the Washington *National Intelligencer*. In an editorial on March 12, 1814, the *Aurora* lamented the fact that, with the nation at war with Great Britain, Congress had to concern itself again with "the transcendent iniquity of the Yazoo speculation." Yet William Duane's *Aurora,* evidently weary of the subject, engaged in no more than mild opposition to the compensation bill, just enough to satisfy the conscience of its outspoken editor. On March 15 the *Aurora* commented on an editorial in the anti-Yazoo *Baltimore Whig* which had expressed wonderment "at the silence of the republican papers on the subject." Although, the Philadelphia newspaper replied, its opinion of "the old affair" remained unchanged, "we only hope that the Yazoo question will now in some shape or other be settled forever." [31] The influential *National Intelligencer,* a paper closely identified with Madison's administration, took an essentially similar position. It characterized the Yazoo claims as "suspicious," but saw some good in the impending settlement of the issue:

. . . we shall at least have to congratulate ourselves that it no longer shall be, as it has for years been, the apple of discord in the national legislature. It is impossible to think without the utmost abhorrence on the corruption in which this transaction was engendered. We find, however, among the supporters of this bill in the Senate, many names of those who have in time past been decidedly adverse to [compensation]. . . . On their votes the decision in the supreme court has probably had considerable effect. [32]

The last of the many Yazoo debates took place in the House during March, 1814, and it followed predictable lines. Once again George Troup, who led the resistance to the Senate bill, covered familiar ground. [33] The New Englanders, he charged, lied in claiming to be innocent purchasers. Not only were they well aware of the original fraud, which automatically voided the sale act, but they should have realized that, corruption or no corruption, the Georgia legislature never had authority to sell in the first place. American government, Troup argued, is limited government, and the Georgia constitution of 1789 simply did not authorize the legislature to sell the state's western lands.[34] The Yazoo purchasers should have known that the sale was inherently unconstitutional, for all Americans were expected to be instant constitutional experts on both the federal and state constitutions. "Every man," he asserted, "is presumed to carry the Constitution in his head or in his pocket, that he may at all times be ready to compare the acts of Government with the Constitution."

As for the Supreme Court decision, Troup argued that *Fletcher* v. *Peck* was a feigned case worthy of no respect from Congress. If the Yazoo bill passed, it would confirm the "shocking" doctrine that, in a case made up between the speculators, the public property of the United States could be taken away. And it would do also "that which the God of Heaven himself cannot do—legalize fraud and corruption." In a passage worthy of the fallen John Randolph, Troup depicted the circle of fraud which anti-Yazooists saw at every turn of the ancient dispute: "Do not believe, sir, that the corruption in which this transaction was engendered was a corruption of any ordinary character; it was a corruption without example in history; may it never find a parallel! Not merely were the corrupted corrupted by the corrupters—the corrupters cheated the corrupted—the corrupters cheated one another, and the corrupters, as they say, cheated these claimants." Another congressman who sided with Troup, John W. Eppes, of Virginia, declaimed that "Polyphemus in his den, wallowing in human gore, was not a more odious and detestable animal than a Yazoo speculator."[35]

Those who defended the compensation bill spoke less

emotionally and made their points systematically. Robert Wright, of Maryland, argued that it would be ridiculous to reject a compromise costing in effect five million acres when the Supreme Court had ruled that the entire Yazoo tract belonged to the claimants. He also called attention to the special importance of compensating the claimants because of their geographical concentration in New England, and he noted that the compromise had been recommended by James Madison, now President of the United States.[36] William Irving, of New York, argued the desirability of promoting the settlement of the Mississippi Territory. He also made the novel suggestion that, contrary to the arguments of Randolph and Troup, the Yazoo claims had shed their sinful origin: because of their transfer to new purchasers and to the descendants of the original claimants, the claims were becoming "more and more innocent, more and more entitled to relief." [37] In two speeches, the territorial delegate from Mississippi, William Lattimore, urged passage of the Senate bill, insisting that the future of Mississippi was at stake because the disputed claims covered two-thirds of its territory. Lattimore predicted that there would be actions of ejectment as soon as a court with federal jurisdiction began operation; the claimants, he feared, "will harass us by law, and ultimately evict us of our lands." [38]

On March 26, 1814, the Yazooists' long patience, or what Troup called their "teasing and worrying" of Congress,[39] was finally rewarded. By a small majority of 81 to 76 the compensation bill passed the House. Sixteen southern and border state representatives voted with 65 northerners, including 38 New Englanders, in favor of compensation. Forty-six representatives from the southern and border states and 30 northerners, but only 1 New Englander, opposed the bill.[40] The Senate concurred in some minor House amendments, and on March 31, 1814, President Madison signed the compensation bill into law.

A comment is in order concerning the 30 anti-Yazoo

votes from northern states. Twenty of these were supplied by Pennsylvania, and this continued a pattern that began in 1800, when a majority of congressmen from the Keystone State voted against the Yazoo claimants.[41] The reason for this striking deviation from the overwhelming support for the claimants demonstrated by all other northern states is not absolutely clear, but the explanation probably lies in two circumstances. First, Pennsylvania was the most consistently Republican of the northern states. Its dominant Republican party was primarily built around skilled workingmen within Philadelphia and farmers in the rural areas; neither group was likely to have much sympathy for the difficulties of land speculators. Second, William Duane's staunchly anti-Yazooist Philadelphia *Aurora,* one of the most important Republican newspapers in the country (the other was the Washington *National Intelligencer*), exerted a strong influence on Pennsylvania politics. Duane was allied with another state leader, Michael Leib, and between them they largely dominated the faction-ridden Pennsylvania Republican party in the early 1800's. Both men saw themselves as embodiments of the Republican spirit of '98, as men who at no small risk had fought for liberty in the trying days of the Alien and Sedition Acts, and they were sympathetic to John Randolph. Although Duane and Leib never quite dared to follow Randolph into opposition against Jefferson (this would have played into the hands of their local opponents), they were undisguised enemies of the Pennsylvanian Albert Gallatin, who figured prominently in the Jefferson and Madison administrations and, as federal commissioner, had recommended compensating the claimants. Eventually, too, the Duane-Leib faction opposed President Madison. The state's political currents, however, are not easily fathomed. Between 1804 and 1806 Duane's *Aurora* violently attacked Postmaster General Gideon Granger for his Yazooist lobbying. Yet in 1814, Granger, who was on the verge of dismissal from

Madison's cabinet, appointed Leib to the important post-mastership of Philadelphia, a move warmly applauded by Duane.[42]

To George Troup the passage of the Yazoo bill marked the triumph of the "arch-fiend," but to the *Columbian Centinel* it was, as summarized in a small headline, an act "Reviving Justice." [43] After twenty years the issue which John Randolph once called "the Alpha . . . the head of the divisions among the republican party" had been settled.[44] There was, finally, an underlying North-South *quid pro quo* written into the Yazoo settlement: New England, as Henry Adams wrote, received a "palliative" to assuage its economic suffering caused by the War of 1812; [45] and the South, now that the confused titles in the Mississippi Territory had been cleared up, was rewarded with the addition of a new slave state, as Mississippi entered the Union in 1817.

Under the terms of the compensation law the claimants were required to file legal documents releasing their claims to the former Georgia lands.[46] Five million dollars' worth of United States stock certificates, obtained by the sale of the five-million-acre tract of Yazoo land reserved for possible compensation in the Georgia–United States agreement of 1802, were reserved for the claimants. Yazooists who might still have a hankering for actual land in the region were allowed to exchange their stock certificates for holdings in the Mississippi Territory.[47] Finally, the law designated the Secretary of State, the Secretary of the Treasury, and the Attorney General as a board of commissioners to administer the settlement.

Four years after the passage of the law the Treasury Department issued a final statement of the awards made by the commissioners. A total of $4,282,151.12 was disbursed, most of it going to persons and interests based in New England.[48] The New England Mississippi Land Company received $1,077,561.73 for redistribution among its shareholders. The Union Bank of Boston was awarded $82,354.21, and the trustees of another Boston enterprise received $157,959.95. Sums of varying size were also granted directly to prominent Massachusetts Yazooists. Thus George Blake received $2,857.14; James Lloyd, $9,150.27; Samuel Dexter, $67,104.22; and William Sullivan, $14,880.94; the estate of Samuel Sewall was awarded $13,771.45; and that of James Sullivan, $9,150.47. Massachusetts merchants were not the only ones to reap the long-awaited compensation: among the successful claimants were such prominent New England businessmen as John C. Nightingale and William Williamson, of Connecticut, and Jonathan and Welcome Arnold and Samuel Ward, of Rhode Island.

Although the enactment of the compensation law ended the stormy dispute, the Yazoo issue left a significant imprint on the American Constitution. Great political conflicts often stimulate a sort of constitutional fallout which gives a new veneer to the Constitution's provisions. And, in turn, the new constitutional meanings help to shape the outcome of subsequent disputes that find their way into the judicial arena. The struggle between James Jackson and the Yazoo land companies and later between John Randolph and the New England Mississippi Land Company was of course involved with personal and political motives, not with an abstract concern for constitutional theory. Yet because of this conflict—and particularly because the Yazooists correctly perceived that they could obtain a favorable judicial ruling which would be a useful weapon for their side—the Supreme Court of Chief Justice John Marshall was given the opportunity to decide *Fletcher* v. *Peck*. The resulting interpretation of the contract clause, as well as the assumptions underlying Marshall's opinion, was for a long time a sturdy influence in the law and politics of the American Constitution.

VII

Fletcher v. *Peck* and American Constitutional Law

Chief Justice Marshall's interpretation of the contract clause in the decision in *Fletcher* v. *Peck* provided the first great constitutional mechanism for protecting vested property rights. During the Marshall period the contract clause became, to use one scholar's apt phrase, a vital "link between capitalism and constitutionalism."[1] The entrepreneurial capitalists, with their banking and corporate ventures, sought legal protection against legislative interference; for many years they found it in Article I, section 10, of the Constitution. Until near the end of the nineteenth century the contract clause was the major constitutional limitation on state legislatures in a period when the states were the source of most laws regulating business interests.[2] Between 1810 (the year of *Fletcher* v. *Peck*) and 1889 the contract clause was invoked in almost 40 per cent of all cases challenging the validity of state legislation. In seventy-five decisions, nearly half of the total number voiding state laws, it was the justification for declaring the legislation unconstitutional.[3] Constitutionally, the nineteenth century was the century of the contract clause.

The historical significance of *Fletcher* v. *Peck* is not only that it was first in a long line of contract cases, but that its assumptions fathered the key doctrines under which its successors were decided. Specifically, *Fletcher* v. *Peck* contained three conclusions that became dogma in the subsequent cases.

The first was that public grants, as well as contracts between purely private parties, were subject to the limitations of the contract clause. On this point the Constitution was silent, and there is little evidence in either the proceedings of the Constitutional Convention of 1787 or the state ratifying conventions that those who framed and adopted the contract clause were thinking of legislative grants when they forbade the states to pass laws "impairing the obligation of contracts." [4] In fact, the evidence, which is sketchy, points the other way: the clause was intended to prevent states from changing the terms of private contracts by allowing debtors to pay their creditors with something less than the hard currency in which the debt had been contracted. [5] John Marshall's opinion, however, interpreted the constitutional silence to mean not the exclusion of state contracts but their inclusion. The words of the Constitution, he argued, contain no distinction between public and private contracts, and to make one would do "violence . . . to the natural meaning of words." [6] "Contract," moreover, was in Marshall's view defined broadly. It included not only *executory* contracts to do something in the future but also *executed* contracts, such as past legislative grants that could not be subsequently undone.

The second major assumption of *Fletcher* v. *Peck,* although implicit, was nevertheless unmistakably clear. The Court's decision elevated vested property to a position of primacy in the hierarchy of American constitutional values. In the eyes of Marshall and his colleagues the sin of the Georgia repeal act was its attempt to take away property already vested in private hands. It was constitutionally sinful because, in adopting the Constitution, "the people of the United States . . . manifested a determination to shield themselves and their property from the effects of those sudden and strong passions to which men are exposed." [7] The shield of course—"a bill of rights for the people of each state," Marshall called it—was Article I, section 10, with its prohibitions against bills of attainder, *ex post facto* laws, and laws impairing the obligation of contracts. Property rights and human liberty, in short, were inseparable. The idea was made even clearer in Justice Johnson's concurring opinion, where he spoke of private property as being an intimate part of the owner's existence, "as essentially so as the blood that circulates through his system." [8]

In consequence, legislative acts interfering with an individual's property or diminishing its value were constitutionally suspect, and this led to the third main contribution of *Fletcher v. Peck,* the instrumental conclusion that courts had a duty to void state laws tampering with either private or public contracts. Marshall's opinion, to be sure, made much of the great "delicacy" of voiding a law, but it did not flinch from the "solemn obligation" to declare the repeal act unconstitutional. Together, these three assumptions —the inclusion of public grants under the limitations of the contract clause, the primacy of vested property as a constitutional value, and the judicial duty to void legislative impairments of contract rights—summarize one of the most influential doctrines of American constitutionalism. Edward S. Corwin called it the "Doctrine of Vested Rights." "Setting out with the assumption that the property right is fundamental," Corwin wrote, it "treats any law impairing *vested rights,* whatever its intention, as a bill of pains and penalties, and so, void." [9] This doctrine, which was fully asserted for the first time in the case that grew out of the Yazoo land fraud, dominated American constitutional law during much of the nineteenth century and the first third of the twentieth.

For approximately a decade after *Fletcher* v. *Peck* it seemed as if the contract clause would be expanded infinitely. In 1812 the Marshall Court ruled that a tax exemption granted by New Jersey on a tract of land, which the state had conveyed to a band of Delaware Indians in return for their relinquishing claims to other lands, could never be alienated. Although the Indians later sold the land to white purchasers and moved on to New York, the Court unanimously held that the tax exemption had the status of a contractual right; it attached to the land, and a New Jersey law repealing the exemption was unconstitutional.[10] A further expansion of the contract clause occurred in the *Dartmouth College Case*. Speaking through Chief Justice Marshall, the Court in 1819 declared unconstitutional a New Hampshire law that changed the terms of the college charter granted by the King of England in 1769 and established a new college government more subject to state control. Charters of incorporation, Marshall's opinion declared, were contracts whose terms could not be changed by the state without violating the Constitution.[11] More important than the fate of the small college in the wilderness was the utility of the *Dartmouth College* doctrine to the new corporate enterprises: it provided corporate property with a valuable constitutional guarantee against legislative interference.

The same year as the *Dartmouth College* decision the Marshall Court also held that, while the states might enact bankruptcy laws, such laws could not free bankrupt debtors of obligations contracted *prior* to the passage of the laws. To rule otherwise, Marshall claimed, would allow debtors to break contracts at the expense of their creditors.[12] And in *Green* v. *Biddle* (1823) the Court pushed the contract clause yet further. It ruled that a "compact" entered into between Kentucky and Virginia under the provisions of the Constitution was a "contract" that in effect limited a state's sovereignty. Kentucky's land was overlaid with contradictory claims, many of which were in the hands of absentee Virginians who had acquired their titles in the days when Virginia

AMERICAN CONSTITUTIONAL LAW

owned the land and casually sold it and resold it to its citizens. Although the Virginia-Kentucky Compact, which the two states signed when Kentucky became a separate state, recognized the validity of the earlier Virginia land titles, the new state confronted a land situation so chaotic that it soon felt compelled to enact a series of occupying claimants laws favoring those claimants actually settled on Kentucky land. These laws, the Supreme Court declared when a Virginia claimant challenged them, violated the "contract" between Virginia and Kentucky and were therefore invalid, a ruling which stimulated great bitterness in Kentucky.[13]

Green v. *Biddle* represents the furthest expansion of the principles first enunciated in *Fletcher* v. *Peck*, but it also marks the beginning of limitations on the contract clause. Kentucky effectively defied the ruling, and within a few years the Court itself changed course and recognized the validity of the occupying claimants laws.[14] Similarly, in 1827 the Court refused to follow the implications of *Sturges* v. *Crowinshield* by ruling that a state could legitimately adopt bankruptcy laws which applied to contracts entered into *after* the passage of the laws. In such cases, it held by a 4-to-3 vote in *Ogden* v. *Saunders*, the laws were in effect a part of the contract, for the creditor and the debtor knew that their agreement was governed by the bankruptcy laws.[15] Chief Justice Marshall dissented: it was his first and only dissent in a constitutional case, and it symbolized his diminished power on the Court, which by the 1820's was dominated by Republican justices. Even the 1819 ruling in *Sturges* v. *Crowinshield* had been at most a limited victory for Marshall's expansive interpretation of the contract clause. Justice Johnson, who voted with the majority in *Ogden* v. *Saunders*, revealed that in the earlier case Marshall had wanted to deny absolutely any state power to pass laws freeing bankrupt debtors from their financial obligations. Since he was unable to carry a unanimous Court for this proposition, Marshall agreed to a decision that prohibited only bankruptcy laws affecting previously negotiated contracts and left open the question of whether the Constitution forbade state bankruptcy laws affecting anterior contracts. That judgment, Johnson said in 1827, partook "as much of a compromise as of a legal adjudication." [16]

By 1830 the new trend was clear. Marshall himself announced the decision in *Providence Bank* v. *Billings,* holding that a tax exemption could not be inferred from the fact that a state had granted a charter of incorporation to a bank; the vital power of taxation, he wrote, could be relinquished only by express statutory declaration.[17] Seven years later, after Roger B. Taney had replaced John Marshall as chief justice, the Supreme Court added a major qualification to the *Dartmouth College* doctrine. Following in the steps of the *Providence Bank* case, the new Taney Court took the position that corporate charters were to be construed strictly so as to preserve the public interest. Only those rights *explicitly* granted by the state in the charter of incorporation, it declared, were constitutionally protected against contractual impairment. The case, *Charles River Bridge* v. *Warren Bridge,* had presented a clear-cut issue. The Charles River Bridge held a charter of incorporation from Massachusetts, authorizing it to collect tolls from those using its facilities. But in 1828 the state granted a charter for the construction of a second bridge not far from the first one. It further provided that the new bridge, the Warren Bridge, was to operate as a free public highway once the construction costs had been paid off. This of course undercut the toll system of the Charles River Bridge Company, which argued that the Massachusetts legislature had violated contractual rights implied in its charter of incorporation. The Court, however, rejected what it called "this doctrine of implied contracts," stating instead: "In charters of this description, no rights are taken from the public, or given to the corporation, beyond those which the words of the charter by their natural and proper construction, purport to convey."[18]

Although the *Charles River Bridge* decision modified the expansive interpretations for which John Marshall had contended in *Fletcher* v. *Peck, New Jersey* v. *Wilson,* and *Dartmouth College* v. *Woodward,* it by no means repudiated the basic holdings of those cases. The Taney Court, no less than the Marshall Court, believed that the contract clause applied to state contracts. Indeed, in the twenty-eight years of the Taney Court (1836–64) eighteen state laws fell under the contract clause, while in the thirty-four years of the Marshall Court (1801–35) the clause claimed only eight state laws.[19] Not only did the Taney Court, a tribunal staffed by Jacksonian Democratic justices, apply the clause to laws changing the obligations of debtors to creditors, but it repeatedly struck down state legislation taxing or regulating banks on the ground that the laws contradicted exemptions granted in the charters of incorporation. It even applied the contract clause to an agreement between the federal government and the states. "The simple fact," the foremost authority on the subject has written, "is that the contract clause was a more secure and a broader base for property rights in 1864 than it had been in 1835."[20]

During the post-Civil War period the clause was held to govern the bond issues of cities and towns, and in almost all of approximately two hundred municipal bond cases the Court ruled that municipalities violated the contract clause when they attempted to repudiate their debts.[21] But these years also marked the gradual demise of the contract clause as a leading tool of constitutional limitation. To begin with, the Supreme Court of the seventies and eighties refused to construe the contract clause as a limitation on the national government. Since federal regulation of corporate and other property was increasing and would eventually surpass that of the states, the restriction of the clause to state cases only began to limit its significance.[22] At the same time, aside from the municipal bond cases, the Waite Court (1874–88) adopted an increasingly strict interpretation of the contract clause in state cases. Despite the argument that the states were violating their contractual agreements, the Court allowed them to change the terms of state bond issues and to regulate the rates of railroads and other corporations.[23] And in the important case of *Stone* v. *Mississippi* (1880) it went well beyond the holding of the old *Charles River Bridge* case by affirming that a state could outlaw lotteries, even though a lottery company possessed a charter, for which it had made cash payments, authorizing it to operate within the state for twenty-five years. Chief Justice Morrison R. Waite declared, however, that a legislature cannot bargain away the state's fundamental police power to regulate in defense of the public health and morality.[24]

These developments were hastened by the rise of the due process clause as a limitation on government regulation. Unlike the contract clause, it applied to both the federal and the state governments (through the Fifth and Fourteenth Amendments), and its potential protection was far broader. The contract clause, after all, dealt only with contracts. No matter how broadly these were defined, the notion of "contract" could never match the virtually limitless scope of substantive "fairness" that became part of the due process clause. From at least 1895 until the judicial acceptance of the New Deal in 1937, the due process clause was the primary vehicle for nullifying federal and state social and economic regulation.[25]

As a consequence, the decline of the contract clause after 1890 was pronounced. Prior to that year it figured in nearly 40 per cent of all cases challenging the constitutionality of state laws, but during the 1890's and early 1900's the clause was at issue in less than 25 per cent of the state cases.[26] The percentage dropped even further in succeeding years, and today the contract clause is of negligible constitutional significance. Two cases in particular epitomize its decline and fall. The first is *Illinois Central Railroad Company* v. *Illinois* (1892), in which the Supreme Court ruled that Illinois was within its police power rights in repealing a grant of more than 1,000 acres of submerged lands in Lake Michigan made to the railroad by an earlier legislative act. Although attorneys for the Illinois Central cited the obvious precedent, *Fletcher* v. *Peck,* the Court took the position that "there can be no irrepealable contract in a conveyance of property by a grantor in disregard of a public trust, under which he was bound to hold and to manage it." [27] *Fletcher* v. *Peck,* which the majority studiously ignored, was in effect overruled and its holding that public grants are constitutionally inviolate relegated to the status of a judicial relic.

The second case epitomizing the fall of the contract clause is *Home Building and Loan Association* v. *Blaisdell* (1934), decided during the Depression years. [28] Informally known as the *Minnesota Moratorium Case,* it upheld the legitimacy of a state law extending the period in which debtors could pay off their mortgages. The Court insisted that the Minnesota law did not impair the ultimate integrity of mortgages, but it could not explain away the fact, as the dissenters passionately urged, that the statute "materially delays enforcement of the mortgagee's contractual right of ownership and possession." [29] The majority's position, which undoubtedly seems sensible to us, was that the Constitution must be interpreted flexibly in the light of changing public needs, and this led it to the conclusion that "the reservation of the reasonable exercise of the protective power of the state is read into *all* contracts." [30] Even private contracts—the original concern of the men who framed the contract clause —are therefore no longer insulated from the state police power. To put it bluntly, the clause once so dear to John Marshall no longer belongs to the living Constitution.

In certain ways, however, *Fletcher* v. *Peck* is still very much a part of the Constitution. If its main legal doctrine is obsolete, its political lessons are not, for *Fletcher* v. *Peck* demonstrates one of the enduring characteristics of our constitutional system, the role of interest groups in soliciting valuable constitutional decisions from the Supreme Court. Traditionally, it has always been a point of commentary among legal and political scholars that American constitutional law is in large measure a product of the haphazard conflict of private parties. But in recent years political scientists have developed a substantial literature showing that modern constitutional law is increasingly less a product of random private disputes and more and more a consequence of carefully planned maneuvers by well-organized interest groups.[31] For one thing, the activities of government today are far more pervasive and systematic than they were in the nineteenth century. They touch virtually all aspects of life, and this in turn provokes organized groups to seek, also systematically, favorable decisions on matters vital to their interests from the administrative, executive, legislative, *and* judicial branches of government. For another, law and politics are uniquely fused in the American system of government, and the leaders and representatives of modern interest groups have a sensitive appreciation of the political significance of judicial decisions.

Those who stress the interest group nature of most contemporary Supreme Court litigation are undoubtedly correct; yet they may well exaggerate the newness of their discovery. As early as 1908, in his classic study, *The Process of Government,* Arthur F. Bentley argued that legal decisions, like all political decisions, were a product of interest group activity.[32] For many years his views made little impact on scholarly opinion. Then, in the 1950's, the interest group theory of American politics gained wide currency after it was brought up to date and forcefully restated by David B. Truman.[33]

It is also an unspoken assumption of much of the recent interest group literature that organized solicitation of Supreme Court decisions as part of an over-all political strategy is an essentially twentieth-century phenomenon. To be sure, serious students have long recognized that, in the period roughly from 1865 to 1937, corporations and their lawyers expected the Court to decide cases in ways favorable to business and vested property interests. But the idea of systematically plotting a judicial-political strategy—supporting a test case, framing it so as to elicit particular judicial answers based on an astute calculation of how the justices are likely to respond, and translating the judicial currency into political advantage—is customarily regarded as a contribution of the National Association for the Advancement of Colored People in its quest for full civil rights for the American Negro. While the conservative Liberty League was, until 1937, moderately successful in fighting President Franklin Roosevelt's New Deal in the courts, the literature of the Supreme Court portrays the NAACP as the pioneer in the manipulation of test cases and the acquisition of desired constitutional pronouncements. Beginning in the 1930's and culminating most dramatically in the Supreme Court's historic ruling on May 17, 1954, that officially sanctioned racial segregation violates the Constitution, the NAACP has justifiably gained a reputation as a champion of the judicial process.[34]

In fact, while there can be no question that the judicial politics of today is largely interest group politics, a study of the origin and consequences of *Fletcher* v. *Peck* makes it clear that the calculating use of Supreme Court decisions as an instrument of interest group politics began in the earliest years of the new republic. The New England Mississippi Land Company planned and staged the case of *Fletcher* v. *Peck,* and it seems most likely that intensive study of the nineteenth-century Court would reveal many similar illus-

trations of concerted interest group activity.[35] Moreover, even
though the precise impact of *Fletcher* v. *Peck* cannot be
measured, it clearly affected the outcome of the long dispute
over the Yazoo compensation bill. Whereas a decision
against the claimants would surely have killed their chances
of obtaining compensation, the opinion in their favor gave
the Yazooists valuable legal and moral leverage. They were
aided by the pressures for Mississippi's admission into the
Union and the Madison administration's desire to appease
New England in the face of its economic discomfort over
the War of 1812, but no explanation of the compensation
bill's passage in 1814 can neglect the significance of *Fletcher*
v. *Peck*. In the congressional debates of 1813 and 1814 both
opponents and proponents of the compensation bill made
the Court's decision one of the central issues. Yazooists ag-
gressively cited it as proof that compensation was due; anti-
Yazooists defensively disparaged it as fraudulent and un-
sound; neither side ignored it.[36] Its mere prominence in the
congressional debates does not prove its influence, but within
the context of the entire Yazoo controversy it seems reasonable to conclude that *Fletcher* v. *Peck* was an essential
ingredient in the ultimate victory of the New England Mississippi Land Company. At the very least it can be said that
John Marshall's opinion provided congressmen with a convenient rationale for a pro-Yazooist vote and that a contrary
decision would have made a compensation law an impossibility.

In another sense, too, *Fletcher* v. *Peck* demonstrates
something that is basic and enduring in the American constitutional system. If it is to succeed, an interest group demand must harmonize (or at least not conflict) with the
values generally dominant on the Supreme Court, just as
the Court's decisions, if they are to be translated into effective
public policy, must in turn be compatible with the national
consensus. Debtors with a radical program for paying off

their creditors in worthless currency, for example, could not have won favorable decisions from John Marshall's Court, no matter how carefully they chose their attorneys and planned their cases. Nor would the Ku Klux Klan succeed today were it to launch a judicial counterattack comparable to that of the NAACP in the 1940's and 1950's: the values represented by the Klan are those of a tiny minority of the population; those of the NAACP, while controversial in certain respects, are more closely attuned to what, for want of a better phrase, may be called "the spirit of the age."

The Yazooists succeeded in their legal appeal because the case of *Fletcher* v. *Peck* provided the Supreme Court with an opportunity to secure constitutionally, through the contract clause, the vested property rights which the justices valued highly. Even more significant, the Marshall Court's ruling itself was influential in shaping the direction of subsequent constitutional cases and in persuading Congress to enact a compensation law because it harmonized with and, indeed, expressed the political and economic ideology of nineteenth-century America. This point deserves to be pursued briefly, for there are scholars who wonder at the influence of John Marshall on American constitutional law; they are surprised that he has retained his reputation as "the Great Chief Justice." One of Marshall's modern critics explains his influence this way: ". . . Marshall's majestic prose, his premise-obscuring rhetoric and inspired generalizations tend to hide the shabby side of the claims which his great opinions protected. More important, Marshall served well the conservative interests of his day—and for a long while it was conservatives who wrote history books." [37]

The fallacy in this type of argument is that it slides over the fact that Marshall's "premise-obscuring rhetoric" and the "shabby" claims he protected had the favor of a majority of the politically conscious Americans of his day. It is of course true that the decisions of the Marshall Court often provoked harsh criticism and political resistance, most commonly when they went against specific state and local interests. This, however, should not obscure the fact that its major decisions failed to antagonize the political forces dominant in the nation as a whole. Its major decisions—*Marbury* v. *Madison,* affirming judicial power to declare federal laws unconstitutional; *Fletcher* v. *Peck* and the *Dartmouth College Case,* making the contract clause into an instrument of vested property rights; *Martin* v. *Hunter's Lessee* and *Cohens* v. *Virginia,* asserting plenary control over all federal questions arising within state judicial systems; *McCulloch* v. *Maryland,* upholding the constitutionality of the Bank of the United States; and *Gibbons* v. *Ogden,* declaring Congress' paramount power over interstate commerce—may have been "conservative," but they did not do violence to the national political consensus.[38]

On no other grounds can the remarkable influence of the Marshall Court be explained. The decision in *Fletcher* v. *Peck,* reflecting a bias in favor of vested property rights, was in nearly perfect harmony with the attitudes and values of most politically conscious Americans. How else can one explain the fact that this decision by a *Federalist* Supreme Court was influential in persuading an overwhelmingly *Republican* Congress to compensate the Yazoo claimants? How else does one explain the fact that Justice William Johnson, in a way Jefferson's personal representative on the Court, endorsed the doctrine of vested rights as fully as John Marshall? How else does one explain that the Jacksonian Court of Roger Taney, while somewhat qualifying the *Dartmouth College* doctrine, actually invalidated more state actions under the contract clause than did the "conservative" Court of John Marshall, supposedly addicted to "shabby" propertied claims?

As a matter of fact, Benjamin Wright's study of the contract clause shows that before 1801, the beginning of Marshall's term as chief justice, only three state constitutions contained contract clauses similar to the one in the federal Constitution.[39] But by 1835, when the Chief Justice's term ended, nine additional states had adopted such clauses. Their language, moreover, followed the broad, inclusive terminology of the federal clause. During the Taney period fourteen more states adopted contract clauses, and eleven of these states were west of the Appalachians, where ideas about popular democracy were presumably the strongest. Admittedly, many of the states adopting contract clauses also included clauses reserving state power to revise the terms of public grants; they were anxious not to compromise public authority to check the potential abuses of the quickly growing corporations. But this intention was not incompatible with the objective of restricting legislative power to interfere with contractual rights in property. It was, indeed, no coincidence that the contract clauses were placed in the bill of rights section of the state constitutions: to the nineteenth-century American, who, if he was not already, hoped soon to be his own little capitalist, the contract clause protected a fundamental human right, the right of property.

All this is now changed. The social and economic conditions of an industrial-urban society have fostered demands for governmental regulation that very often limits the private use of property. In response to these needs and demands the modern American Constitution no longer regards property as something that is sacred and largely untouchable by the government. In its place other rights have come into constitutional pre-eminence: the right to be free from racial discrimination, the right to speak freely, the right to worship God free from official compulsions, the right to a fair criminal trial.[40] Yet, within the context of nineteenth-century America, *Fletcher* v. *Peck* was intended to protect individual liberty, and it is not straining matters to say that in this general way John Marshall's opinion is linked to twen-

tieth-century constitutional doctrines. For the idea of individual liberty, the belief that certain personal rights deserve special protection, remains at the core of the American
constitutional system. Its content has inevitably changed,
and the doctrine of vested rights no longer protects property.
But the underlying theme has not changed: there is still a
doctrine of vested rights, which, in the second half of the
twentieth century, glorifies and protects the more intan-
gible but very real rights of the criminally accused, those
who belong to unpopular racial minorities, and those who
are identified with unconventional political and religious
causes and ideas.[41] As an illustration of the vitality of the
idea of individual liberty and as one of the earliest demon-
strations of the mechanics of constitutional politics, the case
of *Fletcher* v. *Peck* has both historic and modern significance.

Fletcher v. *Peck* also deserves to be remembered purely
on its own terms as the legal chapter in the fascinating story
of the Yazoo land fraud. Quite aside from constitutional
doctrines and contract clauses, the case was part of a remarkable episode in the law and politics of the new republic.
Even from the perspective of over one hundred and fifty
years, years in which corrupt deals have been part of the
accepted price of democratic politics, and even though one
must take into account the inflation of the dollar, there is
something incredible, and almost amusing, about the bribery of an entire legislature and the sale of 35,000,000 acres,
nearly all of Alabama and Mississippi, for $500,000. No less
fascinating is the parade of characters who were caught up
in the Yazoo issue—Gunn, Harper, Jackson, Marshall, Randolph, Troup, Story—and the way in which the issue confused congressional and party politics.

There was an appropriate conclusion to the unusual
Yazoo fraud: it produced no losers. James Gunn and his
partners in fraud managed to reap the fruits of their bribery

by reselling their purchase at a profit. James Jackson and his political machine acquired an issue that they exploited well in the Georgia politics of the day. In much the same way the strange Randolph of Roanoke found in Yazooism an ideal outlet for his destructive talents. The state of Georgia itself retrieved the land and later sold it to the United States for $1,250,000, more than double the original sale price. The federal government received territory it had long wanted and, because of the constantly rising value of land as the nation grew, was able to sell it at many times its purchase price. The New England Mississippi Land Company and the other second- and third-hand speculators in Yazoo lands received over $4,000,000 in compensation, which was more than they had paid for the land titles.[42] America, then as now, was wealthy enough to afford many excesses.

APPENDIXES

A Note on the Appendixes

These appendixes have been compiled with two purposes in mind. The first is to provide the interested reader with a more thorough background to the Yazoo lands controversy by reprinting its major documents. The second purpose is related to the first. The documents reproduced here are either historically significant or inherently fascinating; some, such as the Georgia repeal act or Abraham Bishop's *Georgia Speculation Unveiled,* are both. Moreover, almost all of the documents (the possible exception is the Supreme Court's decision on *Fletcher* v. *Peck*) are not easily accessible. In short, it is hoped that this selected documentary reconstruction of the Yazoo issue will add greater depth and meaning to the narrative of a remarkable episode in our political and constitutional history.

A few words are in order concerning the editing of the documents. Five are reproduced in their entirety, but there is only an excerpt from Robert Goodloe Harper's pamphlet, and I have pruned some of the verbiage in Bishop's long tract. Notes appear only in those few cases where they seemed absolutely necessary. Each document is preceded by a brief introduction.

JAMES JACKSON'S SKETCH
OF THE YAZOO SPECULATION

Jackson's sketch,[1] probably written no earlier than 1803, has obviously been the primary source for the traditional interpretation of the Yazoo sale. In expanded form, and without being credited to Jackson, it was published in 1849 in George White's *Statistics of the State of Georgia* (Savannah, Georgia). From that secondary source it was passed on to later scholars and writers who uncritically adopted Jackson's own "devil theory" of the Yazoo sale and of all persons and things connected with it. The sketch, of course, is no more than that: it carries events no further than January, 1796, when Jackson chaired the legislative committee which sponsored the repeal of the sale act. Even so, the sketch stands as the best partisan statement of Georgia anti-Yazooist sentiment. General Jackson was casual in the use (or nonuse) of punctuation, and this gives his sketch something of a stream-of-consciousness quality.

The Yazoo Speculation was in embrio almost immediately after the Revolutionary War. Certain characters viewed it as the land of Promise but not for all the Children of Israel but a few only and which shortly was exhibited by a combination of Persons stiling themselves the combined Society where an Oath was exacted from every individual of Secrecy as to their plans and movements & no Citizen was to have a share unless he joined them; the secret however leaked out and the Society became disbanded.

In 1798 the famous Swindler [Thomas] Washington as he called himself but whose real name was Walsh, then in the height of Speculation, who would sell Lands houses Horses Carriages and Negroes before he had a shadow of property in them and who was hanged in Charleston for forgery in 1792 having forged the South Carolina & Georgia State Paper to an immense amount got connected with Alexander Moultrie Suches [?] and others and instigated by the relations of one Sullivan a Captain in the Revolution[ary] Army & who headed the Mob in Philadelphi[a] at the State house which insulted the old Congress & who had to fly to the Mississippi for his conduct to save his life first set the 1789 Speculation a going. Artful & cunning in the extreme tho apparently one of the most open of Men & who under that Cloak took almost every Man in, he persuaded the Virginia Yazoo Company of which the celebrated Patrick Henry was the leader to join in an application. Sullivans description of the Western Country was so extravagant that even in Georgia where Washington began to be well known another Company was formed. Some to be sure of the former combined Society others however of fair & honest Characters never impeached until that moment. Those companies employed Agents who worked on the Legislature & several of its Members were persuaded to be interested, but in no manner of comparison of corruption with the Members of the Legislature of 1795. An Act passed, the Sale was made, the People were roused and demanded a repeal, presentments of Grand Juries succeeded and another Legislature declared the Sale a nullity (Mr Duane had better see Mr Nicholsons report Session 1802 1803 on this subject & insert it.) [2] The fire of the Speculation now appeared to be extinct but the embers remained only smothered for a while but in 1794 it kindled into a blaze and Judges and Senators of the United States took the lead. No artifice, no attempt was left untried to get the leading & influential characters of the State to embark on it. One Gentleman then a Senator of the United States and then certainly of Superior influence to any other Man in Georgia was told he might have any number of acres he pleased to half a Million without paying a Cent provided he would put his name to the application, but that Gentleman, Genl J[ackson], firmly opposed the offers & told the proposers that he, not they had fought for Georgia & the right to that territory, that he fought for the people & it was their right & the right of future generations and if they did succeed he should hold the Sale void and would resign his Seat in the Senate come home and head his Fellow Citizens, and either lose his life or have the act annulled. His duty called him to Congress; the Legislature met at the same time and the Monsters of corruption prevailed. In the lobby was seen the disgraceful scene of a Wilson, Judge of the U. States Supreme Court with 25000 dollars in his hand as a ready Cash payment; there a Pendleton, Judge of the District Court of Georgia, passing off Shares to the Members for their votes; and here again a Gunn, bullying with a loaded Whip & cajoling by turns numerous understrappers in Speculation; a Stith, a Judge & others of Georgia surrounding the Representatives striving to frighten or to persuade them into compliance, and many no doubt who would have resisted were intimidated some who could not be persuaded to vote for them were paid to go home and the virtuous minority were every moment in dread of there lives. To this very minority however did the corrupt majority in a few days owe their lives. The people at large, always right when left to themselves, rose in the vicinity of the capital and were determined to put all who voted for the act to death but were prevented by the very minority whom they had so cruelly treated. The alarm on Governor Matthews's signing the Act became General—he had returned one bill with his objections which would have done him immortal honor if he had not signed the second but the signing that damn[e]d him forever in the opinion of the Citizens of Georgia and he shortly after had to quit the State; indeed Georgia was a dangerous residence for all concerned in the Speculation. Roberds Thomas Senator from Hancock County to avoid being publickly tied up to a Sapling and whipped fled to South Carolina but was followed and killed; most of the others one or two Counties excepted, did not dare to appear in publick. At this time the whole State was in a tumult. Presentments of Grand Juries, Resolutions and petitions of the people against the act were almost universal. A Convention for altering the State Constitution had been called to meet in May 1795, but the Members had been chosen at the same election with the corrupt Legislature; of course little was to be expected from them; many of them were the same Men & others of the same kidney; the Presentments, Resolutions and petitions crowded so fast on them that a revision of the Constitution was relinquished and referring the Papers to the next Legislature, the Convention with a trifling alteration as to the time of meeting, broke up in confusion.

The Main Spring of Speculation Genl Gunn having accomplished his ends returned to Congress the last day of February 1795 three days before the Constitutional close of the Session and immediately set his engines at work in Congress to interest the Members and many of whom became so. There is more than reason to believe that Mr Morris Mr Burr & Mr Bingham were among them, from certain resolutions supported by them at that day at the instigation of Gunn & which were prevented from being carried by the negative of the other Georgia Senator the rules of the Senate admitting no bill or joint resolution to be read twice the same day without unanimous consent. The two Georgia Senators came to high words & the opposing Senator told Senate of the wickedness & villainy of the whole Speculation.[3]

By the same vessel Gunn came in as well as by Post the opposing Senator received numbers of letters from different parts of the State requesting him to return to go into the Convention, and he embarked as soon as he could get a passage which he did for Charleston; but after being a Month at Sea, the vessel had reached no further than Cape Hatteras little more than halfway and the Southwest winds then growing daily stronger and the vessel built for the Amsterdam trade not calculated to beat to windward, and the British treaty being to be laid before Senate in June, the election for the Convention being then over and the Convention itself to be held in another Months time May & no prospect of the Ship John reaching her port in that time, so as to give that Senator an opportunity to be so early at the Convention as to be able to do any good and considering the Magnitude of the British treaty which might depend on a single vote, he thought his duty required his return, which with Mr. Bohlen Owner of the Ship was determined on on falling in with the Ship Commerce bound from Charleston to New York & where they arrived in less than three days a greater distance than had been one Month in gaining in the John.

When Senate met on the British treaty, Mr Gunn took no part in its favor but held himself aloof until within two or three days before the decision and until he had ensured the Majority to support the Yazoo measures, when he came out furiously on the British side, and the Southern Negroes carried off by the British during the War & every other disadvantage to the United States were but as trifles not to be mentioned in comparison to benefits to be reaped from the treaty. Indeed it was well the

opposing Georgia Senator returned to the Senate or in all probability the Citizens of the United States would not even now be
permitted to export a single pound of the first staple of the Southern States if not of the United States Cotton in their own bottoms,
the [blank] article of the treaty declaring &c see it. It was then
planted & exported from Georgia only, and altho the same Senator had whilst a Member of the house of Representatives in the
first Congress, got a protecting duty for it. Mr Jay Chief Justice
of the United States whose duty as a Judge as well as an Ambassador required him to be acquainted with all the revenue laws,
knew neither that Cotton was planted nor a protecting duty laid
for it in the United States. The Article would have been amended in some shape by the Mercantile Members but Cotton would
have remained but for the opposing Senator of Georgia and Major
Butler Senator from S Carolina who warmly seconded the Georgia Senator on that head. Gunn however, after he had his terms
was willing to swallow all and without those terms had been
acceded to that curse had never been entailed on the U. States.
His vote, if disinterestedly given, would have rejected it, the
Senate on division being 20 for the treaty and ten against it exactly two thirds; if his vote as he threatened had been the other
way, it would have been constitutionally rejected 19 to 11, wanting three of two thirds; thus one Curse begat another and Yazoo
carried the British treaty which ought eternally to make those
who abominate the British treaty to abominate the vile Yazoo
Speculation, altho that is only a single evil consequence which the
Monster has produced.

On the return of the two Senators the publick indignation was
turned towards the one and the publick approbation by all but
Yazoo partizans bestowed on the other. Genl Gunn was burnt in
effigy and in many parts of the Country did not dare to appear in
publick, whilst Genl Jackson if possible had added to his former
influence. He had before his return written a series of letters addressed to the Citizens of Georgia under the signature of Sicilius,
proving the Sale to be invalid and unconstitutional, calling on
the people to beware of the next election the operation was great
they were every where read with avidity and followed with dili-
gence and determination. The British treaty being decided on, no

object in the Senate appeared to require his presence as much as the Legislature at this crisis at home; he was solicited from all quarters more especially from the Mechanics and planters of Chatham County wherein Savannah lays to resign and gratify there wishes by serving in the Legislature for that County. He acceded to it and was elected by an immense majority. The people notwithstanding the favorable elections to their own wishes in nine Counties out of ten gave instructions to their representatives charging them to annul the abominable act bartering their rights and to restore them to posterity; petitions on petitions Remonstrances Resolutions and presentments against the speculation again crowded from every quarter of the State and a day was assigned to consider the State of the Republick when after full debate those petitions Remonstrances Resolutions & presentments with those laid before the Convention were referred to a Committee of which Genl Jackson was chosen Chairman.

THE GEORGIA REPEAL ACT OF 1796

The repeal act,[1] which codified James Jackson's anti-Yazooist policy, is also a perfect illustration of how the Jackson party masked its essentially conservative position in the language of extreme popular democracy. Over and over again the preamble affirms that the sovereign power resides in "the good people of this State," who stand as a final court of appeal above even the people's elected representatives. Indeed, in the light of the extended scholarly discussion over the growth of American judicial review, it is pertinent to note the casual assumption of the repeal legislature that there were such things as "unconstitutional" laws and that they could and should be voided. The mechanism in this case was the legislature itself, much as it was two years later when the Kentucky and Virginia Resolutions of 1798 and 1799 attempted to declare the federal Sedition Act unconstitutional. In retrospect it seems clear that *legislative* declarations of unconstitutionality were doomed to failure; the separation of powers doctrine, which roughly divided executive, judicial, and legislative functions among three distinct branches of government, was already an American political fixture by the 1790's. If legislation were to be declared unconstitutional, it would have to be done—as it soon was—*judicially*, by courts alone. Ironically, this Georgia repeal act became the first piece of major state legislation voided by the United States Supreme Court.

From another angle, the repeal act should be read as a sort of dissenting opinion to the Supreme Court's decision in *Fletcher* v. *Peck*. Since Georgia's position, which in the argument before the Court was nominally represented by Luther Martin, was so poorly presented, this lengthy preamble provides a dissenting answer to John Marshall's opinion.

AN ACT declaring null and void a certain usurped act, passed by the last Legislature of this State, at Augusta, on the seventh day of January, one thousand seven hundred and ninety-five, under the pretended title of "An act supplementary to an act, entitled 'An act for appropriating a part of the unlocated territory of this State for the payment of the late State troops, and for other purposes therein mentioned,' declaring the right of this State to the unappropriated territory thereof, for the protection of the frontiers, and for other purposes," and for expunging from the face of the public records the said usurped act, and for declaring the right of this State to all lands lying within the boundaries therein mentioned.

Whereas, the free citizens of this State, or, in other words, the community thereof, are essentially the source of the sovereignty of the State, and no individual or body of men can be entitled to, or vested with, any authority which is not expressly derived from that source, and the exercise or assumption of powers not so derived, become, of themselves, oppression and usurpation— which it is the right and duty of the people, or their representatives, to resist, and to restore the rights of the community so usurped and infringed.

And whereas, the will or constitution of the good people of this State is the only existing legal authority derived from the essential source of sovereignty, and is the only foundation of the legislative power or government thereof, and, so far as that will or constitution expressly warrants, the Legislature may go, but no further; and all constructive powers, not necessarily deduced from that expressive will, are violations of that essential source of sovereignty and the rights of the citizens, and are, therefore, of no binding force or effect on the State, or the good people thereof, but null and void.

And whereas, the last Legislature of this State, not confining itself to the powers with which that body was constitutionally invested, did usurp a power to pass an act on the seventh day of January, one thousand seven hundred and ninety-five, entitled "An act supplementary to an act, entitled an act for appropriating a part of the unlocated territory of this State for the payment of the late State troops, and for other purposes therein mentioned, declaring the right of this State to the unappropriated territory thereof, for the protection and support of the frontiers, and for other purposes," by which an enormous tract of unascertained millions of acres of the vacant territory of this State was attempted to be disposed of to a few individuals, in fee simple, and the same is not only unfounded, as being without express constitutional authority, but is repugnant to that authority, as well as to the principles and form of government, the good citizens of this

State have chosen for their rule, which is democratical, or a government founded on equality of rights, and which is totally opposed to all proprietary grants or monopolies in favor of a few, which tend to build up that destructive aristocracy in the new, which is tumbling in the old world; and which, if permitted, must end in the annihilation of democracy and equal rights—those rights and principles of government, which our virtuous forefathers fought for and established with their blood.

And whereas, the fourth section of the fourth article of the constitution of the United States declares, "The United States shall guaranty to every State in this Union a republican government," which could never have been intended to be a republican aristocracy, and which such extravagant grants tend to establish, the constitution of the United States expressly acknowledging a republican democracy as the foundation of the people, it receiving all its force and power from their hands or their gift, which is manifest from its context, "We, the people of the United States."

And whereas, as beforementioned, the said usurped act is repugnant to the constitutional authority, inasmuch as that by the sixteenth section of the first article of the constitution of this State, it is declared "That the General Assembly shall have power to make all laws and ordinances which they shall deem necessary and proper for the good of the State, which shall not be repugnant to this constitution." And the said usurped act is opposed to the good of the State, and it is self-evident that the Legislature which assumed the power did not deem it for the good of the State—

1st. Because self-preservation, or the protecting itself, is the greatest good and first duty of every Government; and, as has been shown, immense monopolies of land, by a few individuals, under the sanction of the Government, are opposed to the principles of democracy or the fundamental laws the citizens of this State have chosen for their rule, which, so far from being for the good or self-preservation of the democratical or equal government, is most manifestly for its destruction and injury.

2d. Because the expression "good of the State" embraces the good of the citizens composing the State, and the good of the citizens consists in the peaceable pursuit of happiness, and the enjoyment of all rights, natural or acquired, not expressly delegated for the purposes of government; and a sale of such an enormous tract to a few speculators, which was and is the common right of all the good citizens of this State, is contrary to those rights, and, therefore, to their manifest injury, and, of course, to the injury of the State.

3d. Because, even supposing constitutional authority to have been vested in the Legislature, for the purpose of such disposal, the Legislature was not vested with power to transfer the sovereignty and jurisdiction of the State over the territory attempted to be disposed of, which it has done, by opening a door for sale to foreign Powers, and a relinquishment of the powers of taxation, until the proprietors choose to be represented; which is, in fact, dismembering the State, and which transfer and relinquishment of taxation cannot be for the good of the State.

4th. Because there was no necessity or pressing urgency for the sale of such an immense tract of territory, equal to some European kingdoms, to carry into execution and operation the extinguishment of the Indian claims to the lands between the Oconee and Ocmulgee, contemplated by the act, entitled "An act for appropriating a part of the unlocated territory of this State for payment of the late State troops, and for other purposes therein mentioned;" the subterfuge on which the said usurped act of the seventh of January, one thousand seven hundred and ninety-five, was founded, when the whole amount of the appropriation for that purpose was but thirty thousand dollars, and funds to a greater amount were then in the treasury unappropriated; and because no State or nation is justified in wantonly dissipating its property or revenues, and a legal alienation of which can only take place from the most pressing necessity; and the territory attempted to be disposed of (was the said usurped law valid) was wantonly dissipated, it being disposed of for the trifling sum of five hundred thousand dollars, a sum not adequate to the annual quit-rents such lands were charged with previously to the Revolution, by the British King; which wanton dissipation cannot be for the good of the State.

5th. Because, exclusive of the immense loss of revenue to which the State is exposed, from the relinquishment of taxation, the sum of five hundred thousand dollars was accepted as the consideration money for the sale, and the sum of eight hundred thousand dollars offered by persons of as large a capital, and as much respectability and credit, and on terms more advantageous to the State, was refused; which, as it was (should the said usurped act have been considered valid) a clear loss of three hundred thousand dollars to the revenues of the State, it is evident that the law authorizing the sale was not deemed by the Legislature for "the good of the State," which must have consisted in obtaining the highest price and the most advantageous terms.

6th. For the very excellent reasons given by his excellency the Governor, in his dissent to the first bill for the disposal of the said territory, delivered to the House of Representatives on the twenty-ninth of December, one thousand seven hundred and ninety-four, and which bill was not materially different from the act in question, and which reasons prove that his excellency, as a negative branch of the Legislature, although he concurred in the law, did not deem it for "the good of the State," and which dissent was in the words following:

1st. I doubt whether the proper time is arrived for disposing of the territory in question.

2d. If it was the proper time, the sum offered is inadequate to the value of the land.

3d. The quantity reserved for the citizens is too small, in proportion to the extent of the purchase.

4th. That greater advantages are secured to the purchasers than to the citizens.

5th. That so large an extent of territory being disposed of to companies or individuals, will operate as monopolies, which will prevent or retard settlements, population, and agriculture.

6th. That, should such disposition be made, at least one-fourth of the lands should be reserved for the future disposal of the State.

7th. That if public notice was given that the land was for sale, the rivalship in purchasers would most properly have increased the sums offered.

8th. The power given to the Executive by the constitution, the duty I owe the community, and the sacredness of my oath of office, will, I flatter myself, justify this dissent in the minds of the Legislature, and of my other fellow-citizens.

And whereas, the said usurped law, passed on the seventh day of January, one thousand seven hundred and ninety-five, is also repugnant to the aforerecited sixteenth section, inasmuch as it is repugnant to the seventeenth or subsequent section of the said first article, which declares, "They (the Legislature) shall have power to alter the boundaries of the present counties, and to lay off new ones, as well out of the counties already laid off, as out of the other territory belonging to the State. When a new county or counties shall be laid off out of any present county or counties, such new county or counties shall have their representation apportioned out of the number of representatives of the county or counties out of which it or they shall be laid out; and when any new county shall be laid off in the vacant territory belonging to the State, such county shall have a number of representatives, not exceeding three, to be regulated and determined by the General Assembly;" and the territory disposed of not lying within the limits of any county already laid off, and a sale and grant thereof, should the said usurped law be deemed valid, having been made, it could not be defined the vacant territory belonging to the State, whereby the constitutional powers vested in the General Assembly, by the said seventeenth section, would be barred and prevented, and, consequently, the settlers on the territory sold be deprived of the constitutional right of representation, and is not only thus repugnant to the said sixteenth and seventeenth sections, but thereby, and by the relinquishment of the right of taxation, until the settlers were represented, which they cannot constitutionally be, is also repugnant to the whole letter and spirit of the constitution, it operating as a dereliction of jurisdictional rights, and a virtual dismemberment of the State.

And whereas, in and by the articles of confederation entered into and finally ratified on the first day of March, one thousand seven hundred and eighty-one, by the then thirteen States of America, the territory within the limits of each of the said States is, to each of them, respectively, confirmed and guarantied, first by the second article, to wit: "Each State retains its sovereignty, freedom, and independence, and every power, jurisdiction, and right, which is not by the confederation expressly delegated to the United States in Congress assembled." And second, by the last clause of the second section of the ninth article, "No State shall

be deprived of territory for the benefit of the United States."
And in and by the first clause of the sixth article of the federal
constitution of the United States, "All engagements entered into
before the adoption of the said constitution, shall be as valid
against the United States under the said constitution as under
the confederation;" and by the twelfth article of the amendments
to the said constitution, ratified and adopted, "The powers not
delegated to the United States by the constitution, nor prohibited
by it to the States, are reserved to the States, respectively, or to the
people."

And whereas, in and by the definitive treaty of peace signed at
Paris, on the third of September, one thousand seven hundred and
eighty-three, the boundaries of the United States were established,
and the said United States fully recognized and acknowledged
by the first article thereof, in the words following: "His Britannic
Majesty acknowledges the said United States, viz: New Hampshire, Massachusetts-bay, Rhode Island, Connecticut, New York,
New Jersey, Pennsylvania, Delaware, Maryland, Virginia, North
Carolina, South Carolina, and Georgia, to be free, sovereign, and
independent States; that he treats with them as such, and for himself, his heirs and successors, relinquishes all claims to the government, proprietary, and territorial rights of the same;" and by the
second article it is declared, "And that all disputes which might
arise in future on the subject of the boundaries of the said United
States may be prevented, it is hereby agreed that the following
are, and shall be their boundaries." And those boundaries thereby
declared, which limit the westwardly and southwardly parts of
this State, are thus defined: "Along the middle of the Mississippi,
until it shall intersect the northernmost part of the thirty-first
degree of north latitude; south, by a line drawn due east from
the termination of the line last mentioned, in the latitude of
thirty-one degrees north of the equator, to the middle of the river
Appalachicola or Chattahoochee; thence along the middle thereof, to its junction with Flint river; thence straight to the head of
St. Mary's river; and thence along the middle of St. Mary's river,
to the Atlantic ocean:" and the King of Great Britain did, by
proclamation dated the 7th day of October, in the year 1763, annex
to the then province of Georgia all the lands lying between the

said river St. Mary's and the Altamaha, its former boundary, claimed by South Carolina under her charters; and the State of South Carolina, in and by a convention held and concluded between the commissioners of the said States, at Beaufort, under the authority and articles of the confederation, on the 28th day of April, 1787, did confirm to the State of Georgia the southward and westwardly boundaries described in the said treaty of Paris, by a cession and relinquishment of all right, title, and claim, which the said State possessed from the original charter thereof, to the Government, sovereignty, and jurisdiction in and over the same, and also the right of pre-emption of the soil from the native Indians, and all other the estate, property, and claim, in or to the said land; and the boundaries so described also coincide with the boundaries of this State as described by the land act of this State now in force, passed at Savannah, the 17th of September, in the year 1783, (except as to the northern boundary of the State) which by the said convention is thus established and ratified by the first article thereof: "The most northern branch or stream of the river Savannah, from the sea or mouth of such stream, to the fork or confluence of the rivers now called Tugaloo, or Keowee; and from thence to the most northern branch or stream of the said river Tugaloo, till it intersects the north boundary of South Carolina, if the said branch or stream of Tugaloo extends so far north, reserving all the islands in the said rivers Savannah and Tugaloo to Georgia; but if the head, spring, or source of any branch or stream of the said river Tugaloo does not extend to the north boundary of South Carolina, then a west line to the Mississippi."

And whereas, until the formation of the confederation, there could possibly belong no territorial rights to the United States, nor after such formation within the chartered limits of any State, but such as were specially ceded and relinquished by the respective States; and the people of the State of Georgia have by no act of theirs, or in any manner or shape whatever, transferred or alienated, or delegated a power to transfer or alienate the territory attempted to be disposed of by the said usurped act passed on the 7th of January, in the year 1795; and the same and every part thereof is hereby declared to be vested in the State and people thereof, and inalienable, but by a convention called by the people for that express purpose, or by some clause of power expressed by the people delegating such express power to the Legislature in the constitution.

And whereas, divested of all fundamental and constitutional authority which the said usurped act might be declared by its advocates, and those who claim under it, to be founded on fraud, has been practised to obtain it and the grants under it; and it is a fundamental principle, both of law and equity, that there cannot be a wrong without a remedy, and the State and the citizens thereof have suffered a most grievous injury in the barter of their rights by the said usurped act and grants, and there is no court existing, if the dignity of the State would permit her entering one, for the trial of fraud and collusion of individuals, or to contest her sovereignty with them, whereby the remedy for so notorious an injury could be obtained; and it can no where better lie than with the representatives of the people chosen by them, after due promulgation by the grand juries of most of the counties of the State, of the means practised, and by the remonstrances of the people of the convention, held on the 10th day of May, in the year 1795, setting forth the atrocious peculation, corruption, and collusion, by which the said usurped act and grants were obtained.

And whereas, the said petitions and remonstrances of the good people composing the State, to the said late convention, held at Louisville on the said 10th day of May, 1795, produced a resolution of that body in the following words: "*Resolved,* That it is the opinion of this convention that, from the numbers, respectability, and ground of complaint stated in the sundry petitions laid before them, that this is a subject of importance, meriting legislative deliberation: *Ordered, therefore,* That such petitions be preserved by the Secretary, and laid before the next Legislature at their ensuing session." Which resolution invests this Legislature with conventional powers, *quoad hoc,* or, in common terms, for the purpose of investigating the same, and which gives additional validity to legislative authority, were the powers of one Legislature over the acts of another to be attempted to be questioned.

And whereas, it does appear from sundry affidavits and a variety of proofs satisfactory to this Legislature, as well as from the presentments of the grand juries, on oath, of a considerable majority of the counties of the State, and by the aforerecited petitions and remonstrances of the good people thereof to the convention, and by numerous petitions to this present Legislature to the same purport, as also from the self-evident proof of fraud, arising from the rejection of eight hundred thousand dollars, and the acceptance of five hundred thousand dollars, as the consideration money for which the said territory was sold; that fraud and corruption were practised to obtain the said act and grants, and that a majority of those members of the Legislature who voted in favor of the aforesaid act were engaged in the purchase; and a majority of one vote only appeared in favor of this said usurped act in Senate, and on which majority in that branch the same was passed, and corruption appears against more than one member of that body; which, exclusive of the many deceptions used, and the inadequacy of price for such an immense and valuable tract of country, would be sufficient in equity, reason, and law, to invalidate the contract, even supposing it to be constitutional, which this Legislature declares it is not.

Be it therefore enacted, That the said usurped act, passed on the 7th day of January, in the year 1795, entitled "An act, supplementary to an act, entitled An act for appropriating a part of the unlocated territory of this State, for the payment of the late State troops, and for other purposes therein mentioned, declaring the right of this State to the unappropriated territory thereof, for the protection of the frontiers, and for other purposes," be, and the same is hereby, declared null and void; and the grant or grants, right or rights, claim or claims, issuing, deduced, or derived therefrom, or from any clause, letter, or spirit of the same, or any part of the same, is hereby also annulled, rendered void, and of no effect; and, as the same was made without constitutional authority, and fraudulently obtained, it is hereby declared of no binding, force, or effect, on this State, or the people thereof; but is and are to be considered, both law and grants, as they ought to be *ipso facto,* of themselves void, and the territory therein mentioned is also hereby declared to be the sole property of the State, subject only to the right of treaty of the United States, to enable the State to purchase, under its pre-emption right, the Indian title to the same.

2. *And be it further enacted,* That, within three days after the passing of this act, the different branches of the Legislature shall assemble together; at which meeting, the officers shall attend, with the several records, documents, and deeds, in the Secretary's, Surveyor General's, and other public offices; and which records and documents shall then and there be expunged from the face and indexes of the books of record of the State, and the enrolled law or usurped act shall then be publicly burnt, in order that no trace of so unconstitutional, vile, and fraudulent a transaction, other than the infamy attached to it by this law, shall remain in the public offices thereof; and it is hereby declared the duty of the county officers of record, where any conveyance, bond, or other deed whatever, shall have been recorded, relating to the sale of said territory, under the said usurped act, to produce the book wherein the said deed, bond, or conveyance may be so recorded, to the superior court, at the next session of the court after the passing this law, and which court is hereby directed to cause such clerk or keeper of the public records of the county to obliterate the same in their presence; and if such clerk or keeper of records neglect or refuse so to do, he shall be, and is hereby, declared incapable of holding any office of trust or confidence in this State, and the superior court shall suspend him; and, from and after the passing of this act, if any clerk of a county, notary public, or other officer keeping record, shall enter any transaction, agreement, conveyance, grant, law, or contract, relative to the said purchase under the said usurped act on their books of record, whereby claim can be derived of authority of record, he or they shall be rendered incapable of holding any office of trust or profit within this State, and be liable to a penalty of one thousand dollars, to be recovered in any court within and under the jurisdiction of this State; one half thereof to be given for the benefit of the informer, and the other half to be lodged in the treasury for the use of the Commonwealth.

3. *And be it further enacted,* That the said usurped law, passed on the 7th of January, in the year 1795, shall not, nor shall any grant or grants, issued by virtue thereof, or any deed or convey-

ance, agreement or contract, scrip or paper relative thereto, be received as evidence in any court of law or equity of this State, so far as to establish a right to the said territory, or to any part thereof: *Provided,* That nothing herein contained shall be construed to prevent such deed or conveyance, agreement or contract, between individuals, scrip issued by the pretended purchasers, or other paper, from being received as evidence in private actions for the recovery of any moneys given, paid, or exchanged, as the consideration for the pretended sales by the original pretended purchasers, or persons claiming and selling by and under them.

4. *And be it further enacted,* That his excellency the Governor be, and he is hereby empowered and required to issue warrants on the Treasurer, after the expiration of sixty days, in favor of such persons as may have *bona fide* deposited moneys, bank bills, or stock, in the funds of the United States, or warrants, in part or in whole payment of pretended shares of the said [p]retended purchased territory: *Provided,* The same shall be now therein, and not otherwise: *And provided, also,* That the risk attending the keeping the sum or sums so paid in, be deemed, and is hereby declared to lie entirely with the persons who deposited them; and that any charge of guards or other expenses for safe keeping thereof be deducted therefrom; and in case of neglect of application to his excellency therefor, within eight months after the passing this act, the same shall be, and is hereby, deemed property derelict, and escheated to and for the use of this State.

5. *And be it further enacted,* That any pretended power assumed, usurped, or intended by the said act, or any clause or letter of the same, or which may or can be construed to that purpose by the said usurped act, grant or grants under it, or from the Journal of the Senate or House of Representatives, to apply to the Government of the United States, for the extinguishment of the Indian claims to the lands within the boundaries in the said usurped act mentioned, and the holding any treaty by the said General Government, in consequence of any application therefor, by the company purchasers, under the said usurped act, so far as may effect the rights of this State to the lands therein described, is, and are hereby also declared, null and void; and the

right of applying for, and the extinguishment of Indian claims to, any lands within the boundaries of this State, as herein described, being a sovereign right, is hereby further declared to be vested in the people and Government of this State, to whom the right of pre-emption to the same belongs, subject only to the controlling power of the United States to authorize any treaty or treaties for, and to superintend the same.

6. *And be it further enacted,* That, in order to prevent future frauds on individuals, as far as the nature of the case will admit, his excellency the Governor is hereby required, as soon as may be after the passing of this law, to promulgate the same throughout the United States.

Concurred, February 13th, 1796.

THOMAS STEPHENS, *Speaker of the House of Representatives.*
BENJAMIN TALIAFERRO, *President of the Senate.*
JARED IRWIN, *Governor.*

ROBERT GOODLOE HARPER'S
THE CASE OF THE GEORGIA SALES
ON THE MISSISSIPPI CONSIDERED

Robert Goodloe Harper (1765–1825), one of the prominent organizers of the Yazoo land companies, had a rich and varied career as a land speculator, lawyer, and politician. He began his public career in 1795 as a Republican congressman from South Carolina, but soon shifted his loyalties to the Federalist party. Like many converts, Harper became a zealous proselytizer for Federalism, enthusiastically advocating war with France and a strict enforcement of the Sedition Act. He—and Federalism—became unpopular in South Carolina, and in 1801 Harper moved to Baltimore, Maryland, where he established a well-deserved reputation as one of the outstanding lawyers in early nineteenth-century America. Although he often resorted to cheap demagoguery, Harper deserves credit as a flexible and skillful political leader who contributed to the construction of the pragmatic Federalist party that challenged the Republicans during the early nineteenth century.[1]

In 1816 Harper was elected to the United States Senate, and that year he also appeared as a vice-presidential candidate on the last national ticket of the Federalist party. Among Harper's contributions to Americana is the slogan, "Millions for defense, but not a cent for tribute," which he coined at a dinner given in honor of John Marshall in 1798. Marshall was just returned from France as one of the three American envoys whom Talleyrand, the French foreign minister, had unsuccessfully sought to bribe through secret agents X, Y, and Z.

Harper's pamphlet, *The Case of the Georgia Sales on the Mississippi Considered*,[2] which he wrote in the summer of 1796, is a brief defending the legality of the Yazoo sale and attacking the repeal act of 1796. It includes a detailed examination of Georgia's title to the land at the time of the sale, which Harper naturally affirmed, and is supported by a documentary appendix containing seventeen items. The excerpt published here is the full text of Harper's statement dealing with the question which he posed as "Whether those [Yazoo land] purchases can be affected by the act of the Georgia legislature, passed February 13, 1796, and commonly called the repealing act?" Harper, of course, had a chance to repeat his arguments in 1809 and 1810, when he appeared as one of the attorneys on the side of the Yazooists in the case of *Fletcher* v. *Peck*.

The claims of the United States, which opened the first, and far the most extensive field of inquiry, having been thus surveyed, the repealing act of Georgia, now presents itself for consideration.

This act, it is to be observed, in the first place, does not profess to *repeal* the act of January 7th, 1795, but declares it void. The reasons for this mode of proceeding, are obvious. The act of January 7th, had produced its whole effect. The sales which it directed, had been completely made, the money paid, and grants passed. It could not, therefore, have been at all affected by a repeal; for it is a well known principle, that to repeal a law, far from undoing what has already been done under it, can only prevent its future operation. In order to destroy these sales, therefore, which was the object aimed at by the legislature, it was necessary to do something more than repeal the law: it was necessary to declare it originally void.

A single observation, which presents itself here, might decide the question on this repealing law. It is this; that the force, validity, or meaning of a legislative act, is purely a judicial question, and altogether beyond the province of the legislature. It is the province of the legislative power to make laws, to give them their existence; but to expound and enforce them, belongs to the judiciary. The judicial power is to declare, what the *law is;* the legislative, what it *shall be*. The legislature, therefore, may repeal one of its own acts; that is, may declare, that it shall not hereafter be law: but should it go further, and declare that it is void, that it is not now law, it steps beyond its powers, and its proceedings become null.

This is a fundamental principle of all our constitutions which declare, that the judicial and legislative powers shall be distinct and separate. It results also from the very existence of a written constitution; which, by its necessary operation, prescribes limits to the legislative body, and confides the protection and maintenance of those limits, to the judicial power. As well might the legislature try causes, or hear appeals, as attempt to expound, enforce, or declare void, one of its own acts; except so far as might relate to the *future* operation of such act. Its validity, so far as might relate to its former operation, to acts already done under its authority, is a question which the courts of justice alone, not the legislature, are competent to decide.

These sales moreover were contracts, made with the utmost solemnity, for a valuable consideration, and carried deliberately into complete execution. It is an invariable maxim of law, and of natural justice, that one of the parties to a contract, cannot by his own act, exempt himself, from its obligation. A contrary principle would break down all the ramparts of right, dissolve the bonds of property, and render good faith, to enforce the observance of which, is the great object of civil institutions, subservient to the partiality, the selfishness, and the unjust caprices of every individual. There is no reason why governments, more than private persons, should be exempt from the operation of this maxim; nor are they considered as exempt by our constitution or our laws. The state of Georgia, being a party to this contract, could no more relieve itself from the obligation, by any act of its own, than an individual, who had signed a bond, could relieve himself from the necessity of payment. If there were sufficient grounds for relief in either case, the state, or the individual must resort to the courts of justice, where it would be afforded: but the acts of the one, and the other, for relieving themselves, would be equally and essentially nugatory.

The act of Georgia, therefore, can have no legal effect.[3] It can be regarded only as a declaration, stating the grounds on which that state conceives itself entitled to relief, from the contract in question. As such a declaration however, from so respectable a body as the legislature of a state, cannot fail to make a strong impression, it will not be improper to examine these grounds a little more minutely, in order that a better judgement may be formed about their sufficiency.

The sales are declared void by this act, on two grounds. First, that the legislature had not constitutional power to make them. Secondly, that in passing the act for that purpose, it was influenced by fraudulent and corrupt motives.

As to the first, it is not improper to repeat that it is purely an object of judicial inquiry. Had the state of Georgia, as it might have done, filed a bill in the supreme federal court, against the purchasers, to set aside the sales, one object of inquiry in that court would have been, whether they were made by sufficient authority: and if it had found that they were not, they must have been set aside. But who ever heard, till this act was passed, that the legislatures under our constitutions have not power to sell the public property or give it away? This has always been considered as one of the most essential branches of legislative authority. It has been exercised by every legislative body in the Union; and by that of Georgia, in numerous instances. If the legislature has a right to dispose of the public lands, which cannot be denied, it may dispose of them in what quantities and on what conditions it thinks fit: for the right being unrestricted, so must be its exercise.

The second ground, the ground of fraud and corruption, was equally a subject of judicial inquiry. There cannot be a doubt, that if a legislative body, in making a contract, has been imposed on, it will, equally with an individual, be entitled to relief; but, like an individual, it must seek this relief in a court of justice. In a bill filed in this case for setting aside the sales, the allegation of fraud would have been inquired into, and, if supported by proper proof, would no doubt have been a sufficient ground for relief. This course the state might have pursued. In this manner it might have obtained whatever remedy it is entitled to, in law and justice.

But what is the nature of the fraud complained of; and by what proof is the charge supported?

The act does not pretend that the legislature which made these sales was deceived, was imposed on; but that some individuals among them were corrupted. Do the circumstances alledged amount to corruption? Can the motives of individual members be inquired into, in order to invalidate the acts of a legislative body?

It is alledged by the act "That a majority of those members of the legislature who voted in favour of the sales, were engaged in the purchase." There are various other vague and general charges, but this is the only specific fact alleged. It is not even pretended that a majority of the legislature was concerned, but only "a majority of those who voted for the sales." Admitting this to be true, was it an act of corruption? It might be considered perhaps as an impropriety; but on what ground can it be stigmatized as corrupt? It is not stated that those persons were bribed; that they were to receive money for their votes, or even to have part of the land without paying for it; but simply, that they were concerned in the purchase. But are there no other corrupt motives, which could induce a member to vote for a sale of public property, in which he himself was concerned? Might he not regard the sale, especially as it was of lands, the benefit of which to the public depends on their being cultivated, as advantageous to the state as well as to the purchasers? Might it not in fact be so? It is a rule of law, that if an act can be fairly accounted for on proper motives, corrupt ones shall not be presumed.

But it is believed that a legislative act, can never be invalidated on account of the motives, from which it may have been agreed to by individual members: that those motives can never be brought into question. Could such inquiries be instituted, where could be the end of them? By what mode of proof should they be conducted? What a door would be opened to fraud and uncertainty of every kind! The very foundations of legislative authority would be shaken; and all its acts might be nullified by the fraud or the artifices of individuals. If the legislature, considered as an individual, have been imposed on, like an individual it may be relieved: if it have exceeded the bounds of its authority, its acts are null; but the motives of its members can never be questioned without striking at the root of law, and introducing scenes of confusion a thousand times more intolerable, than any evils which it could be intended to remedy.

The proofs of this corruption, which come next to be considered, are stated by the act under four heads: affidavits; presentments of grand juries; petitions and remonstrances; and the circumstance of a larger sum having been rejected for the same property.

It is well known that the presentments of a grand jury are never admitted as evidence in courts of justice. Even the testimony on which they are founded is, for the most part, of such a nature that it could not be received there. They serve as the foundations of inquiry, but never as proof of a fact. Such of the presentments in question as have been seen, even if they were admitted as evidence, would prove nothing; for they either denounce the sales in general terms, as injurious to the public, and improperly obtained, or merely state the fact of some members having been concerned, or requested to be so, in the purchase.

Still less can remonstrances and petitions be relied on in the decision of legal rights. The means by which they are frequently obtained, and the slight grounds whereon they sometimes rest, are too well known to need any observations.

As to the rejection of a large offer, it may have been a very wise step. The security may have been deemed insufficient. The offer may have been considered as delusive. It is not known by the counsel, much less insinuated, that this was the case; but it is sufficient that it may have been so considered by the legislature, and, therefore, may have furnished them with a very upright, though perhaps ill-judged motive for their rejection. The fact is, that the offer was made by only four or five individuals; while the companies who purchased consisted of a very considerable number. The latter also paid a large sum in advance, which it is not understood that the former proposed. Under these circumstances, surely it is not necessary to resort to corrupt motives for the preference.

On the subject of the affidavits, all of which have been carefully examined, several important observations occur.

In the first place, they were ex parte, taken in private, before a committee of the house of representatives; the witnesses not confronted with those persons against whom their testimony was to operate; not subjected to cross-examination. The admission of testimony taken in this manner is no less contradictory to the practice of every court known to the American constitutions, than to the plain principles of natural justice. Had those witnesses been cross-examined, it is impossible to tell what circumstances might have appeared to give a different complexion to the whole case. In testimony too not delivered from the mouth of the witness himself, but taken in writing, and taken by one side only, it is natural to presume that whatever makes in favour of that side, will be more particularly dwelt on, and more strongly expressed; while such parts as seem opposed to it are apt to be either omitted or stated imperfectly. This arises from the natural imperfection of the human mind, from the effect of our passions on our understanding, and our conduct. Hence has resulted a rule which is invariably observed in all our courts; that testimony is never admitted, unless both parties have had an opportunity of joining in the examination.

In the case of these affidavits, it is affirmed, that the examining committee refused to take down material parts of the testimony actually given by the witnesses, and tending to exculpate the members accused of corruption.[4] In the uncertainty that there is, whether this fact may not have been misunderstood, the respect due to such a body as the committee of a legislative assembly, represses those remarks, to which, if true, it must give rise.

But the evidence itself, if properly taken, is liable to many strong objections.

In some instances it is contradictory,[5] and conjectural?[6] It depends in a great degree on hearsay,[7] which the best known rules of law, and the dictates of common justice, concur in rejecting. It consists almost wholly of the confessions of members made, not to the legislature, or the committee, but to the witnessess, about the impropriety of their own conduct; and finally, the whole scope of it is to prove that certain members, who voted for the law, were actuated by corrupt motives; a point which it has been shown, can never be inquired into, for the purpose of invalidating a legislative act.

It is worthy of remark also, that the members who appear, by these affidavits, to have been concerned in the contract, were to pay their portion of the purchase money.[8] There is, indeed, one instance of the contrary; but it is proved by the hearsay confession, not of the member himself, but of a person, who declared himself to be one of the purchasers.[9]

This testimony, therefore, whether its substance be regarded, or the manner of its being taken, appears equally defective.

But, if it were less so, if the proofs of corruption in the legislature, were not only admissible but strong, they would be greatly counterbalanced, by the conduct of the governor. He has never been accused, or even suspected, of corruption. It can hardly be conceived, that, pure himself, he would have aided the corruption of others; would have sanctioned an act which he knew to have originated in motives so flagitious. Had these practices existed, it is next to impossible that they should have escaped his knowledge: for he was not only on the spot, and well acquainted with all the actors in this business, but lived in the closest connection and intimacy, with some of its warmest opposers.[10]

It cannot be pretended that the governor countenanced this act through deference for the legislature; for the same motive would have led him to concur in the first bill, which, however, was rejected. He must, therefore, have assented to the second, because he found it free from those objections which had operated against the first; and considered it as conducive to the public good. Why may not the legislature be conceived to have acted from the same motives? Must corruption be resorted to in order to find a reason for their doing an act, which the governor, equally enlightened with them, was led to by a sense of duty?

Thus it seems clear that the legislature of Georgia was wholly incompetent to set aside this act, even had there been sufficient grounds; because this is a judicial, not a legislative function, and because the sale was a contract to which the state itself was a party: that had the legislature been competent, the evidence on which it proceeded was not only inconclusive, but altogether inadmissible: And that, since to dispose of the public land is one of the most undeniable powers of the legislature, and the motives of members, even if corrupt, which in this case is far from being established, cannot be alledged against the validity of a legislative act, there was no ground, either of unconstitutionality or corruption, upon which, even in a competent tribunal, this act could have been declared void.

It is proper to add that even if this contract could be set aside, an essential condition of doing so must be the repayment of the purchase money. It is one of the most obvious improprieties in the repealing act, that it attempts to destroy the purchase without making the least provision, or even stipulation, for their repayment.[11] If, as it has been asserted, the legislature which passed the repealing act made an appropriation of part of this money, it was a complete confirmation, as far as depended on them, of the contract which they avowed an intention of annulling.

From this view of the two points submitted, taken under all those aspects which were deemed important, the undersigned counsel is led to the following conclusion, which he certifies as his opinion: 1. That the United States never had a right to any part of the lands in question, above a line drawn due east from the mouth of the Yazoo: 2. That, under the circumstances of the case, they will probably be considered, in the courts of equity, as bound by the sales which have been made by the state of Georgia below that line: And 3. That the title of the purchasers, either above or below, can in no degree be affected by the repealing act of that State.

ROB. G. HARPER

New-York, Aug. 3rd, 1796.

ALEXANDER HAMILTON'S OPINION
ON THE GEORGIA REPEAL ACT

This legal advice,[1] which the Yazoo land companies solicited from Alexander Hamilton, is the first recorded suggestion that the federal contract clause prohibited not only state interference with private contracts but also with public contracts. Hamilton, in other words, argued that a state was constitutionally barred from breaking contractual agreements into which it had entered. Like his views on judicial review and the broad construction of Congress' power, Hamilton's opinion on the scope of the contract clause found its way into the constitutional decisions of the Marshall Court.

CASE

The legislature of the State of Georgia, by an act of the 7th January, 1795, directed a sale to be made of a certain tract of land, therein described to James Gunn and others, by the name of the Georgia Company, upon certain conditions therein specified. The sale was made pursuant to the act: the conditions of sale were performed by the purchasers, and a regular grant made to them, accordingly, of the said tract of land. Subsequent thereto, the said legislature has passed an act, whereby, on the suggestion of unconstitutionality, for various reasons, (prout the act,) and also of fraud and corruption, in application to the legislative body, the first act, and the grants thereupon, are declared null and void.

On the foregoing case, the opinion of counsel is desired, whether the title of the grantees and their assigns, the latter being *bona fide,* purchasers of them, for valuable considerations, be valid? Or, whether the last mentioned act be of force to annul the grant?

ANSWER

Never having examined the title of the State of Georgia to the lands in question, I have no knowledge whether that state was, itself, entitled to them, and in capacity to make a valid grant. I can, therefore, have no opinion on this point. But, assuming it, in the argument, as a fact, that the state of Georgia had, at the time of the grant, a good title to the land, I hold that the revocation of it is void, and that the grant is still in force.

Without pretending to judge of the original merits or demerits of the purchasers, it may be safely said to be a contravention of the first principles of natural justice and social policy, without any judicial decision of facts, by a positive act of the legislature, to revoke a grant of property regularly made for valuable consideration, under legislative authority, to the prejudice even of third persons, on every supposition, innocent of the alledged fraud or corruption; and it may be added, that the precedent is new, of revoking a grant on the suggestion of corruption of a legislative body. Nor do I perceive sufficient ground for the suggestion of unconstitutionality in the first act.

In addition to these general considerations, placing the revocation in a very unfavourable light, the constitution of the United States, article first, section tenth, declares that no state shall pass a law impairing the obligations of contract. This must be equivalent to saying, no state shall pass a law revoking, invalidating, or altering a contract. Every grant from one to another, whether the grantor be a state or an individual, is virtually a contract that the grantee shall hold and enjoy the thing granted against the grantor, and his representatives. It, therefore, appears to me, that taking the terms of the constitution in their large sense, and giving them effect according to the general spirit and policy of the provisions, the revocation of the grant by the act of the legislature of Georgia, may justly be considered as contrary to the constitution of the United States, and, therefore null; and that the courts of the United States, in cases within their jurisdiction, will be likely to pronounce it so.

(Signed)   ALEX. HAMILTON
March 25, 1795.[2]

ABRAHAM BISHOP'S
GEORGIA SPECULATION UNVEILED

Abraham Bishop (1763–1844) was a minor Connecticut politician.[1] He came from a well-to-do family, graduated from Yale in 1778 at the age of sixteen, but for some years it seemed as if Bishop would fritter his life away. He made a desultory and unsuccessful start as a lawyer, involved himself in an unhappy marriage, traveled in Europe, and taught school. By the mid-1790's, however, he settled down in his native New Haven to a life-long career built around Jeffersonian principles and political patronage. Bishop served as clerk of various local courts in the New Haven area and was an active Republican. In 1801 President Jefferson replaced the Federalist collector of the port of New Haven with Bishop's aging father, an appointment intended to benefit the son. Two years later his father died, and Bishop officially became the collector, holding the position until ousted in 1829 by another patronage-conscious President, Andrew Jackson.

Bishop's modest fame rests principally on a number of political pamphlets written near the turn of the century. These ridiculed the Federalists—"ye well-fed, well-dressed, chariot-rolling, caucus-keeping, levee-revelling federalists," he called them in one tract—and argued for Jeffersonian values. He wrote against the alliance of church and state, the marriage of business and government, and, as he saw it, the Federalists' reverence for class privileges and outmoded traditions.

The pamphlets were effective because Bishop had a talent for combining straightforward English with the hard-hitting satirical phrase. These qualities are very evident in *Georgia Speculation Unveiled* (1797),[2] interesting both as the most literate of the anti-Yazooist writings and as a perfect illustration of why anti-Yazooism, despite its inherent appeal to Republican purists, divided the Jeffersonian party. The tract affirms the supremacy of the legislature as the direct and ultimate expression of the democratic impulse, denies the power of the United States Supreme Court to void the repeal act, and generally insists on the sovereignty of the individual states. Yet, although all Jeffersonian Republicans should have been united in opposition to the Yazoo interest, they were not. Instead, the anti-Yazooist positions were largely manned by such southern Republicans as John Randolph and George Troup. The reason most northern Republican politicians failed to keep the faith is of course owing to the fact that they were compromised by their involvement (or that of their constituents) in the Yazoo speculation.

Abraham Bishop himself is a prime example. A careful reading of his pamphlet reveals his special concern with the question whether or not innocent purchasers of Georgia lands are obligated to pay those who deceived them.[3] Bishop frequently writes as if he were one of the aggrieved innocent purchasers; this implication is particularly strong in his closing line, where he tells the speculators: ". . . if the day of your total poverty, contempt, and despair, can be hastened by what is here written, I shall have paid to you, who deserve this character, the only debt, which in equity and good conscience I owe you."

In fact, the best anti-Yazooist tract was written by a speculator in Yazoo lands: in October, 1795, Abraham Bishop, along with his father and seven other residents of Connecticut, had purchased 550,000 acres of Georgia lands for $44,000. The Bishops' share was 200,000 acres at a cost of $16,000, which they paid for by giving two Georgia speculators $4,000 and promissory notes for the remainder, to be paid within twenty-four months. When Georgia repealed the sale, Bishop wrote his angry pamphlet and also sued the two sellers, John C. Nightingale and Phinehas Miller, for a return of the $4,000 and a release from the terms of the promissory notes. Nightingale and Miller in turn sued the Bishops for their failure to pay the promissory notes. These two cases were started in the federal Circuit Court for Connecticut in 1797 and dragged on inconclusively until 1805, when they were dismissed by mutual consent of the parties.[4] Interestingly, there is no record that after 1797 Abraham Bishop ever again did battle with the Yazooists, and the report of the United States Secretary of the Treasury in 1818 on the payments made to the claimants under the compensation law shows that he received a sum of $5,719.02.[5]

Abraham Bishop's venture into the Yazoo speculation is consistent with all that is known about him. The sketch of Bishop's life in the *Dictionary of American Biography* notes that his appointment as collector of New Haven "quieted his radical tendencies" and that "he spent the rest of his life acquiring respectability, a belief in the protective tariff, and a fortune, apparently with marked success in each endeavor." [6] In many ways, then, *Georgia Speculation Unveiled* is a more revealing commentary on the Yazoo speculation than its author intended.

This Pamphlet is an actual, though not a literal answer to the "STATE OF FACTS," published by the Georgia Companies. It contains the outlines of the present state of the Georgia business, and a brief sketch of the arguments on both sides, with such Commentaries as the compass of the work would allow. The general tenor of it, especially that part which treats of the Chancery powers of our Courts, will be found applicable to the cases of all, who have suffered by any kind of Land speculation.

NO. I

Let the buyer look out, is a maxim supposed applicable to all contracts where land is named; but to the northern sales of Georgia land it can have no application; for these are not sales of *land,* as facts now shew; and by the sellers were not intended to be sales of *land,* but a mere floating imaginary right to buy land —which partakes no more of reality than a right to buy goods or horses. The right to buy Indian land is at best no more than a chattel, and is a perfect non-descript, unknown to all the writers upon real estate. It originated in avarice and power, and never, *in this instance,* has gained any other existence than on paper.

The State of Georgia claimed a right in fee to certain lands, —which lands were in fact subject to an absolute fee-simple, in the right owners,—and said state acknowledged this fee, subject to a particular kind of usufruct—which usufruct was the absolute undisputed dominion and possession of these owners, with an ancient, inherent and interminable right of doing with it as they pleased, without any hindrance or molestation from this claimant:—and this fee, dominion and possession of the right owners, guaranteed by the United States, and secured by severe laws from all fraud and force on the part of the preemptors:— and to crown all, this same preemption claimed over the heads of this same state of Georgia by the United States, who have an uncontrolable right to decide by judicial officers of their own creation on the right of preemption:—and again, this usurped preemption of the state of Georgia, secured from invasion by their own constitution and positive laws, and guarded against fraud and deceit by all those general maxims which obtain and are recognized in all sovereign states.

The mind of man can proceed but one step further, and yet retain one idea of lands or claims; and this step is presented in the kind of right, which the Georgia companies claim to these lands. By the force of fraud and corruption (as I shall shew hereafter) they have broken through all the barriers, which so perfectly secured the fee and possession of the right owners—and after obtaining the semblance of a granting act, came forward, and by a printed pamphlet, entitled, *"State of Facts,"* &c. declared to all the world, that they were the true and lawful assignees of the *fee* of those lands, and to all the uses of it, except a particular kind of usufruct, called a right of hunting and fishing of the Indians. Not one of the attributes of their claim was of necessity a matter of record; and the land could not from its situation promise to any purchaser under them an office of record, where he might resort for evidence of title;—therefore every thing inducing a sale must be from the seller, and in all such cases, *let the seller look out, that he deceive not the buyer.* 'Tis a maxim of common sense and reason, that whatever inducements the seller improves to draw money from the buyer he shall make true, or suffer the inconvenience of their proving false; for if he has taken money for his own falshoods, he ought to refund it, whenever equity and good conscience demand it.—And if this rule is not in the books, it ought to be placed there, by the side of *caveat emptor.* Both parties are to look out; all men are to look out; *but courts are especially to look out, and see that men get no gain by cheating their neighbours;*—and if in every case they cannot find a precedent for doing right, let them, as Lord Hardwicke did, make a precedent.

The frauds practised in the negociation and sales of these Georgia lands, have been as numerous and complicated as the heart of man could conceive; and the property now resting for decision of the courts in consequence of them, is to an immense amount. The rescinding act of the state of Georgia has brought all these matters to a crisis, and one decision of the supreme court of the United States, may probably influence the decisions of lower courts. I shall therefore proceed to discuss,—1st. the validity of this rescinding act—2d. the impossibility of affecting it by any court or power in the United States—and 3d. the consequence upon all the notes depending on the sales under the granting act.

1. The validity of the rescinding act depends on the power which passed it.—This is the sovereign independent state of Georgia, having a right to make or repeal their own laws at pleasure, and this right wholly uncontrolable. When individuals deal with each other, there are courts to compel compliance with their contracts:—how far the policy of the United States will sustain a citizen in a dispute against a state, for monies due on state notes, or otherwise acknowledged; and whether a marshall may safely commit to prison the governor, treasurer or secretary of the state for a state debt, is beside my present object. This was a grant said to be standing on records, whereof the legislature had the control. These records do not now exist;—they are burnt, and the reasons are assigned on new records for destroying the same. I ask, what remedy have the Georgia companies? They cannot bring a writ of ejectment; for none but the Indians are in possession.—They cannot sue for the lands, but in the state where the lands lie;—and whatever court tries the cause, must try it by the existing laws of the state of Georgia; and no law exists in favor of the companies.—Copies of record will not answer: if they would, a secretary might certify what on trial would eject all the people of a state from every foot of their land. The existing laws must be such as are recognized by the people, legally represented; and the legal representatives must have a right to declare their sense of the laws.

In various cases a legislature may declare a pretended act void —as whenever 'tis contrary to constitution—as where a less number was present at passing it, than is required to form a house— or where the speaker or president of the council was bribed to declare that a vote, which was not a vote; or where the voters in favor of an act were interested in the passing of it; or where it was passed by members not having taken the necessary oaths; and in all cases, where fraud and deceit are combined between those who compose the legislature, and those who are to be benefited by any particular act. Take this power from a legislature, and where is the sovereignty of the state?—Such a powerless state would be left open to the ravages of all the unprincipled men in the universe, and their property and rights might be bartered for bribes. All contracts with sovereign states must be made in confidence that power and integrity will be united; and he who approaches a sovereign people for grants, must do it with clean hands. The maxims of honor and honesty, which form a part of the policy of all enlightened sovereignties, are a sufficient guarantee to those who deal uprightly with governments. Let those who maintain a different doctrine, go prosecute the national assembly of France to make good their assignats, or the United States for their continental bills.—Where is the power to try the cause?—Or let such point out the power, which can control the state of Georgia in the enaction of their laws, or the management of their records. Can the congress of the United States do it? Certainly no:—this would destroy the confederation. Can the court of the United States? Clearly they cannot judge what laws ought to exist.

All the arguments of the opposers to the rescinding act would be more plausible, if they had in view real estate in fee and possession; and had honestly paid a fair consideration for it.—In such a case the law might stretch its force to obtain them justice; but this being an unsubstantial thing the law cannot reach it, and could not do it, even if the question was between two individuals. As in case A owns a large farm, divided into 16 lots, and has a right to keep it and use it as long as he lives, and then to leave it to his heirs forever, B, C, D, and so on, to the number of 16; knowing that competition of buyers raises the value of farms, and disposed for their own advantage to deprive A of this benefit, agree among them that B shall alone bid on lot No. 1, C on No. 2, so that A may sell to no other.—B sells his right of preemption in lot No. 1 to S for 10 dollars—S sells it to T for 100—T to U for 1000. Now B declares that he was cheated out of it,—that he never delivered the deed, &c. and that he holds himself a bidder for the land as much as ever. A is still in possession, and likely so to continue. Can U sustain an action against B? All men will agree that B has done U no damage, and U has gained nothing by his money; but U has given his notes to T, and they are put in suit.—He petitions for relief, stating that T pretended that he owned the fee, and that it was the most valuable part of the farm; and that this was his inducement to give 1000 dollars; that there were no records to resort to, and that he relied solely on T's word. T owns it all—and that in fact *he did not own the land, but had a right to buy it*. Will a court doubt what equity and good conscience demand in this case?—To apply this, the land in question is merely a right to buy land, which perhaps may never be for sale; which consideration alone, separate from the doctrine of state sovereignty, is an invincible intrenchment for the state of Georgia, and the northern purchasers.

Some say they may restore the records. Am I to lie out of my money for an age, waiting to see whether the sovereign state of Georgia will pity me for having been cheated by those who cheated her? But say others, she may grant it to another company, and then we may try the title. Perhaps ages may pass before this sovereign state will grant it again, and then neither of us can try the title to the lands, 'till the Indian title is extinguished.— That can't be done, but by liberty to hold a treaty; and this liberty cannot be granted to those whom the state of Georgia denies as her grantees, without violating her sovereignty; unless by a suit at law the title should be determined;— and this title can never be made a law question, 'till the fee and possession of the right owners is extinguished. Suppose a suit brought for the preemption, what marshall could levy the execution?—on what could he levy it? Whatever might be the judgment, it would be an idle one, founded on nothing, and no one could carry it into effect.

Others say we have fairly bought it, *and will have it*—and under this grant, rescinded and burnt, negociations are now making on the Mississippi lands. Vain new editions of Mississippi dreams! Such managers might as well have used force without a grant; but when force is used, the reign of law and argument has ceased.

Those who have not cheated nor been cheated in this business, feel dispassionate; they utter no deprecations against Jackson and his party, but calmly view the state of Georgia, exercising a sovereign right in a sovereign and righteous manner. A great class of people comfort themselves with a hope of trying the question in the federal court, in some one of the northern states, whether the rescinding act is valid. As well might you try it before a justice's court: the judgment of both would be equally powerless. Can you put at issue in a distant state the sovereignty of Georgia? Can you obtain judgment that her legislature has been distracted; and what will you do with your execution? All the propositions which have been made to render the rescinding act of no validity are equally unpromising, as to the present claimants under the granting act.—All common-law principles attempted to be applied to the subject are lost; and the greatest lawyer is as the weakest peasant, when attempting to discuss it. As preemptive claims were never founded on law or right, they are not a subject of law-books; as they are peculiar to this country, they are not understood elsewhere; and as no cases such as that of the rescinding act have ever before occurred, we are not to wonder, that men should be confounded at the operation of it.

But take the nature of their claims, as it is explained—the rule of equity, which applies to the transfer of them—the sovereignty of the state—the rescinding of the act—the impracticability of trying the legality or equity of it, and it will fairly appear that *the present purchasers have nothing, and have no prospect of any thing for their money or their notes.*

2d. These things being true, what is the consequence upon the notes, depending on the sales under the granting act? My answer is, that they ought not to be paid. What forms the courts may think proper to adopt in rendering them void is not material. If it be once ascertained that they ought to be void, courts will adopt or invent means proper for the end.

I begin then by taking the three following positions—1st. *That where a man has been deceived in a contract, and in consequence has deceived another, he shall gain nothing by the transfer: if he escape without loss, it is the most he can desire.—2d. If he knew of the deceit practised on him previous to his selling, and yet made use of the deceit to induce a bargain, the least he can expect is the total loss of the price agreed on.—3d. If he were a partaker in the original deceit, he ought to lose the whole and be severely punished.* All the sellers of Georgia land have been within these classes; for there was deceit at the bottom;—and the many insidious arts practised by many of the sellers, give good reason to believe that they were the *original* deceivers.

The whole transaction has all the air and appearance of a deep-laid and thoroughly executed plan of swindling.—The management of it proves that in the plan some southern people were to be gainers, and a great number of the northern people to be losers. I venture to predict, that some southern people will be bankrupts, and that the northern people will, after much vexation and delay, escape from loss. The rescinding act has struck a deadly blow at these first deceivers, and has arrested their career at the very moment when they were about to be loaded with wealth.

In this precise stage of the business, the granting act being rescinded—the preemption resumed—no fee of lands in existence —the sellers greedy for payment, crouding for it at the bar of our courts—hosts of lawyers in their pay, on great wages—notes all in suit, and petitions for relief pending:—What can our courts do? I answer, they are courts of law and equity, and are instituted for the purpose of doing right between man and man; and this they are to do as far as may be, according to the principles and practice of law and equity in the books. I think it has been shewn abundantly, that this case could not have been contemplated in the books;—it will follow then that this must form the basis of a precedent, and must be determined on its own merits.

The first natural enquiry of the courts therefore, is—the character of the parties and their respective claims on the justice or equity of the law.—Not their private character; but that which they wear in relation to this new and unprecedented cause. The plaintiffs in these causes when asked this question may safely answer—"We are of those, who contrived and colluded with several members of the legislature of the state of Georgia, to procure an act, violating their constitution and alienating the property of the people.— By promises of gain, by bribes, we led them to violate their oaths and those principles of honor and fidelity to their constituents, which all laws command them to maintain.—We succeded in our plan—procured a grant—we published not single pages, but pamphlets of lies—circulated them with our own hands—supported them by our own affirmations—swore to them on our honor.—We thus enlisted men of integrity on our side— caused them to betray their neighbours—opened subscriptions for the land—headed with names of men, whose permission had never been obtained.—We entrapped the unwary—committed heads of families for more than they were worth—pretended that we were selling under the influence of embarrassment, for less than half what we might get, had we time to seek purchasers.—We hastened our bargains, lest the rescinding act should overtake us;—and to crown all, after we knew the act was passed, we employed emissaries from Philadelphia to ride express to complete bargains already projected, and to open contracts at all hazards;—and when all this was known, we cursed Jackson and his party, in the language of fallen Lucifer to Michael.—We then secretly employed lawyers to write treatises against the rescinding act, as their *voluntaries,* upon such an unprincipled measure.—We circulated these to convince the dupes of our management, that Jackson was an enemy to fair dealing, and that the sovereign state of Georgia was a miserable subjected province, whose laws wanted no other confutation than our contempt:—but when conviction begun to operate on the public mind, and even on our own, that this rescinding act was serious and conclusive,—we employed hosts of lawyers, with enormous fees, to abet our cause; —and by their combined influence, and the aid of law-books, we hope to bear all before us. Tho' we knew that the men whom we had deceived, retained only the miserable shadows of land, which we pretended to sell them, and were willing to give up their deeds, and to suffer loss for their delusion—we haughtily refused; and to shew our power, loaded them with attachments —put them to all manner of expense, and are determined that wide-spread ruin and desolation shall follow those who have dealt with us,—for which object we approach the altar of justice, and pray the aid of this honorable court to carry our purposes into effect.—And if the court doubt this our character, we refer them to the rescinding act, containing 64 depositions in proof of it—to our pamphlets, and to our uniform conduct." To which character, well may the court say—Hail Lucifer, son of the morning!

The other characters are plainly those, who have been the subjects of all this deceit, imposture, falshood and vexation; and who come before the court to obtain relief against a system of fraud and swindling—perhaps more complicated in its machinery, and varied in its operations, than any which has disgraced the character of man in this or any other age.

I have put language into the mouths of the plaintiffs, which they would not be apt to use—*for 'tis the language of truth,*—not fancied, but thorougly proveable; and with all the varnishes and apologies, which this age of reason, refinement and revolutions, can put upon their conduct, the result of a fair investigation will produce just such a conclusion.—To overdraw the character, or distort the cause in this stage of it, would be a prejudice to the end which is aimed at. I have therefore presented them as they must appear, when record, evidence and substantial testimony shall be combined in the proof;—which will infallibly take place before the conclusion of this business. Let not those judge chimerical, this mode of introducing characters, who have observed in courts of chancery every thing brought forward, which forms the characters of the parties, in direct relation to the cause in question.—This is always admitted, and no more is contended.

.   .   .   .

NO. II

From the premises in my first number, I open this with the following questions, and answers:—

1. Did the state of Georgia ever own the right in fee to the lands described in the granting act?—Answer—No.

2. Did not the pretended claimants under the granting act publish and circulate a pamphlet, entitled,—"STATE OF FACTS,"—declaring the right of the state to have been a right in fee, and the sale of the state to have been fair and constitutional?—Answer—They did.

3. Was there any truth in these declarations?—Answer—No.

4. Was it not generally represented to the purchasers in these northern states, verbally as well as by said pamphlets, that the state of Georgia would not, and could not, rescind said grant?—Answer—It was.

5. Was there any truth in this representation?—Answer—No.

6. Is not the grant rescinded in such manner, that the pur-

chasers are wholly foreclosed of all possible benefit from their purchases, 'till the same sovereign will and power which rescinded the act, shall be united to restore it?—Answer—Yes.

7. Is there any probability that they will ever voluntarily do this?—Answer—Not the least.

8. Can they be compelled to do it by any court or power in the United States?—Answer—No.

9. Has not the state of Georgia by their rescinding act, put at great hazard the property, limbs and life of any man or body of men, who within the limits of said state shall in any way attempt to contravene said act, or any clause of it?—Answer—Yes.

10. Have they not a sovereign right to make such laws as they judge proper for the well ordering of the state?—Answer—They have.

11. If the declarations of the sellers and of their pamphlets had been true, would not the purchases have been profitable to the purchasers?—Answer—They probably would.

12. Falshood having been substituted in the place of truth, and the purchasers having relied on the declarations of the sellers, and those declarations having proved uniformly deceitful—shall it be in the mouth of the sellers to say to the purchasers—"You ought to have looked out that we did not cheat you?"—Answer—No.

If any person is disposed to give a different answer to any of these questions, the question and answer shall be made the subject of a separate discussion.

Several powerful delusions have been improved to crown the first delusion.

1st. That a grant is in its nature irreversible.

2d. That provided the purchasers will ever have any claim on the sellers, they must first try the title which they have acquired; and if that fails, then they may come upon the sellers.

3d. That these lands were purchased as lottery tickets are, and if they had turned out fortunately, it would have been well with the purchasers: otherwise they must bear the loss.

4th. That all the book-principles relating to real estate and to notes are in favor of the sellers, and that contesting the payment will be vain.

5th. That our courts will decide against the rescinding act, and then the lands may be sold in Europe, for a dollar per acre.

6th. That the rescinding act was made in the tumult of the people, and that there is good chance of its being repealed, and the grant restored.

7th. That if this rescinding act is good, the state of Connecticut may rescind the act granting the reserve, and Massachusetts their act granting the Chenessee country.

By such chimeras, the advocates of the sales are addressing themselves to the hopes and fears, to the reason and to the weakness of the purchasers; and are thus endeavoring to wheedle them out of further payments. But be not deceived;—for this irreversible grant is actually reversed, beyond the power of man; and all the comparisons between the sovereign state of Georgia, granting their lands, and the province of New-Hampshire, then subject to Great-Britain, granting their lands, will be found vain. The distinction must be sustained, that a dependant power has a power above them, to compel them to make good their grants and contracts; and that *an independent power can make, or unmake grants at will; because no power can decide on the morality, equity, or policy of their measures.* If the granting act had been constitutional, fair and honorable, and the rescinding act ever so unfair and immoral,—yet the consequence to the purchasers would be equally fatal. The power which has deprived them of the lands, is beyond their control; and all the advocates in favour of the sellers, never have and never can suggest one practicable mode of even beginning to attack the validity of the rescinding act.—That of deciding against it in these northern states, has been already shewn to be futile. Some have been disposed to maintain, that if the first act could be void at all, it must have been so in its own nature; and therefore the rescinding act, notwithstanding the first, stands to be discussed on its own merits:—But this is only a re-production of the first delusion;—for the granting act does not stand at all: it is burnt, and that power alone, which could declare definitively on the validity of it, has put it beyond the reach of discussion. The power itself is first to be disscussed, and if you can once discuss that out of existence, you well know that the granting act will be good enough.—You have the parch-

ments, 'tis true, large as dining-tables, certified by the secretary.—
Vain shadows of a grant!—Dare you produce them in the state
of Georgia, to support the title which you pretended to sell us?
Of little worth are they, if they cannot be produced on a trial,
where if we obtain judgment, the execution will invest us with
the title which you sold us. A condition of wrong without redress,
or of right without power, is very undesirable to a landholder.
Your own wrongs, your own frauds and violations of morality,
have led up this act, against which you so vehemently cry—shame,
wickedness, immorality!—Go cry them in the streets of Georgia,
plead them in their courts, ring them in the ears of their legislators,—there alone will they answer our purpose. If this is all a fair
transaction, as you declared to us by words and pamphlets, make
it appear so to the world, and let us have the benefit of your
exertions.—While it appears unfair and wicked, we shall with-
hold from you payment—courts will sustain us in withholding
it:—and the certain event of the breaking of the bubble, will be
your own bankruptcy, which is even now at the doors. I have not
rested entirely on the ground of power, thro' any idea that the
granting act would be valid on its own merits. If any man judges
that it was valid, and that the sellers have conducted with a due
portion of integrity, let him assert it; and I am willing to take
the burden of proving the act bad, and unfairly obtained,—and
the conduct of a number of the sellers to have been thoroughly
abandoned.—In this number I include all those who were themselves deceived, and who in consequence deceived their neighbours, and who are demanding any profits in the trade. This
fact of demanding *profits* in such a business, accompanied by a
few acknowledged principles and deductions, will fix the character of such beyond a vindication.

I have thus answered the two first delusions, and pray you to
reflect, that the grant is really reversed and revoked, and that you
can never try your title to any purpose—that you have lost all
shadows of the land—and that if you have any defence to make,
any money to save, any notes to avoid, or any redress to obtain,
—now is your time; and the time to avail yourselves will be short.

Next, as to the similitude between these sales, and those of
lottery tickets, so often introduced, it may be just as respects a

number of the Georgia bargains, so far as it can apply; but if a man proposes to me to purchase of him a 100 tickets in the Savannah fire lottery, and shews me a scheme of the lottery, and assures me that it will be drawn in 60 days, and I buy them, and give him my note for the payment—and it afterwards appears that there was neither lottery, managers, nor any scheme published, or that there was a lottery without a prize, or one which could never be drawn,—am I to pay my note?—Certainly not —especially not, if I can prove that this same man contrived with several others, to make out a scheme of a lottery, which could not in its nature answer any other purposes than those of imposture. But this comparison with lottery tickets is not just: for in lottery tickets, every man buys with known hazard of loss or gain. In these bargains every man bought with the greatest certainty of gain, provided the pamphlets and declarations which he bought with his deeds, proved true.—He could not calculate upon loss, except from those circumstances of treachery and fraud on the part of the sellers, which would wholly vacate the contract.

But 4th. Those who have given notes, are to be frightened by the books! !—Unfortunately for the sellers, the books give no comfort, no support. Courts have been trammelled by books at the opening of this business.—Judge Chafe was trammelled with books in the opening of the famous Connecticut state cause; but after four days digestion, his mind was relieved, and he declared that the books did not apply, and that there was *no such thing as sustaining an analogy between protections granted by a sovereign independent state, and those granted by the dependant courts of Westminster-Hall.* By citing books and authorities, and covering the green cloth with folios, the advocates may persuade their Georgia clients, that much good may come out of evil; but on thorough canvassing, it will be found, that (strange to tell) the books can afford no light on a subject of which the compilers had no conception.

5th. Let purchasers be guarded against being amused by the prospect of *our* courts deciding against the rescinding act.—If all the courts in the United States should decide against it, and all the marshalls and deputy-marshalls, sheriffs and deputy-sheriffs, should be employed to carry their judgments into effect,—the whole would still be a miserable farce and delusion;—for they would not in the least prejudice the rescinding act, nor benefit our title, and the state of Georgia would care nothing about them.

6th. As to the rescinding act being made in the tumult of the people, and that there is good chance of its being repealed—there is not one word of truth, nor symptom of probability about it: —and this pretence is a mere continuation of the false and swindling measures, which have been practised on you.

And 7th. As to the hypothetical reasoning, that if Georgia could rescind this act, then Connecticut and Massachusetts can rescind theirs—it ought to be otherwise stated, viz.—That Georgia has rescinded her granting act, and if Connecticut and Massachusetts should rescind theirs, they would do as Georgia has done; —and what would the claimants do in any such case, where the Indian title is not extinguished? In a situation wholly remediless, as to title or preemption, are you who have thought yourselves purchasers of Georgia lands; and your situation is brought on you by your confidence in those, who sold to you;—and this situation is aggravated by the persecutions and law perplexities, with which these deceivers are hunting you. Your time is devoted, and your property subjected to the apparent rapacity of the Georgia sellers; but they in reality, are now only the puppets of the farce—there is not one chance in a thousand of their eventually gaining any thing; but still the farce must be carried on, for the emolument of the craftsmen. Of great importance is it in this situation, that you possess yourselves of facts—that you give way to no delusions—and that you compose yourselves under these complicated abuses. If you get rid of your notes, yet the land deeded to you is not worth a thousandth part of what you have paid—be that sum ever so small.

.   .   .   .

Happily our courts are not destitute of chancery powers, sufficient to carry the equitable objects of the rescinding act into full effect: and when the doctrines of chancery are introduced—when the original principles of right are contemplated—when this bubble is compared with other bubbles—when the parties and the causes are known, and the rescinding act is duly plead,—if courts can hesitate about pronouncing against the notes, it will be only that one fiat of the national legislature, may put a perpetual end to the convulsions and distress caused by the Georgia, Virginia, Susquehannah, Canada, and all other baseless speculations.

It will be well seen, that I have not left these notes to depend on the contingence of such a national measure. The defence of those, who are sued on their notes, stands most substantially on the chancery powers vested in our courts:—and the means of calling those powers into effectual exercise, have been just shewn to be abundant.

But merely to get rid of the payment of the notes is not the sole object.—Large sums of money have been paid, which in equity and good conscience ought to be refunded.—In addition to these, great damages have been sustained, by reason of the falshood and swindling practised in these sales. The lands or deeds in the hands of the purchasers, are not worth a farthing, —and would be worth the meerest trifle, if the rescinding act should now be burnt, and the granting act restored:—for the granting act restored would not invest you with the fee of the lands, subject to the right of hunting and fishing, &c.—which fee you thought yourselves to have bought: and the violent parties, which have been created in the confusion of this business, would probably prevent your ever obtaining a right to extinguish the Indian title.—Indeed the commotions about the Georgia lands, have led up a serious claim of congress,—which otherwise would have been as dormant as their claim to the Chenessee country.— This claim, however originated, will not be easily relinquished.

But if all obstacles were removed, your right to hold a treaty, is merely a right to buy the land at the full value of it,—and this you are to do under the eye of sworn commissioners and interpreters. This treaty is to be opened with great expense: and your agents are to meet not a few ignorant straggling Indians, but the powerful, opulent and enlightened nations of the Creeks, Chactaws and Chickasaws—headed by chiefs of great fame, information and influence.—The object of this treaty is, to buy from them the place of their birth, their conquests and their residence:—and you come to them under the fascinating character of men, representing a horde of impostors, who cheated the repre-

sentatives of the state of Georgia, out of their usurped and imposing right of alone bidding on these lands: and you apply to
them, after blood has been repeatedly and unsuccessfully shed, to
force them to retreat.—You apply to them for their lands—not as
a place of refuge from persecution—not as a soil, where you wish
to labour, and to introduce agriculture, and the arts of civilized
life—not as a place, where you wish to embrace and treat them
as a band of brothers;—but as a frontier, where you may erect
forts, establish garrisons, stretch the strong arm of the union, and
fill, with their ancient and implacable opressors and enemies.—
With a council such as these nations will present to you,—rum,
whisky and rusty nails, will not be considered as conclusive arguments:—truth, sincerity and a sufficiency of property to enable
them to remove where they may do better, will alone go down.
Will you tell them, that you have already paid large sums of
money, to prevent others from bidding on their lands—and that
therefore you cannot give the full value of them?—Will you
desire the commissioners to inform them, that you expect to
make immense fortunes out of their lands, and that there is no
way of your doing it, but by purchasing them for far less than
they are worth?—Shall your interpreters expound to them the
whole history of this business?—Or will you smoke with them
the calumet of peace, exchange your baubles for theirs, and call
them friends and brothers? Will you tell them, that you came
from a land flowing with milk and honey, abounding in corn
and green pastures, and overflowing in all the conveniences and
luxuries of life—from a land, where every industrious man may
gain wealth—and that for their sakes you are come up thither?
They know better than all this,—they have lately told us, at lake
Erie, that they know the arts of the white men:—and the Georgia commissioners, but last year, with as much parade as could
attend a treaty, and as plausible talks as you can hold with them,
got for answer, that they would not sell.—And suppose you get
the same answer, after all your expenses, what is your preemption
worth?—Or suppose they should offer the lands to you, at such
price as you have repeatedly declared them worth, if free from
incumbrance, what would your preemption be worth? As respects the Indians, the lands are theirs in fee, with all the uses

belonging to them;—and they care not for preemptive rights—they can disencumber them at pleasure—and they feel and know themselves entitled to as much in value, as the lands are worth to any purchaser,—and there is no propriety in their giving you 9-10ths of the whole land for selling the remainder:—and yet a less commission for doing this business, is hardly contemplated. Perhaps fraud or force may deprive these nations of their lands, within a few years; but I have no idea, that within a century they will voluntarily sell them:—for they are not a miserable handful, as the Georgia sellers represented, constantly decreasing in numbers, and rather inclining to retreat than to maintain their ground; but just the contrary.

Shall it be said, that the purchasers knew or ought to have known all these things?—The best answer will be, that they did not know them, and had not the means of knowing them, and the whole representation was as I have before stated—that there was only an usufruct between the purchasers and a complete possession of the lands,—which usufruct might be easily extinguished, as there were immense tracts farther to the westward and northward, where the Indians would find better hunting and fishing than on these lands.—The commotions respecting the sales have been such, that a restoration of the granting act, if such an event could be conceived, would be very far from restoring to the present claimants, what they supposed they had purchased:—so far from it, that the incumbrances then existing upon the claim, would in all probability be insurmountable. I have not even taken into my calculation, the influence which the state of Georgia, or any party among them, might use against you in case of a treaty,—nor the probable existence of a great interference of titles, by fraudulent and multiplied deeds, resting merely on detached paper or parchment, without any record to support them or discover their fallacy;—but we have a fair right to believe, that men who will take unprincipled means to get rich, will not be less abandoned in the means of extrication, when the gulph of bankruptcy is before them.

In view of the premises, I fully believe, that a restoration of the granting act, would not only wrong the people of Georgia, —but would prove a serious evil to the present claimants, and a dreadful misfortune to all who might be after purchasers.—It would open a new scene of delusive hopes to the world, and furnish new daggers to aim at the vitals of morality, fair dealing and confidence between man and man. Long enough have friends stabbed friends, neighbours betrayed neighbours—and the wealth of centuries been wasted by the delusions of a moment.—Truth, honesty and commercial credit have suffered wounds deep enough: and all the friends of society feel grateful to the legislature, which arrested in its progress the destructive pestilence. Formerly the enemies of man frequented the public roads—put pistols to the breasts of unsuspecting travellers, and robbed them of the valuables they had about them; but the sufferers could return to their houses and lands, and by industry repair the loss. —We live to see robbery in a more refined stile. Men who never added an iota to the wealth or morals of the world, and whose single moment was never devoted to making one being wiser or happier throughout the universe—riding in their chariots—plotting the ruin of born and unborn millions—aiming with feathers to cut throats, and on parchments to seal destruction,—these are the robbers of modern days.—They bring desolation among our farmers—they spread distress in towns—they scorn the paltry plunder of pocket-books, and watches—they aim at houses and lands—strike at the foundation of many generations,—and would destroy families, root and branch. Long enough have fraud, falshood and swindling stalked our streets:—often enough have our farmers left their fields and wrecked the industry of painful and honest years upon the mountains of Virginia:—often enough have our jails and dockets witnessed the ruined hopes of the dupes of Newtown and Stockbridge speculations.—These last are not imputable to the Georgia sellers,—unless by their superior address, and the wider ruin they have caused, they may claim the honor of ingurgitating these lesser robberies.

I am not distorting this subject; but am drawing likenesses of which the originals exist. The indignation of an incensed public, is fast gathering over you who have sat for this picture.—The advocates of your impostures, begin to discover, that they have been led to abet measures which they abhor. The means of paying fees are nearly exhausted—the funds to which you look for help, will prove as deceitful as the eyes of those, whom you have injured, will be dreadful to you, after your ruin shall be complete. Your characters, your hopes of wealth, your all, are tumbling into the pit, which you have digged for others:—and if the day of your total poverty, contempt and despair, can be hastened by what is here written, I shall have paid to you, who deserve this character, the only debt, which in equity and good conscience I owe you.

A. B.

New-Haven, Oct. 14, 1797.

JOHN RANDOLPH AND MATTHEW LYON'S DEBATE IN THE HOUSE OF REPRESENTATIVES

The polemical exchange[1] between John Randolph and Matthew Lyon typifies the bitterness and emotionalism which enveloped the Yazoo issue. At this stage in the twenty-year dispute Randolph was highly effective in his opposition to a compensation law. Randolph's speech on January 29, 1805, reveals in sharp outline the main elements of his political style. He insisted that "true" Republicanism was exclusively on his side and skillfully used literary allusions and rhetorical appeals, all the while directing stinging personal attacks against those who opposed him. In this instance he heaped abuse on Postmaster General Gideon Granger and Representative Matthew Lyon. According to Randolph, Granger, a prominent lobbyist for the New England Mississippi Land Company, was using his official position to buy Yazoo votes in favor of the compensation bill. The Postmaster General, he claimed, was bribing congressmen with the lure of mail-carrying contracts, a charge that directly implicated Matthew Lyon, who held such contracts.

In attacking Lyon, however, Randolph had fastened on an opponent who could answer him in kind. Matthew Lyon, in fact, was one of the most outspoken and pugnacious men ever to sit in Congress.[2] A businessman, politician, and soldier, Lyon first attained distinction during the Revolutionary War as a colonel in Ethan Allen's Vermont militia. Although busy in a variety of entrepreneurial activities, Lyon also found time for politics in his native Vermont. He was elected to Congress in 1797 as a Republican and became a national celebrity because of a violent fight with Roger Griswold, a Federalist congressman from Connecticut. When Griswold spoke disparagingly of his military record, Lyon responded by spitting in Griswold's face. Fifteen days later, after the House had refused to expel Lyon, Griswold revenged himself by caning the "spitting animal," as the Federalist press labeled the Vermont Republican.[3] Lyon was soon in trouble again for violating the Sedition Act; when he was imprisoned, he became renowned as a Republican hero. His constituents returned him to Congress in 1800 with a huge majority, but one year later he moved his business interests westward to Kentucky. Lyon remained in politics, however, and sat in the House from 1803 to 1811 as a representative from the new state.

RANDOLPH AND LYON'S DEBATE

Since both Randolph and Lyon had bona fide credentials as charter Jeffersonian Republicans, their clash in a sense exemplifies the split that the Yazoo issue caused in the Republican ranks. Randolph's and Lyon's flair for personal polemics should not obscure the fact that their hot debate reflected some severe tensions in the governing party.

THE GENTLEMAN FROM VIRGINIA: MR. RANDOLPH

The facts which I am about to mention are derived from such a source that I could almost pledge myself for their truth: When the agent of the Georgia Mississippi Company (under whom the New England Land Company claim) arrived in the Eastern States, he had great difficulty in disposing of his booty. The rumor of the fraud by which it was acquired had gone before him. People did not like to vest their money in this new Mississippi scheme. He accordingly applied to some leading men of wealth and intelligence, offering to some as high as 200,000 acres, to others less, for which they were neither to pay money, nor pass their paper, but were to stand on his books as purchasers at so much per acre. These were the decoy-birds to bring the ducks and geese into the net of speculation. On the faith of these persons, under the idea that men of their information would not risk such vast sums without some prospect of return, others resolved to venture, and gambled in this new land fund, laid out their money in the Yazoo lottery and have drawn blanks. And these, sir, are the innocent purchasers by whom we are beset; purchasers without price, who never paid a shilling, and never can be called upon for one; the vile panders of speculation. And in what do their dupes differ from the losers in any other gambling or usurious transaction? The premium was proportioned to the risk. As well may your buyers and sellers of stock, your bulls and your bears of the alley, require indemnification for their losses at the hands of the nation. There is another fact, too little known, but unquestionably true, in relation to this business. This scheme of buying up the Western Territory of Georgia did not originate there. It was hatched in Philadelphia and New York, (and I believe Boston; of this, however, I am not positive,) and the funds with which it was effected were principally furnished by moneyed capitalists in those towns. The direction of these re-

sources devolved chiefly on the Senator who has been mentioned.[4]
Too wary to commit himself to writing, he and his associates
agreed upon a countersign. His re-election to the Senate was to
be considered as evidence that the temper of the Legislature of
Georgia was suited to their purpose, and his Northern confederates were to take their measures accordingly. In proof of this
fact, no sooner was the news of his reappointment announced at
New York, than it was publicly said in a coffee house there,
"then the Western Territory of Georgia is sold." Does this require
a comment? Do you not see the strong probability that many of
those, who now appear in the character of purchasers from the
original grantees named in the act of 1795, are in fact partners,
perhaps instigators and prime movers of a transaction in which
their names do not appear? Amidst such a complication of guilt,
how are you to discriminate; how fix the Proteus? The chairman
of the Committee of Claims,[5] who brought in this report, under
the lash of whose criticism we have all so often smarted, that he
is generally known as the pedagogue of the House, will give me
leave on this subject to refer him to an authority. It is one with
which he is no doubt familiar, and, however humble, well disposed to respect. The authority which I am about to cite is Dill-
worth's Spelling Book, and if it will be more grateful to the
gentleman, not our common American edition, but the Royal
English Spelling Book. In one of the chapters of that useful ele-
mentary work it is related, that two persons going into a shop on
pretence of purchase, one of them stole a piece of goods and
handed it to the other to conceal under his cloak. When challenged with the theft, he who stole it said he had it not, and he
who had it said he did not take it. Gentlemen, replied the honest tradesman, what you say may all be very true, but, at the
same time, I know that between you I am robbed. And such
precisely is our case. But I hope, sir, we shall not permit the
parties, whether original grantees who took it, or subsequent
purchasers who have it, to make off with the public property.

The rigor of the Committee of Claims has passed into a proverb. It has more than once caused the justice of this House to
be questioned. What, then, was our surprise on reading their
report, to find that they have discovered "Equity" in the preten-

sions of these petitioners. Sir, when the war-worn soldier of the Revolution, or the desolate widow and famished offspring of him who sealed your independence with his blood, ask at the door of that Committee for bread, they receive the statute of limitation. On such occasions you hear of no equity in the case. Their claims have not the stamp and seal of iniquity upon them. *Summum jus* is the measure dealt out to them. The equity of the Committee is reserved for those claims which are branded with iniquity and stamped with infamy. This reminds me of the story of a poor, distressed female in London applying for admittance into the Magdalen Charity. Being asked who she was, her wretched tale was told in a few words—"I am poor, innocent, and friendless." "Unhappy girl, replied the director, your case does not come within the purview of this institution. Innocence has no admission here; this is a place of reception for prostitutes; you must go and qualify yourself before you can partake of our relief." With equal discretion the directors of the Committee of Claims suffer nothing to find support in their asylum but what is tainted with corruption, and stamped with fraud. Give it these properties and they will give it "equity."

But we are told that the United States gave even less for these lands than the price paid by the several companies of 1795. Admitting the fact, (which is unquestionably false,) did Georgia sell to the Union for pounds, shillings and pence? Did North Carolina and Virginia, in their acts of cession of even more extensive countries, look to pecuniary profit? Are we become so grovelling that public spirit and the general good, go for nothing? The money which we engaged to pay out of the proceeds of the land, although more than double the amount paid by the four companies in 1795 constitutes but a small part even of the pecuniary consideration. We are, moreover, pledged to the extinguishment of the Indian title to an immense territory within the present limits of Georgia. It has been whispered in my ear that the fate of a late treaty with the Creeks is to depend on the decision of this question, and as the British Treaty and the Yazoo were made to stand or fall together in 1795 so the Creek Treaty and the Yazoo are to stand or fall together in 1805. But those who hold out this threat to the members from Georgia, should know them better, should be told that they are made of the sternest stuff of republicanism, and can neither be coaxed nor intimidated out of their principles. Of those who talk of the Western lands being acquired for nothing, I would ask if that be an argument for throwing them away upon flagitious men? But were the toils, and dangers, and treasures of the Revolution nothing? The bloody battles, the burning and devastations of the Southern and Western countries? Was the expedition of the brave and intrepid Clarke, which wants only a Polybius to rival the march of Thrasymene; were the exploits of this American Hannibal, who secured the Western country to you, nothing? Were your Indian wars and massacres nothing?

This Government, let me remind you, has acquired the confidence of the public by the disinterestedness of its measures. The repeal of the internal taxes is not the least conspicuous among them. How long will you retain that well-earned confidence, if you lavish on a band of speculators a landed capital whose annual interest is more than equivalent to the whole proceeds of those taxes? I will not go into petty details now, but I pledge myself that, whoever makes the calculation, will find the value of the land, together with the expense of extinguishing the Indian title, at the rate of our last treaty in that quarter, to yield a clear perpetual annuity, equal to the receipt from the internal taxes. What would you say to a proposition to revive those taxes and mortgage them for the payment of the interest on a Yazoo stock? Do you wonder that we shrink from such a precipice? Shall a republican House of Representatives sanction this wanton waste of the public resources to nourish the bane of every Republic? Are you simple enough to believe that the five millions will quiet them? Yes, as the tribute of the Roman world satisfied their barbarian enemies. You only whet their appetite and increase their means for extorting more. Like the Gauls, after the sack of Rome, they will make their second attempt upon the Capitol, before they have divided the plunder acquired in the first. When I see the formidable front displayed by this band of broken speculators, I am irresistibly impelled to inquire, what would have been their force if their attempt on the western country of Georgia had not been baffled by the virtue and patriotism of that

State? What is there in this Government that could have coped with them? Sir, you must have built another wing to your Capitol, for the third branch of your Legislature. You would have had a Yazoo estate in your empire, not with a qualified negative, but an absolute veto on all your proceedings. Scarcely would they have left you the initiative.

I have said, and I repeat it, that the aspect in which this thing presents itself, would, alone, determine me to resist it. In one of the petitioners I behold an Executive officer, who receives and distributes a yearly revenue of $300,000, yielding scarcely any net profit to Government,[6] Offices in his disposal to the annual amount of $94,000, and contracts more lucrative making up the residue of the sum. A patronage limited only by the extent of our country. Is this right? Is it even decent? Shall political power be made the engine of private interest? Shall such a suspicion tarnish your proceedings? How would you receive a petition from the President of the United States, if such a thing can be supposed possible? Sir, I wish to see the same purity pervading every subordinate branch of administration, which, I am persuaded, exists in its great departments.—Shall persons holding appointments under the great and good man, who presides over our councils, draw on the rich fund of his well-earned reputation, to eke out their flimsy and scanty pretensions? Is the relation in which they stand to him, to be made the cloak and cover of their dark designs? To the gentleman from New York, (Mr. Root.) who takes fire at every insinuation against his friend, I have only to observe, on this subject, that what I dare to say, I dare to justify. To the House I will relate an incident, from which it may judge how far I have lightly conceived or expressed an opinion to the prejudice of any man. I owe an apology to my informant for making public what he certainly did not authorize me to reveal. There is no reparation which can be offered by one gentleman and accepted by another, that I shall not be ready to make him; but I feel myself already justified to him, since he sees the circumstances under which I act. A few evenings since, a profitable contract for carrying the mail was offered to a friend of mine who is a member of this House. You must know, sir, that the person so often alluded to maintains a jackall, fed, not (as you would suppose) upon the offal of contract, but with the fairest pieces in the shambles; and, at night, when honest men are in bed, does this obscene animal prowl through the streets of this vast and desolate city, seeking whom he may tamper with. Well, sir, when this worthy plenipotentiary had made his proposal, in due form, the independent man to whom it was addressed, saw at once its drift. "Tell your principal, said he, that I will take his contract, but I shall vote against the Yazoo claim, notwithstanding." Next day, he was told that there had been some misunderstanding of the business, that he could not have the contract, as it was previously bespoken by another!

Sir, I well recollect, when first I had the honor of a seat in this House, we were members then of a small minority; a poor, forlorn hope; that this very petitioner appeared in Philadelphia, on behalf of another great land company on Lake Erie. He then told us, as an inducement to vote for the Connecticut reserve (as it was called) that if that measure failed, it would ruin the republicans and the cause in that State. You, sir, cannot have forgotten the reply he received: "That we did not understand the republicanism that was to be paid for; that we feared it was not of the right sort, but spurious." And, having maintained our principles through the ordeal of that day, shall we now abandon them, to act with the men and upon the maxims which we then abjured? Shall we now condescend to means which we disdained to use in the most desperate crisis of our political fortune? This is, indeed, the age of monstrous coalitions; and this corruption has the quality of cementing the most inveterate enmities, personal as well as political. It has united in close concert those, of whom it has been said, not in the figurative language of prophecy, but in the sober narrative of history: "I have bruised thy head, and thou hast bruised my heel." Such is the description of persons who would present to the President of the United States an act to which when he puts his hand, he signs a libel on his whole political life. But he will never tarnish the unsullied lustre of his fame; he will never sanction the monstrous position, (for such it is, dress it up as you will,) "that a legislator may sell his vote, and a right, which cannot be divested, will pass under such sale."

Establish this doctrine, and there is an end of representative Government; from that moment republicanism receives its death-blow.

The feeble cry of Virginian influence and ambitious leaders, is attempted to be raised. If such insinuations were worthy of reply, I might appeal to you, Mr. Speaker, for the fact, that no man in this House, (yourself, perhaps, excepted.) is oftener in a minority than I am. If by a leader he meant one who speaks his opinion freely and boldly; who claims something of that independence of which the gentleman from New York so loudly vaunts; who will not connive at public robbery, be the robbers whom they may, then the imputation may be just; such is the nature of my ambition; but, in the common acceptation of words, nothing can be more false. In the coarse, language of the proverb, " 'tis the still sow that sucks the draff." No, sir, we are not the leaders. There they sit, and well they know it, forcing down our throats the most obnoxious measures. Gentlemen may be silent, but they shall be dragged into public view. If they direct our councils at least let them answer for the result. We will not be responsible for their measures. If we do not hold the reins we will not be accountable for the accidents which may befall the carriage.

But, sir, I am a denunciator! Of whom? Of the gentlemen on my left? Not at all; but of those men and their principles whom the people themselves have denounced: on whom they have burnt their indelible curse, deep and lasting as the lightning of Heaven. But, you are told, not to regard such idle declamation. I would remind the gentleman from New York that, if to declaim be not to reason, so neither is it to be argumentative to be dull. Warmth is the creature of the heart, not of the head. A position, in itself just, can lose no part of its truth from the manner in which it is uttered, whether by the driest and most stupid special pleader, or bellowed with the lungs of a Stentor. Are our opponents ashamed of their cause, that they devolve its defence on the little ones by whom we are beset?

Mr. Speaker, I had hoped that we should not be content to live upon the principal of our popularity; that we should go on to deserve the public confidence and the disapprobation of the gentlemen over the way. But, if everything is to be reversed, if official influence is to become the handmaid of private interest, if the old system is to be revived with the old men, or any that can be picked up, I may deplore the defection, but never will I cease to stigmatize it. Never shall I hesitate between any minority, far less that in which I now find myself, and such a majority as is opposed to us. I took my degrees, sir, in this House, in a minority, much smaller, indeed, but of the same stamp. A minority, whose every act bore the test of rigorous principle, and with them to the last I will exclaim, *fiat justitia, ruat cælum.*

THE GENTLEMAN FROM KENTUCKY: MR. LYON

After having taken a view of the subject now before the House, during the last session, in all its shapes and bearings, and after having, in a very ample and explicit manner, given the reasons which governed my vote at that time, it was my intention to have given a silent vote on this occasion. The hope of changing the mind of a single member does not now call upon me to rise; no, sir, the uncandid insinuations, the undeserved reproaches and criminations from a member from Virginia have caused me to break through that silence I had imposed upon myself. Yet, since I am up, permit me to remind you, sir, of that view, and in a very brief manner of those reasons which will in every stage of this business induce me to adhere to the contemplated compromise. It seems that the government of Georgia, in 1792, made an agreement with certain companies which was not fulfilled by the grantees, nor consummated by the government of Georgia, for the sale of a large part of their western lands; accordingly, the Legislature again offered those lands for sale, and by solemn legislative and executive acts, did sell, and by deed convey forty millions of acres of those lands to certain other companies, for which they received the compensation agreed on. That those grantees, having it in their power to show to purchasers the best possible evidence of a good and authentic title, did sell the property thus purchased to other purchasers, who had the best right imaginable to put faith in the authenticated documents and title papers presented to them—documents and title papers as good as any ever obtained from an individual by another, or from a State or a nation by a purchaser. Notwithstanding which the succeeding Legislature, not liking the bargain, assumed or attempted to assume the power of reclaiming the property, and passed an act purporting their intention of invalidating the title given by their predecessors, as well as for the destruction of the records and every evidence of the title given by them.

It appears that the purchasers, when they found Georgia offering to cede those lands to the United States, gave warning and notice of their claims to the Chief Magistrate of the Union; in consequence of which, or for some other cause, a provision for a compromise with the claimants was made in the law which authorized the holding a treaty with Georgia respecting the cession of those lands. Commissioners of the United States, agreeably to the powers vested in them by that provision, have met the claimants, and have, it seems, agreed on terms of compromise, which in my opinion are very advantageous to the United States; which compromise is now before this House for their sanction.

I stated last year that, under my impression of the validity of the title of the claimants, the compromise was more advantageous to the nation than could be expected; more advantageous to be sure than I had previously expected could have been made. I still think it an advantageous bargain, on account of the revenue which will arise from the sale of the residue of the lands—seven-eighths of forty millions, to which an unexceptionable title can then be given, a title which good farmers and useful settlers will not fear to improve under. Advantageous, I say also, on account of the benefit to be derived from the early settlement of some of the best lands, and in the best situation of any the Government claims—a country intersected by many navigable waters, and through which the road goes from almost every State in the Union to Natchez and New Orleans; a road which, in the present state of things, is frequently infested with murderers and freebooters.

Nothing could be more surprising to me than the opposition this, in my opinion, reasonable, necessary and profitable compromise has met with, both last session and this. I say profitable, because it takes not a cent out of the Treasury, nor from any other fund but the land itself; which, however wrong it was to purchase it, knowing it to be sold to others, whose claim was in a measure recognised by the contemplated compromise at the very outset of the negotiation—however wrong, I say, it might have been for the United States to have become the purchasers, they have not paid, nor are they bound to pay a shilling from any other fund than the land itself, notwithstanding all this clamor about robbery. Such has ever been my opinion of public faith, that although I doubt not that bribery was used in the Legislature of Georgia in the transaction of 1795, to a certain degree, their successors and the State were bound to abide by the solemn contract. I say solemn, because it appears to be confirmed by the Executive of the State, against whom I do not recollect any charge of bribery to have been made. Had that Executive (who was on the spot, and must have been a better judge of the corruption talked of than we can be) arrested, by his withholding hand, the completion of the contract, and refused his signature to those papers which enabled the purchasers to convey their purchase to others, I should now say, the title being incomplete, we have nothing to fear from it, we want no compromise. This no doubt would have been done had the Executive supposed that the people of Georgia were injured, and that they would support him in that refusal. But, sir, the honors and preferments retained by and conferred on so many of those persons charged with the bribery, leads me to believe that there were causes unknown to me which led to the uneasiness on the part of the people of Georgia, with regard to the sale in 1795, and led to the attempt at resuming the right to the lands in 1796.

In the course of this discussion, we who wish for a compromise of this perplexing business—this business which seems to be kindling the greatest discord in the nation—have been charged with an intention of committing a robbery which is far to exceed all the petty larcenies of the former Administration, and such of us as have aided to depose the former and support the present Administration, are threatened with being for the future considered as Federalists, let our professions be what they may. For my part, I can assure the member who threatens us, that it never in my life gave me pain to be called a Federalist, in the true sense of that word—in the sense in which the word was used by the great man who said, "We are all Federalists, we are all Republicans;" but, sir, it really gives me pain to hear and to see the character of the head of one of the Departments of our Government lugged into this debate, and so illiberally treated. The man I respect highly both for his integrity and talents—in the first of which, in my opinion, he stands behind no man in this nation; and although he has the misfortune to suffer the censure of the member from Virginia, I believe he enjoys almost universal applause for the great zeal, fidelity, and sound discretion with which he has discharged the important functions entrusted to him.

From the drift of the speeches delivered by the member from Virginia, from his call for the Postmaster General's report of a list of his contracts, and from the invitation he has given to an examination of that report, I am led to consider it a duty I owe to myself, in this House, and in the face of the world, to take up that report, and explain the nature of the contracts which there appear in my name. I find my name seven times mentioned in that report: the first is in the 12th page, for a contract for carrying the mail from Cincinnati to Detroit; the second in the same page, and is from Marietta to Cincinnati; these two contracts I never solicited or bid for, but the Postmaster General having advertised for proposals, and having received none that he thought reasonable, they being new routes and to be for one year only, he wrote to me offering the price they stand there at, and I undertook to get the business done. For the performance of the latter contract I gave every cent I received, and without saving one penny for a great deal of trouble, risk, and perplexity, I had taken upon myself to get it effected. From the other I saved a few dollars toward paying me for the care, trouble, and responsibility I had sustained on the occasion. Long before these contracts were out, I informed the Postmaster General that I should take neither of them again, and the contract from Cincinnati to Detroit was let to another person at $105.60 more than was given to me; this may be seen in the 22d line of page 20 of the same report.

The third time my name is mentioned is in the same 12th page, and is from Hartford to Fort Massac, a distance of about 180 or 190 miles, for which $654.75 is paid; out of this $65 is to be paid for ferriage. For some parts of this route I am obliged to give much more than a proportionate share of what I receive; some other parts I give a trifle less; sometimes my own horses carry the mail. I cannot with precision tell what is lost or gained in it, but it cannot be $50 either way. The fourth contract is also in the same page, it is from Russelsville to Eddygrove, or, rather, Eddyville; it is 80 miles, for which $240 is paid; this is as low if not lower than the price given anywhere south or west of this place, and I give to the person who performs it the whole amount of what I receive. The fifth and sixth time my name is mentioned in that report is in the 28th page—those are merely a renewal of the two last mentioned contracts, which had expired in 1803; all of those contracts were made before I was elected to my present seat in this House, before I had the pleasure of a personal acquaintance with the present Postmaster General, and before I ever spoke with him.

The seventh contract is noticed in the last page of the Postmaster General's report, which is from Massac to New Madrid, from Kaskaskias to Girardeau, from Cahoka to St. Louis, a distance of more than 200 miles, for $515, out of which more than $150 must be paid for ferriage, at the rate ferriages stood at the time of the contract.

This is the true history of the contracts by which it is insinuated that the Postmaster General has bribed me. I never was bribed, sir; it is not all the lands and negroes my accuser owns that could tempt me to do a thing which honor or conscience dictated to me to avoid. I could, sir, if it was pertinent, show how the over-vigilance of the present Postmaster General has deprived me of the benefit of the only profitable contract I ever made with the Government—a contract made with his predecessor—which he very improperly, in my opinion, considered void on account of some words in it not being exactly consonant with the intention of the contracting parties; believing, however, that the Postmaster General designed to do what he thought right, he has not lost my esteem, nor do I think his character can be injured by the braying of a jackall or the fulminations of a madman. But, sir, permit me to inquire from whom these charges of bribery, of corruption, and of robbery, come. Is it from one who has for forty years, in one shape or other, been intrusted with the property and concerns of other people, and has never wanted for confidence—one whose long and steady practice of industry, integrity, and well doing, has obtained him his standing on this floor? Is it from one who sneered with contempt on the importunity with which he was solicited to set a price on the important vote he held in the last Presidential election? No, sir; these charges have been fabricated in the disordered imagination of a young man whose pride has been provoked by my refusing to sing *encore* to all his political dogmas. I have had the impudence to differ from him in some few points, and some few times to neglect his fiat. It is long since I have observed that the very sight of my plebeian face has had an unpleasant effect on the gentleman's nose—for out of respect to this House and to the State he represents, I will yet occasionally call him gentleman. I say, sir, these charges have been brought against me by a person nursed in the bosom of opulence, inheriting the life services of a numerous train of the human species, and extensive fields, the original proprietors of which property, in all probability, came no honester by it than the purchasers of the Georgia lands did what they claim. Let that gentleman apply the fable of the thief and the receiver, in Dilworth's Spelling Book, so ingeniously quoted by himself, in his own case, and give up the stolen men in his possession.

I say, sir, these charges have come from a person whose fortune, leisure, and genius, have enabled him to obtain a great share of the wisdom of the schools, but who in years, experience, and the knowledge of the world and the ways of man, is many, many years behind those he implicates—a person who, from his rant in this House, seems to have got his head as full of British contracts and British modes of corruption as ever Don Quixotte's was supposed to have been of chivalry, enchantments, and knight errantry—a person who seems to think no man can be honest and independent unless he has inherited lands and negroes, nor is he willing to allow a man to vote in the people's elections, unless he is a landholder.

I can tell that gentleman, I am as far from offering or receiving a bribe as he or any other member on this floor; it is a charge that no man ever made against me before him, who from his insulated situation, unconversant with the world, is perhaps as little acquainted with my character as any member of this House, or almost any man in the nation; and I do most cordially believe that, had my back and my mind been supple enough to rise and fall with his motions, I should have escaped his censure.

I, sir, have none of that pride which sets men above being merchants and dealers; the calling of a merchant is, in my opinion, equally dignified, and no more than equally dignified with that of a farmer or a manufacturer. I have a great part of my life been engaged in all the stations of merchant, farmer, and manufacturer, in which I have honestly earned and lost a great deal of property, in the character of a merchant. I act like other merchants, look out for customers with whom I can make bargains advantageous to both parties; it is all the same to me, whether I contract with an individual or the public; I see no Constitutional impediment to a member of this House serving the public for the same reward the public gives another. Whenever my constituents or myself think I have contracts inconsistent with my duties as a member of this House, I will retire from it.

I came to this House as a representative of a free, a brave, and a generous people. I thank my Creator that he gave me the face of a man, not that of an ape or a monkey, and that he gave me the heart of a man also, a heart which will spare to its last drop in defence of the dignity of the station my generous constituents have placed me in. I shall trouble the House no farther at this time, than by observing that I shall not be deterred by the threats of the member from Virginia, from giving the vote I think the interest and honor of the nation requires; and by saying if that member means to be understood that I have offered contracts from the Postmaster General, the assertion or insinuation has no foundation in truth, and I challenge him to bring forward his boasted proof.

THE SUPREME COURT'S DECISION IN *FLETCHER* V. *PECK*

John Marshall's opinion settled, in purely legal terms, the constitutional questions surrounding the Georgia land issue, and it assisted the claimants in their political campaign for a compensation law. The Court's decision,[1] therefore, is one of the primary events in the Yazoo dispute. It should also be read as a leading and influential statement on the contract clause and the rights of vested property. While the Marshall opinion is the historically important one, Justice Johnson's concurring opinion provides an interesting contrast, since it was written by a Jeffersonian judge.

March 16, 1810. MARSHALL, C. J., delivered the opinion of the court as follows:

The pleadings being now amended, this cause comes on again to be heard on sundry demurrers, and on a special verdict.

This suit was instituted on several convenants contained in a deed made by John Peck, the defendant in error, conveying to Robert Fletcher, the plaintiff in error, certain lands which were part of a large purchase made by James Gunn and others, in the year 1795, from the State of Georgia, the contract for which was made in the form of a bill passed by the legislature of that State.

The first count in the declaration set forth a breach in the second covenant contained in the deed. The covenant is, "that the legislature of the State of Georgia, at the time of passing the act of sale aforesaid, had good right to sell and dispose of the same in manner pointed out by the said act." The breach assigned is, that the legislature had no power to sell.

The plea in bar sets forth the constitution of the State of Georgia, and avers that the lands sold by the defendant to the plaintiff, were within that State. It then sets forth the granting act, and avers the power of the legislature to sell and dispose of the premises as pointed out by the act.

To this plea the plaintiff below demurred, and the defendant joined in demurrer.

That the legislature of Georgia, unless restrained by its own constitution, possesses the power of disposing of the unappropriated lands within its own limits, in such manner as its own judgment shall dictate, is a proposition not to be controverted. The only question, then, presented by this demurrer, for the consideration of the court, is this, did the then constitution of the State of Georgia prohibit the legislature to dispose of the lands, which were the subject of this contract, in the manner stipulated by the contract?

The question, whether a law be void for its repugnancy to the constitution, is, at all times, a question of much delicacy, which ought seldom, if ever, to be decided in the affirmative, in a doubtful case. The court, when impelled by duty to render such a judgment, would be unworthy of its station, could it be unmindful of the solemn obligations which that station imposes. But it is not on slight implication and vague conjecture that the legislature is to be pronounced to have transcended its powers, and its acts to be considered as void. The opposition between the constitution and the law should be such that the judge feels a clear and strong conviction of their incompatibility with each other.

In this case the court can perceive no such opposition. In the constitution of Georgia, adopted in the year 1789, the court can perceive no restriction on the legislative power, which inhibits the passage of the act of 1795. They cannot say that, in passing that act, the legislature has transcended its powers, and violated the constitution.

In overruling the demurrer, therefore, to the first plea, the circuit court committed no error.

The 3d covenant is, that all the title which the State of Georgia ever had in the premises had been legally conveyed to John Peck, the grantor.

The 2d count assigns, in substance, as a breach of this covenant, that the original grantees from the State of Georgia promised and assured divers members of the legislature, then sitting in general assembly, that if the said members would assent to, and vote for, the passing of the act, and if the said bill should pass, such members should have a share of, and be interested in, all the lands purchased from the said State by virtue of such law. And that divers of the said members, to whom the said promises were made, were unduly influenced thereby, and, under such influence, did vote for the passing of the said bill; by reason whereof the said law was a nullity, &c., and so the title of the State of Georgia did not pass to the said Peck, &c.

The plea to this count, after protesting that the promises it alleges were not made, avers, that until after the purchase made from the original grantees by James Greenleaf, under whom the said Peck claims, neither the said James Greenleaf, nor the said Peck, nor any of the mesne vendors between the said Greenleaf and Peck, had any notice or knowledge that any such promises or assurances were made by the said original grantees, or either of them, to any of the members of the legislature of the State of Georgia.

To this plea the plaintiff demurred generally, and the defendant joined in the demurrer.

That corruption should find its way into the governments of our infant republics, and contaminate the very source of legislation, or that impure motives should contribute to the passage of a law, or the formation of a legislative contract, are circumstances most deeply to be deplored. How far a court of justice would, in any case, be competent, on proceedings instituted by the State itself, to vacate a contract thus formed, and to annul rights acquired, under that contract, by third persons having no notice of the improper means by which it was obtained, is a question which the court would approach with much circumspection. It may well be doubted how far the validity of a law depends upon the motives of its framers, and how far the particular inducements, operating on members of the supreme sovereign power of a State, to the formation of a contract by that power, are examinable in a court of justice. If the principle be conceded, that an act of the supreme sovereign power might be declared null by a court, in consequence of the means which procured it, still would there be much difficulty in saying to what extent those means must be applied to produce this effect.

Must it be direct corruption, or would interest or undue influence of any kind be sufficient? Must the vitiating cause operate on a majority, or on what number of the members? Would the act be null, whatever might be the wish of the nation, or would its obligation or nullity depend upon the public sentiment?

If the majority of the legislature be corrupted, it may well be doubted, whether it be within the province of the judiciary to control their conduct, and, if less than a majority act from impure motives, the principle by which judicial interference would be regulated, is not clearly discerned.

Whatever difficulties this subject might present, when viewed under aspects of which it may be susceptible, this court can perceive none in the particular pleadings now under consideration.

This is not a bill brought by the State of Georgia, to annul the contract, nor does it appear to the court, by this count, that the State of Georgia is dissatisfied with the sale that has been made. The case, as made out in the pleadings, is simply this. One individual who holds lands in the State of Georgia, under a deed covenating that the title of Georgia was in the grantor, brings an action of covenant upon this deed, and assigns, as a breach, that some of the members of the legislature were induced to vote in favor of the law, which constituted the contract, by being promised an interest in it, and that therefore the act is a mere nullity.

This solemn question cannot be brought thus collaterally and incidentally before the court. It would be indecent, in the extreme, upon a private contract, between two individuals, to enter into an inquiry respecting the corruption of the sovereign power of a State. If the title be plainly deduced from a legislative act, which the legislature might constitutionally pass, if the act be clothed with all the requisite forms of a law, a court, sitting as a court of law, cannot sustain a suit brought by one individual against another founded on the allegation that the act is a nullity, in consequence of the impure motives which influenced certain members of the legislature which passed the law.

The circuit court, therefore, did right in overruling this demurrer.

The 4th covenant in the deed is, that the title to the premises has been, in no way, constitutionally or legally impaired by virtue of any subsequent act of any subsequent legislature of the State of Georgia.

The third count recites the undue means practised on certain members of the legislature, as stated in the second count, and then alleges that, in consequence of these practices and of other causes, a subsequent legislature passed an act annulling and rescinding the law under which the conveyance to the original grantees was made, declaring that conveyance void, and asserting the title of the State to the lands it contained. The count proceeds to recite at large, this rescinding act, and concludes with averring that, by reason of this act, the title of the said Peck in the premises was constitutionally and legally impaired, and rendered null and void.

After protesting, as before, that no such promises were made as stated in this count, the defendant again pleads that himself and the first purchaser under the original grantees, and all intermediate holders of the property, were purchasers without notice.

To this plea there is a demurrer and joinder.

The importance and the difficulty of the questions presented by these pleadings, are deeply felt by the court.

The lands in controversy vested absolutely in James Gunn and others, the original grantees, by the conveyance of the governor, made in pursuance of an act of assembly to which the legislature was fully competent. Being thus in full possession of the legal estate, they, for a valuable consideration, conveyed portions of the land to those who were willing to purchase. If the original transaction was infected with fraud, these purchasers did not participate in it, and had no notice of it. They were innocent. Yet the legislature of Georgia has involved them in the fate of the first parties to the transaction, and, if the act be valid, has annihilated their rights also.

The legislature of Georgia was a party to this transaction; and for a party to pronounce its own deed invalid, whatever cause may be assigned for its invalidity, must be considered as a mere act of power which must find its vindication in a train of reasoning not often heard in courts of justice.

But the real party, it is said, are the people, and when their agents are unfaithful, the acts of those agents cease to be obligatory.

It is, however, to be recollected that the people can act only by these agents, and that, while within the powers conferred on them, their acts must be considered as the acts of the people. If the agents be corrupt, others may be chosen, and if their contracts be examinable, the common sentiment, as well as common usage of mankind, points out a mode by which this examination may be made, and their validity determined.

If the legislature of Georgia was not bound to submit its pretensions to those tribunals which are established for the security of property, and to decide on human rights, if it might claim to itself the power of judging in its own case, yet there are certain great principles of justice, whose authority is universally acknowledged, that ought not to be entirely disregarded.

If the legislature be its own judge in its own case, it would seem equitable that its decision should be regulated by those rules which would have regulated the decision of a judicial tribunal. The question was, in its nature, a question of title, and the tribunal which decided it was either acting in the character of a court of justice, and performing a duty usually assigned to a court, or it was exerting a mere act of power in which it was controlled only by its own will.

If a suit be brought to set aside a conveyance obtained by fraud, and the fraud be clearly proved, the conveyance will be set aside, as between the parties; but the rights of third persons, who are purchasers without notice, for a valuable consideration, cannot be disregarded. Titles, which, according to every legal test, are perfect, are acquired with that confidence which is inspired by the opinion that the purchaser is safe. If there be any concealed defect, arising from the conduct of those who had held the property long before he acquired it, of which he had no notice, that concealed defect cannot be set up against him. He has paid his money for a title good at law; he is innocent, whatever may be the guilt of others, and equity will not subject him to the penalties attached to that guilt. All titles would be insecure, and the intercourse between man and man would be very seriously obstructed, if this principle be overturned.

A court of chancery, therefore, had a bill been brought to set aside the conveyance made to James Gunn and others, as being obtained by improper practices with the legislature, whatever might have been its decision as respected the original grantees, would have been bound, by its own rules, and by the clearest principles of equity, to leave unmolested those who were purchasers, without notice, for a valuable consideration.

If the legislature felt itself absolved from those rules of property which are common to all the citizens of the United States, and from those principles of equity which are acknowledged in all our courts, its act is to be supported by its power alone, and the same power may devest any other individual of his lands, if it shall be the will of the legislature so to exert it.

It is not intended to speak with disrespect of the legislature of Georgia, or of its acts. Far from it. The question is a general question, and is treated as one. For although such powerful objections to a legislative grant, as are alleged against this, may not again exist, yet the principle, on which alone this rescinding act is to be supported, may be applied to every case to which it shall be the will of any legislature to apply it. The principle is this: that a legislature may, by its own act, devest the vested estate of any man whatever, for reasons which shall, by itself, be deemed sufficient.

In this case the legislature may have had ample proof that the original grant was obtained by practices which can never be too much reprobated, and which would have justified its abrogation so far as respected those to whom crime was imputable. But the grant, when issued, conveyed an estate in fee-simple to the grantee, clothed with all the solemnities which law can bestow. This estate was transferable; and those who purchased parts of it were not stained by that guilt which infected the original transaction. Their case is not distinguishable from the ordinary case of purchasers of a legal estate without knowledge of any secret fraud which might have led to the emanation of the original grant. According to the well-known course of equity, their rights could not be affected by such fraud. Their situation was the same, their title was the same, with that of every other member of the community who holds land by regular conveyances from the original patentee.

Is the power of the legislature competent to the annihilation of such title, and to a resumption of the property thus held?

The principle asserted is, that one legislature is competent to repeal any act which a former legislature was competent to pass; and that one legislature cannot abridge the powers of a succeeding legislature.

The correctness of this principle, so far as respects general legislation, can never be controverted. But if an act be done under a law, a succeeding legislature cannot undo it. The past cannot be recalled by the most absolute power. Conveyances have been made, those conveyances have vested legal estates, and, if those estates may be seized by the sovereign authority, still, that they originally vested is a fact, and cannot cease to be a fact.

When, then, a law is in its nature a contract, when absolute rights have vested under that contract, a repeal of the law cannot devest those rights; and the act of annulling them, if legitimate, is rendered so by a power applicable to the case of every individual in the community.

It may well be doubted whether the nature of society and of government does not prescribe some limits to the legislative power; and if any be prescribed, where are they to be found, if the property of an individual, fairly and honestly acquired, may be seized without compensation.

To the legislature all legislative power is granted; but the question, whether the act of transferring the property of an individual to the public, be in the nature of the legislative power, is well worthy of serious reflection.

It is the peculiar province of the legislature to prescribe general rules for the government of society; the application of those rules to individuals in society would seem to be the duty of other departments. How far the power of giving the law may involve every other power, in cases where the constitution is silent, never has been, and perhaps never can be, definitely stated.

The validity of this rescinding act, then, might well be doubted, were Georgia a single sovereign power. But Georgia cannot be viewed as a single, unconnected, sovereign power, on whose legislature no other restrictions are imposed than may be found in its own constitution. She is a part of a large empire; she is a member of the American Union; and that union has a constitution the supremacy of which all acknowledge, and which imposes limits to the legislatures of the several States, which none claim a right to pass. The constitution of the United States declares that no State shall pass any bill of attainder, *ex post facto* law, or law impairing the obligation of contracts.

Does the case now under consideration come within this prohibitory section of the constitution?

In considering this very interesting question, we immediately ask ourselves what is a contract? Is a grant a contract?

A contract is a compact between two or more parties, and is either executory or executed. An executory contract is one in which a party binds himself to do, or not to do, a particular thing; such was the law under which the conveyance was made by the governor. A contract executed is one in which the object of contract is performed; and this, says Blackstone, differs in nothing from a grant. The contract between Georgia and the purchasers was executed by the grant. A contract executed, as well as one which is executory, contains obligations binding on the parties. A grant, in its own nature, amounts to an extinguishment of the right of the grantor, and implies a contract not to reassert that right. A party is, therefore, always estopped by his own grant.

Since, then, in fact, a grant is a contract executed, the obligation of which still continues, and since the constitution uses the general term contract, without distinguishing between those which are executory and those which are executed, it must be construed to comprehend the latter as well as the former. A law annulling conveyances between individuals, and declaring that the grantors should stand seized of their former estates, notwithstanding those grants, would be as repugnant to the constitution as a law discharging the vendors of property from the obligation of executing their contracts by conveyances. It would be strange if a contract to convey was secured by the constitution, while an absolute conveyance remained unprotected.

If, under a fair construction of the constitution, grants are comprehended under the term contracts, is a grant from the State excluded from the operation of the provision? Is the clause to be considered as inhibiting the State from impairing the obligation of contracts between two individuals, but as excluding from that inhibition contracts made with itself?

The words themselves contain no such distinction. They are

general, and are applicable to contracts of every description. If contracts made with the State are to be exempted from their operation, the exception must arise from the character of the contracting party, not from the words which are employed.

Whatever respect might have been felt for the state sovereignties, it is not to be disguised that the framers of the constitution viewed, with some apprehension, the violent acts which might grow out of the feelings of the moment; and that the people of the United States, in adopting that instrument, have manifested a determination to shield themselves and their property from the effects of those sudden and strong passions to which men are exposed. The restrictions on the legislative power of the States are obviously founded in this sentiment; and the Constitution of the United States contains what may be deemed a bill of rights for the people of each State.

No State shall pass any bill of attainder, *ex post facto* law, or law impairing the obligation of contracts.

A bill of attainder may affect the life of an individual, or may confiscate his property, or may do both.

In this form the power of the legislature over the lives and fortunes of individuals is expressly restrained. What motive, then, for implying, in words which import a general prohibition to impair the obligation of contracts, an exception in favor of the right to impair the obligation of those contracts into which the State may enter?

The State legislatures can pass no *ex post facto* law. An *ex post facto* law is one which renders an act punishable in a manner in which it was not punishable when it was committed. Such a law may inflict penalties on the person, or may inflict pecuniary penalties which swell the public treasury. The legislature is then prohibited from passing a law by which a man's estate, or any part of it, shall be seized for a crime which was not declared, by some previous law, to render him liable to that punishment. Why, then, should violence be done to the natural meaning of words for the purpose of leaving to the legislature the power of seizing, for public use, the estate of an individual in the form of a law annulling the title by which he holds that estate? The court can perceive no sufficient grounds for making that distinction. This rescinding act would have the effect of an *ex post facto* law. It forfeits the estate of Fletcher for a crime not committed by himself, but by those from whom he purchased. This cannot be effected in the form of an *ex post facto* law, or bill of attainder; why, then, is it allowable in the form of a law annulling the original grant?

The argument in favor of presuming an intention to except a case, not excepted by the words of the constitution, is susceptible of some illustration from a principle originally ingrafted in that instrument, though no longer a part of it. The constitution, as passed, gave the courts of the United States jurisdiction in suits brought against individual States. A State, then, which violated its own contract, was suable in the courts of the United States for that violation. Would it have been a defence in such a suit to say that the State had passed a law absolving itself from the contract? It is scarcely to be conceived that such a defence could be set up. And yet, if a State is neither restrained by the general principles of our political institutions, nor by the words of the constitution, from impairing the obligation of its own contracts, such a defence would be a valid one. This feature is no longer found in the constitution; but it aids in the construction of those clauses with which it was originally associated.

It is, then, the unanimous opinion of the court, that, in this case, the estate having passed into the hands of a purchaser for a valuable consideration, without notice, the State of Georgia was restrained, either by general principles which are common to our free institutions, or by the particular provisions of the Constitution of the United States, from passing a law whereby the estate of the plaintiff in the premises so purchased could be constitutionally and legally impaired and rendered null and void.

In overruling the demurrer to the 3d plea, therefore, there is no error.

The first covenant in the deed is, that the State of Georgia, at the time the act of the legislature thereof, entitled as aforesaid, was legally seized in fee of the soil thereof, subject only to the extinguishment of part of the Indian title thereon.

The 4th count assigns, as a breach of this covenant, that the right to the soil was in the United States, and not in Georgia.

To this count the defendant pleads, that the State of Georgia was seized; and tenders an issue on the fact in which the plaintiff joins. On this issue a special verdict is found.

The jury find the grant of Carolina, by Charles II., to the Earl of Clarendon, and others, comprehending the whole country, from 36 deg. 30 min., north lat., to 29 deg. north lat., and from the Atlantic to the South Sea.

They find that the northern part of this territory was afterwards erected into a separate colony, and that the most northern part of the 35th deg. of north lat., was the boundary line between North and South Carolina.

That seven of the eight proprietors of the Carolinas, surrendered to George II., in the year 1729, who appointed a governor of South Carolina.

That in 1732, George II., granted to the Lord Viscount Percival, and others, seven eighths of the territory between the Savannah and the Alatamaha, and extending west to the South Sea, and that the remaining eighth part, which was still the property of the heir of Lord Carteret, one of the original grantees of Carolina, was afterwards conveyed to them. This territory was constituted a colony, and called Georgia.

That the governor of South Carolina continued to exercise jurisdiction south of Georgia.

That, in 1752, the grantees surrendered to the crown.

That, in 1754, a governor was appointed by the crown, with a commission describing the boundaries of the colony.

That a treaty of peace was concluded between Great Britain and Spain, in 1763, in which the latter ceded to the former Florida, with Fort St. Augustin, and the Bay of Pensacola.

That, in October, 1763, the king of Great Britain issued a proclamation, creating four new colonies, Quebec, East Florida, West Florida, and Grenada; and prescribing the bounds of each, and further declaring that all the lands between the Alatamaha, and St. Marys, should be annexed to Georgia. The same proclamation contained a clause reserving, under the dominion and protection of the crown, for the use of the Indians, all the lands on the western waters, and forbidding a settlement on them, or a purchase of them from the Indians. The lands conveyed to the plaintiff lie on the western waters.

That, in November, 1763, a commission was issued to the governor of Georgia, in which the boundaries of that province are described, as extending westward to the Mississippi. A commission, describing boundaries of the same extent, was afterwards granted in 1764.

That a war broke out between Great Britain and her colonies, which terminated in a treaty of peace, acknowledging them as sovereign and independent States.

That, in April, 1787, a convention was entered into between the States of South Carolina and Georgia, settling the boundary line between them.

The jury afterwards describe the situation of the lands mentioned in the plaintiff's declaration, in such manner that their lying within the limits of Georgia, as defined in the proclamation of 1763, in the treaty of peace, and in the convention between that State and South Carolina, has not been questioned.

The counsel for the plaintiff rest their argument on a single proposition. They contend that the reservation for the use of the Indians, contained in the proclamation of 1763, excepts the lands on the western waters from the colonies within whose bounds they would otherwise have been, and that they were acquired by the revolutionary war. All acquisitions during the war, it is contended, were made by the joint arms, for the joint benefit of the United States, and not for the benefit of any particular State.

The court does not understand the proclamation as it is understood by the counsel for the plaintiff. The reservation for the use of the Indians appears to be a temporary arrangement, suspending, for a time, the settlement of the country reserved, and the powers of the royal governor within the territory reserved, but is not conceived to amount to an alteration of the boundaries of the colony. If the language of the proclamation be, in itself, doubtful, the commissions subsequent thereto, which were given to the governors of Georgia, entirely remove the doubt.

The question, whether the vacant lands within the United States became a joint property, or belonged to the separate States, was a momentous question, which, at one time, threatened to shake the American confederacy to its foundation. This important and dangerous contest has been compromised, and the compromise is not now to be disturbed.

It is the opinion of the court, that the particular land stated in the declaration appears, from this special verdict, to lie within the State of Georgia, and that the State of Georgia had power to grant it.

Some difficulty was produced by the language of the covenant, and of the pleadings. It was doubted whether a State can be seized in fee of lands subject to the Indian title, and whether a decision that they were seized in fee might not be construed to amount to a decision that their grantee might maintain an ejectment for them, notwithstanding that title.

The majority of the court is of opinion that the nature of the Indian title, which is certainly to be respected by all courts, until it be legitimately extinguished, is not such as to be absolutely repugnant to seizin in fee on the part of the State.

JOHNSON, J. In this case I entertain, on two points, an opinion different from that which has been delivered by the court.

I do not hesitate to declare that a State does not possess the power of revoking its own grants. But I do it on a general principle, on the reason and nature of things: a principle which will impose laws even on the Deity.

A contrary opinion can only be maintained upon the ground that no existing legislature can abridge the powers of those which will succeed it. To a certain extent this is certainly correct; but the distinction lies between power and interest, the right of jurisdiction and the right of soil.

The right of jurisdiction is essentially connected to, or rather identified with, the national sovereignty. To part with it is to commit a species of political suicide. In fact a power to produce its own annihilation is an absurdity in terms. It is a power as utterly incommunicable to a political as to a natural person. But it is not so with the interests or property of a nation. Its possessions nationally are in nowise necessary to its political existence; they are entirely accidental, and may be parted with in every respect similarly to those of the individuals who compose the community. When the legislature have once conveyed their interest or property in any subject to the individual, they have lost all control over it; have nothing to act upon; it has passed from them; is vested in the individual; becomes intimately blended with his existence, as essentially so as the blood that circulates through his system. The government may indeed demand of him the one or the other, not because they are not his, but because whatever is his is his country's.

As to the idea, that the grants of a legislature may be void because the legislature are corrupt, it appears to me to be subject to insuperable difficulties. The acts of the supreme power of a country must be considered pure for the same reason that all sovereign acts must be considered just; because there is no power that can declare them otherwise. The absurdity in this case would have been strikingly perceived, could the party who passed the act of cession have got again into power, and declared themselves pure, and the intermediate legislature corrupt.

The security of a people against the misconduct of their rulers, must lie in the frequent recurrence to first principles, and the imposition of adequate constitutional restrictions. Nor would it be difficult, with the same view, for laws to be framed which would bring the conduct of individuals under the review of adequate tribunals, and make them suffer under the consequence of their own immoral conduct.

I have thrown out these ideas that I may have it distinctly understood that my opinion on this point is not founded on the provision in the Constitution of the United States, relative to laws impairing the obligation of contracts. It is much to be regretted that words of less equivocal signification had not been adopted in that article of the constitution. There is reason to believe, from the letters of Publius, which are well known to be entitled to the highest respect, that the object of the convention was to afford a general protection to individual rights against the acts of the State legislatures. Whether the words, "acts impairing the obligation of contracts," can be construed to have the same force as must have been given to the words "obligation and effect of contracts," is the difficulty in my mind.

There can be no solid objection to adopting the technical definition of the word "contract," given by Blackstone. The etymology, the classical signification, and the civil law idea of the word, will all support it. But the difficulty arises on the word "obligation," which certainly imports an existing moral or physical necessity. Now a grant or conveyance by no means necessarily implies the continuance of an obligation beyond the moment of executing it. It is most generally but the consummation of a contract, is *functus officio* the moment it is executed, and continues afterwards to be nothing more than the evidence that a certain act was done.

I enter with great hesitation upon this question, because it involves a subject of the greatest delicacy and much difficulty. The States and the United States are continually legislating on the subject of contracts, prescribing the mode of authentication, the time within which suits shall be prosecuted for them, in many cases affecting existing contracts by the laws which they pass, and declaring them to cease or lose their effect for want of compliance, in the parties, with such statutory provisions. All these acts appear to be within the most correct limits of legislative powers, and most beneficially exercised, and certainly could not have been intended to be affected by this constitutional provision; yet where to draw the line, or how to define or limit the words, "obligation of contracts," will be found a subject of extreme difficulty.

To give it the general effect of a restriction of the State powers in favor of private rights, is certainly going very far beyond the obvious and necessary import of the words, and would operate to restrict the States in the exercise of that right which every community must exercise, of possessing itself of the property of the individual, when necessary for public uses; a right which a magnanimous and just government will never exercise without amply indemnifying the individual, and which perhaps amounts to nothing more than a power to oblige him to sell and convey, when the public necessities require it.

The other point on which I dissent from the opinion of the court, is relative to the judgment which ought to be given on the first count. Upon that count we are called upon substantially to decide, "that the State of Georgia, at the time of passing the act of cession, was legally seized in fee of the soil, (then ceded,) subject only to the extinguishment of part of the Indian title." That is, that the State of Georgia was seized of an estate in fee-simple in the lands in question, subject to another estate, we know not what, nor whether it may not swallow up the whole estate decided to exist in Georgia. It would seem that the mere vagueness and uncertainty of this covenant would be a sufficient objection to deciding in favor of it, but to me it appears that the facts in the case are sufficient to support the opinion that the State of Georgia had not a fee-simple in the land in question.

This is a question of much delicacy, and more fitted for a diplomatic or legislative than a judicial inquiry. But I am called upon to make a decision, and I must make it upon technical principles.

The question is, whether it can be correctly predicated of the interest or estate which the State of Georgia had in these lands, "that the State was seized thereof, in fee-simple."

To me it appears that the interest of Georgia in that land amounted to nothing more than a mere possibility, and that her conveyance thereof could operate legally only as a covenant to convey or to stand seized to a use.

The correctness of this opinion will depend upon a just view of the state of the Indian nations. This will be found to be very various. Some have totally extinguished their national fire, and submitted themselves to the laws of the States; others have, by treaty, acknowledged that they hold their national existence at the will of the State within which they reside; others retain a limited sovereignty, and the absolute proprietorship of their soil. The latter is the case of the tribes to the west of Georgia. We legislate upon the conduct of strangers or citizens within their limits, but innumerable treaties formed with them acknowledge them to be an independent people, and the uniform practice of acknowledging their right of soil, by purchasing from them, and restraining all persons from encroaching upon their territory, makes it unnecessary to insist upon their right of soil. Can, then, one nation be said to be seized of a fee-simple in lands, the right of soil of which is in another nation? It is awkward to apply the technical idea of a fee-simple to the interests of a nation, but I must consider an absolute right of soil as an estate to them and their heirs. A fee-simple interest may be held in reversion, but our law will not admit the idea of its being limited after a fee-simple. In fact, if the Indian nations be the absolute proprietors of their soil, no other nation can be said to have the same interest in it. What, then, practically, is the interest of the States in the soil of the Indians within their boundaries. Unaffected by particular treaties, it is nothing more than what was assumed at the first settlement of the country, to wit, a right of conquest or of purchase, exclusively of all competitors within certain defined limits. All the restrictions upon the right of soil in the Indians, amount only to an exclusion of all competitors from their markets; and the limitation upon their sovereignty amounts to the right of governing every person within their limits except themselves. If the interest in Georgia was nothing more than a preemptive right, how could that be called a fee-simple, which was nothing more than a power to acquire a fee-simple by purchase, when the proprietors should be pleased to sell? And if this ever was any thing more than a mere possibility, it certainly was reduced to that state when the State of Georgia ceded, to the United States, by the constitution, both the power of preëmption and of conquest, retaining for itself only a resulting right dependent on a purchase or conquest to be made by the United States.

I have been very unwilling to proceed to the decision of this cause at all. It appears to me to bear strong evidence, upon the face of it, of being a mere feigned case. It is our duty to decide on the rights, but not on the speculations of parties. My confidence, however, in the respectable gentlemen who have been engaged for the parties, has induced me to abandon my scruples, in the belief that they would never consent to impose a mere feigned case upon this court.

NOTES

NOTES

CHAPTER I

1. William Priest, *Travels in the United States of America* (London, 1802), p. 132.

2. Andrew A. Lipscomb (ed.), *The Writings of Thomas Jefferson* (20 vols.; Washington: Thomas Jefferson Memorial Association, 1903), II, 118.

3. U.S. Bureau of the Census, *Historical Statistics of the United States, Colonial Times to 1957* (Washington: U.S. Government Printing Office, 1961), p. 7.

4. Those who purchased titles to land that was misleadingly described were at least getting something. Some of the Pine Barren speculators sold titles to absolutely fictitious tracts. See below, p. 3.

5. E. Merton Coulter, *Georgia: A Short History*, rev. ed. (Chapel Hill: University of North Carolina Press, 1947), p. 198. On the Pine Barren Speculation see Absalom H. Chappell, *Miscellanies of Georgia* (Atlanta: James F. Meegan, 1874), pp. 43–55; Samuel G. McLendon, *History of the Public Domain of Georgia* (Atlanta: Foote & Davies Co., 1924), pp. 60–64; and A. M. Sakolski, *The Great American Land Bubble* (New York and London: Harper & Bros., 1932), pp. 141–46.

6. Ellis P. Oberholtzer, *Robert Morris: Patriot and Financier* (New York: Macmillan Co., 1903), p. 355 and chap. xi, *passim;* see also Eleanor Young, *Forgotten Patriot: Robert Morris* (New York: Macmillan Co., 1950), chaps. xv–xviii.

7. Coulter, *Georgia*, pp. 197–98; McLendon, *Public Domain of Georgia*, pp. 40–52.

8. McLendon, *Public Domain of Georgia*, pp. 57–58.

9. Quoted in Coulter, *Georgia*, p. 194. Coulter gives the signature on the mock statement as "Herachitus," undoubtedly a typographical error. I have changed it to Heraclitus.

10. Charles H. Haskins, "The Yazoo Land Companies," *Papers of the American Historical Association* (5 vols.; New York and London: G. P. Putnam's Sons, 1891), V, Part 4, 64–75. See also Chappell, *Miscellanies*, pp. 63–70, and William B. Stevens, *A History of Georgia* (2 vols.; New York: D. Appleton and Co.; Philadelphia: E. H. Butler and Co., 1847–59), II, 463–67.

11. *Moultrie* v. *Georgia* (1798), an unreported Supreme Court case. See Charles Warren, *The Supreme Court in United States History*, rev. ed. (2 vols.; Boston: Little, Brown and Co., 1923), I, 93n., 99n.

12. Haskins, "Yazoo Land Companies," pp. 80–83. Other useful ac-

counts of the second Yazoo sale appear in Chappell, *Miscellanies,* pp. 90–105, and Stevens, *History of Georgia,* II, 467–77.

13. Quoted in the appendix, Georgia Mississippi Company, *State of Facts Showing the Right of Certain Companies to the Lands Lately Purchased by Them from the State of Georgia* (Philadelphia, 1795).

14. This and many similar statements were elicited under oath by an investigating committee of the Georgia legislature in 1796. Defenders of the Yazoo sale seriously challenged their validity. Most of the statements came from members of the legislature who had voted against the sale, without any opportunity being given the incriminated members to cross-examine the witnesses. Equally important, the chairman of the investigating committee was the highly partisan James Jackson, who used the Yazoo issue to further his political career. See below, pp. 10–12. Yet, despite the fact that they were obtained in a manner offensive to twentieth-century standards of procedural fairness, the statements ring true and are consistent with the practices of land companies in that period. Moreover, they are independently corroborated by documents showing that on January 9 and 10, 1795, the Georgia Company and the Tennessee Company granted shares to many of the legislators who voted for the sale. The going rate appears to have been from 56,000 to 112,000 acres—the amount of land given to such legislators as Richard Carnes, Stephen and Thomas Heard, John King, and Lachlan McIntosh. Although no one was ever convicted in a court of law, it is my view that the charges of bribery were fully justified. The incriminating statements and the supporting documents are in *American State Papers, Public Lands* (8 vols; Washington: Gales and Seaton, 1832–61), I, 140–49.

15. McLendon, *Public Domain of Georgia,* pp. 52–54.

16. These quotations are taken from a picturesque account by James Jackson. Jackson, then a United States senator, was not in Augusta at the time of the sale. His manuscript, published in Lilla M. Hawes (ed.), "Miscellaneous Papers of James Jackson, 1781–1798," *Georgia Historical Quarterly,* XXXVII (1953), 152–56, was reprinted with a few changes in George White, *Statistics of the State of Georgia* (Savannah: W. Thorne Williams, 1849), pp. 48–54. White's description, which he does not attribute to Jackson, is the source of almost all subsequent accounts of the Yazoo sale.

17. Coulter, *Georgia,* p. 197; McLendon, *Public Domain of Georgia,* pp. 65–66.

18. Albert J. Beveridge, *The Life of John Marshall* (4 vols.; Boston: Houghton Mifflin Co., 1916–19), III, 551. A copy of the sale act is published in *American State Papers, Public Lands,* I, 156–58.

19. Typical expressions of this point of view are found in Chappell, *Miscellanies;* Coulter, *Georgia;* Haskins, "Yazoo Land Companies"; and Stevens, *History of Georgia.*

20. Jackson has recently been the subject of a useful, though uncritical,

biography: William Omer Foster, Sr., *James Jackson: Duellist and Militant Statesman, 1757–1806* (Athens: University of Georgia Press, 1960).

21. William Plumer, the New Hampshire politician. Everett S. Brown (ed.), *William Plumer's Memorandum of Proceedings in the United States Senate, 1803–1807* (New York: Macmillan Co., 1923), p. 459.

22. Thomas Gamble, *Savannah Duels and Duellists* (Savannah: Review Publishing and Printing Co., 1932), chap. iv.

23. Hawes, "Miscellaneous Papers of James Jackson, 1781–1798," p. 160.

24. This version of Jackson's behavior, of course, originated with Jackson himself. See above, n. 16.

25. *Annals of the Congress of the United States*, 3rd Cong., February 27, 1795, cols. 838–39; February 17, 1795, col. 1231.

26. Foster, *Jackson*, pp. 108–10.

27. He did not, however, sell much of his real estate, and his biographer is probably correct in saying that Jackson could not "be classed with the active land speculators." Foster, *Jackson*, pp. 32–33. On p. 106 Foster notes Jackson's silence on the land-grabbing schemes prior to 1795; see also McLendon, *Public Domain of Georgia*, p. 56.

28. Haskins, "Yazoo Land Companies," p. 81n.

29. Foster, *Jackson*, pp. 124–26.

30. Thomas N. P. Charlton, *The Life of Major General James Jackson* (Augusta: George F. Randolph and Co., 1809), pp. 154–55.

31. Foster, *Jackson*, pp. 67–68, 144.

32. Coulter, *Georgia*, pp. 238–41.

33. Foster, *Jackson*, p. 114.

34. Stevens, *History of Georgia*, II, 491–92. Jackson was determined to destroy every vestige of the sale. In 1798 Georgia adopted a new constitution, and Jackson was responsible for a provision declaring that "the contemplated purchases of a considerable portion" of the state's western territory are "constitutionally void." Article I, section 24, of the Georgia constitution of 1798, reproduced in House of Representatives, *Sundry Papers, in Relation to Claims, Commonly Called the Yazoo Claims* (Washington, 1809). In 1800 Jackson engaged in a bitter controversy with Colonel Robert Watkins because Watkins, in publishing an official digest of the state's law, had included a copy of the sale act. Jackson was then governor, and he blocked the payment due Watkins for his work and had another digest, minus the hated act, commissioned. Jackson and Watkins, the only legislator to vote for the sale who had not been bribed, were enemies of long standing over the Yazoo issue. On two occasions they fought physically, and in 1802 Watkins wounded Jackson in a pistol duel. See Foster, *Jackson*, pp. 127–30.

35. Joel Chandler Harris, *Stories of Georgia* (New York: American Book Co., 1896), pp. 134–35. Foster, however, believes the incident to be substantially correct. *Jackson*, pp. 118–20.

36. A copy of the act is reproduced in *American State Papers, Public Lands,* I, 156-58.

37. George G. Smith, *Story of Georgia and the Georgia People, 1732 to 1800* (Macon: George G. Smith, 1900), pp. 170-71.

38. Henry Adams, *History of the United States of America* (9 vols.; New York: Charles Scribner's Sons, 1889-91), I, 303.

39. James Gunn continued to serve in the Senate until 1801, when he retired to private life. He died later that year, leaving, according to his onetime Senate colleague, James Jackson, an estate of $45,000 filched from innocent Yazoo purchasers. Foster, *Jackson,* p. 133.

40. It is not clear exactly how many of the original Yazoo purchasers accepted refunds. Coulter, *Georgia,* p. 204, says that "many of the Yazooists declined to call for their money, and insisted on having the land"; and Sakolski, *Land Bubble,* p. 137, declares that "few" of the purchasers took advantage of the repayment offer. But an official report made by the treasurer and controller general of Georgia on August 2, 1802, indicates that $310,695 of the $500,000 purchase price was refunded. *American State Papers, Public Lands,* I, 150.

41. Haskins, "Yazoo Land Companies," pp. 87-88; Sakolski, *Land Bubble,* pp. 135-36.

42. Boston *Columbian Centinel,* March 16, 1796.

43. The resulting legal action, *Derby* v. *Blake* (1799), is discussed below in chap. iv.

44. Statement of George Blake, March 12, 1814, in *American State Papers, Public Lands,* II, 885-87.

45. Benjamin Russell, in the Boston *Columbian Centinel,* October 9, 1799.

46. Chappell, *Miscellanies,* pp. 109-12; Foster, *Jackson,* p. 140. The extent to which the New England purchasers were implicated in the original fraud was a prominent subject in the congressional debates discussed below in chap. iii.

47. Philadelphia *Aurora,* March 30, 1795.

48. The surviving evidence seems to confirm that New England purchasers were well aware that the Georgia sale might be reversed. Thus, nine Connecticut buyers were concerned that Georgia might disavow the sale because of the low price paid by Gunn and his associates and because of the allegation that the legislature had been bribed. Prior to purchasing 550,000 acres in October, 1795, they had the Georgia sellers stipulate that the Georgia title was good, that no fraud had been practiced in getting the legislature to sell, and that there was no likelihood of the state's repudiating the sale. These facts appear in the legal brief filed in the federal circuit court for Connecticut by Abraham and John Bishop in 1797 in a suit against two sellers of Yazoo lands. *Bishop and Bishop* v. *Nightingale and Miller,* Records of the Circuit Court of the United States for the District of Connecticut, Orders and Decrees in Chancery, 1790-1812,

pp. 129–30, 132–33, in the Federal Record Center of the General Services Administration, Boston.

49. Jackson to Jared Irwin, April 7, 1796, in Lilla M. Hawes (ed.), "The Letter Book of General James Jackson, 1788–1796," *Georgia Historical Quarterly,* XXXVII (1953), 326.

CHAPTER II

1. Reprinted in *The American Law Journal,* V (1814), 354–457. An excerpt from the Harper pamphlet appears in Appendix C.

2. D. B. Goebel and J. Goebel, Jr. (eds.), *The Law Practice of Alexander Hamilton,* Vol. I: *Documents and Commentary* (New York: Columbia University Press, 1964). The Hamilton opinion is published on pp. 454–56 of *The American Law Journal* volume that contains Harper's pamphlet. See Appendix D.

3. During the 1780's James Wilson, who served as legal counsel for the Bank of North America in its conflict with the Pennsylvania legislature, had argued that corporate charters ought to be inviolate. Forrest McDonald, *E Pluribus Unum: The Formation of the American Republic, 1776–1790* (Boston: Houghton Mifflin Co., 1965), p. 187n. Hamilton's opinion, however, stands as the first complete argument that the contract clause of the new Constitution extended to public contracts. It was signed on March 25, 1796 (the Harper pamphlet erroneously gives the date as March 25, 1795), preceding by two months an opinion by Justice William Paterson in the United States Circuit Court holding that a Pennsylvania law unconstitutionally violated a "contract" to which the state was a party. *Van Horne's Lessee* v. *Dorrance,* 2 Dallas 304 (1795). The constitutional doctrines involving the contract clause are discussed more fully below in chaps. v and vii.

4. Georgia Mississippi Company, *State of Facts Showing the Right of Certain Companies to the Lands Lately Purchased by Them from the State of Georgia* (Philadelphia, 1795).

5. *Dictionary of American Biography* (22 vols.; New York: Charles Scribner's Sons, 1928–58), XIII, 245–46; Jedidiah Morse, *The American Gazetteer,* 1st ed. (Boston, 1797).

6. At this point Morse cited the Harper pamphlet and the Hamilton opinion. *American Gazetteer,* sigs. Qqq1^v, Qqq2.

7. Abraham Bishop, *Georgia Speculation Unveiled* (Hartford, 1797). The full text of Bishop's pamphlet may be read in Appendix E.

8. Bishop's motives, however, were mixed, for he himself was a disappointed speculator in Yazoo lands. See Appendix E.

9. The Constitution of 1787, which rejected the trappings of monarchy and accepted the liberal suffrage qualifications of the states, must be viewed as an essentially democratic document. Virtually all of its allegedly anti-democratic features (such as the presidential electoral college) are the

products not of aristocratic scheming but of elaborate compromises worked out by the practical politicians who controlled the Constitutional Convention. See John P. Roche, "The Founding Fathers: A Reform Caucus in Action," *American Political Science Review,* LV (1961), 799–816, and Chilton Williamson, *American Suffrage from Property to Democracy, 1760–1860* (Princeton: Princeton University Press, 1960), a study which presents an illuminating picture on the extent of the suffrage in the late eighteenth century.

10. William Nisbet Chambers, *Political Parties in a New Nation: The American Experience, 1776–1809* (New York: Oxford University Press, 1963), chap. vi. During the 1790's, however, Federalism was more a set of doctrines and loose affiliations than an organized political party. Not until Federalism lost its national power in the election of 1800, did a Federalist *party,* modeled on the victorious Republican party, take shape. See David Hackett Fischer, *The Revolution of American Conservatism: The Federalist Party in the Era of Jeffersonian Democracy* (New York: Harper & Row, 1965).

11. A statement such as this is intended as a generalization on Federalist-Republican differences. The Adams administration, by no means sympathetic with France, adopted a moderate foreign policy and conscientiously sought to negotiate a settlement, much to the anger of the Hamilton Federalists, who wanted war with France. See Page Smith, *John Adams, 1735–1826* (2 vols.; New York: Doubleday and Co., 1962), II, chaps. lxx–lxxxiii, *passim.*

12. I am persuaded of the correctness of this observation in Fischer's *The Revolution of American Conservatism,* p. 201: "There was surely no simple symmetry of political conviction and economic interest, no clean-cut cleavage between wealth and poverty, between agriculture and commerce, between realty and personalty holdings, between city-dwellers and countryfolk, between subsistence and commercial farmers, between hardy frontiersmen and effete easterners, between orthodox Calvinists and other religious groups." My summary discussion of the demography of the early parties follows the tentative theory suggested by Fischer in Appendix I of his brilliant revisionist study of the Federalist party.

13. *Ibid.,* pp. 211–18.

14. Chambers, *Political Parties,* pp. 119–21; Fischer, *The Revolution of American Conservatism,* pp. 207–8.

15. Jefferson to Gideon Granger, August 13, 1800, in Paul Leicester Ford (ed.), *The Writings of Thomas Jefferson* (10 vols.; New York: G. P. Putnam's Sons, 1892–99), VII, 450–53.

16. Chambers, *Political Parties,* p. 55.

17. Smith, *Adams,* II, 843.

18. See below, chap. iii.

19. Bishop, *Georgia Speculation Unveiled.* See below, p. 155.

20. *Ibid.,* p. 156.

21. Adrienne Koch, *Jefferson and Madison: The Great Collaboration* (New York: Oxford University Press, 1964), chap. vii. Although the Virginia and Kentucky Resolutions were directed against a federal law, they clearly suggested that legislatures were proper institutions for voiding unconstitutional laws. *Ibid.*, p. 188. Federalist-controlled legislatures in the North responded to the resolutions by affirming that the function of voiding federal laws belonged to the federal Supreme Court. Charles Grove Haines, *The American Doctrine of Judicial Supremacy*, 2nd ed., rev. (New York: Russell & Russell, 1959), pp. 190–91.

22. Philadelphia *Aurora*, March 8, 1796.

23. Everett S. Brown (ed.), *William Plumer's Memorandum of Proceedings in the United States Senate, 1803–1807* (New York: Macmillan Co., 1923), p. 627. The Giles-Plumer conversation took place on February 27, 1807. The French ambassador to the United States in 1795 reported to his government that the Jay Treaty was approved because two senators had been bribed; he named Gunn and Jacob Read, of South Carolina. Smith, *Adams*, II, 873. See also the accusations made in Congress by John Randolph, *Annals of the Congress of the United States*, 8th Cong., January 31, 1805, col. 1104.

24. Senator Gunn was one of but two senators from the states south of Maryland to vote for the Jay Treaty. *Annals*, 3rd Cong., June 24, 1795, col. 862.

25. *Ibid.*, March 2, 1795, col. 844.

26. *American State Papers, Public Lands* (8 vols.; Washington: Gales and Seaton, 1832–61), I, 34–67.

27. *Annals*, 5th Cong., March 20, 1798, cols. 1277–83.

28. *Ibid.*, col. 1280. It was voted on by a voice, not a roll call, vote, and it is therefore not possible to tabulate how Federalist and Republican congressmen voted.

29. Georgia constitution of May 30, 1798, Article I, section 23, in House of Representatives, *Sundry Papers, in Relation to Claims, Commonly Called the Yazoo Claims* (Washington, 1809).

30. *Annals*, 5th Cong., March 20, 1798, col. 1278.

31. *Annals*, 6th Cong., April 16, 1800, col. 161. The italics are mine.

32. *Ibid.*, cols. 161–62. All party identifications of senators and representatives made in this book are derived from the following sources: James Grant Wilson and John Fiske (eds.), *Appleton's Cyclopædia of American Biography* (7 vols.; New York: D. Appleton and Co., 1887–1900); *Biographical Directory of the American Congress, 1774–1961*, rev. ed. (Washington: U.S. Government Printing Office, 1961); *Dictionary of American Biography; The National Cyclopædia of American Biography* (47 vols.; New York: James T. White & Co., 1898–1965).

33. *Annals*, 6th Cong., April 25, 1800, cols. 683–85. Earlier, Sewall had reported to the House the findings of a committee appointed to study the petitions of certain Yazoo claimants who sought compensation. He

recommended that their claims be honored. *American State Papers, Public Lands,* I, 101.

34. *Annals,* 6th Cong., April 25, 1800, col. 686.

35. *Ibid.,* April 23, 1800, col. 681; April 25, col. 685.

36. *American State Papers, Public Lands,* I, 126.

37. William Omer Foster, Sr., *James Jackson: Duellist and Militant Statesman, 1757–1806* (Athens: University of Georgia Press, 1960), p. 188.

38. See above, pp. 10–12.

39. *American State Papers, Public Lands,* I, 134–35.

40. 2 United States Statutes at Large 232 (1803).

CHAPTER III

1. Irving Brant, *James Madison* (6 vols.; Indianapolis: Bobbs-Merrill Co., 1941–61), IV, 237–38.

2. U.S. Bureau of the Census, *Historical Statistics of the United States, Colonial Times to 1957* (Washington: U.S. Government Printing Office, 1961), p. 547.

3. A useful definition is that of David B. Truman: ". . . an interest group is a shared-attitude group that makes certain claims upon other groups in the society. If and when it makes its claims through or upon any of the institutions of government, it becomes a political interest group." *The Governmental Process: Political Interests and Public Opinion* (New York: Alfred A. Knopf, 1951), p. 37.

4. *American State Papers, Public Lands* (8 vols.; Washington: Gales and Seaton, 1832–61), II, 881–84.

5. The acreage holdings are given in a report prepared for the House of Representatives by Secretary of State James Madison in 1805. *American State Papers, Public Lands,* I, 219–46.

6. Bacon to Story, June 1, 1808, in Gerald T. Dunne, "Joseph Story: The Germinal Years," *Harvard Law Review,* LXXV (1962), 738.

7. Diary entries of March 21, 1806, and February 5, 1808, in Charles Francis Adams (ed.), *Memoirs of John Quincy Adams* (12 vols.; Philadelphia: J. B. Lippincott Co., 1874–77), I, 423, 514. That the Yazooists stopped citing Federalist authorities after 1801 was suggested to me by Dunne, "Story," p. 713.

8. William C. Bruce, *John Randolph of Roanoke, 1773–1833* (2 vols.; New York and London: G. P. Putnam's Sons, 1922), II, 203.

9. The wording of this famous remark varies slightly in different accounts; to whom belongs the honor of being its recipient is disputed. Henry Adams, *John Randolph,* 9th ed. (Boston: Houghton Mifflin Co., 1886), p. 289, identifies Henry Clay (with whom Randolph dueled in 1826) as the object of Randolph's spleen; Gerald W. Johnson, *Randolph of Roanoke: A Political Fantastic* (New York: Minton, Balch & Co., 1929), p. 16, believes it was Edward Livingston.

10. William Plumer, Jr., *Life of William Plumer*, ed. Andrew P. Peabody (Boston: Phillips, Sampson and Co., 1857), p. 255.

11. Bruce, *Randolph*, I, 180.

12. It should be noted, however, that in 1803 Randolph, as the administration leader in the House, helped to put through the legislation appropriating money for the purchase of the Louisiana Territory. This, of course, was itself a bold expansion of federal power, and it bothered Jefferson, who would have preferred to justify the Louisiana Purchase with a constitutional amendment but had to give up the idea as impractical. See Bruce, *Randolph*, I, 178–79.

13. William Nisbet Chambers, *Political Parties in a New Nation: The American Experience, 1776–1809* (New York: Oxford University Press, 1963), p. 184.

14. Brant, *Madison*, IV, 232–33.

15. Bruce, *Randolph*, II, 331; chap. ix, *passim*. Despite legitimate doubts about the value of "psychological biographies," a study of John Randolph by a scholar equipped with the tools of psychiatric analysis, yet aware of their limitations, would perhaps lead to new insights into the causes of political behavior.

16. *Annals of the Congress of the United States*, 8th Cong., March 7, 1804, col. 1104.

17. Brant, *Madison*, IV, 233–34.

18. *Annals*, 8th Cong., February 20, 1804, cols. 1039–40.

19. Adams, *Randolph*, p. 106.

20. Quotes in this paragraph are from the *Annals*, 8th Cong., March 7, 1804, cols. 1100–15.

21. *Ibid.*, January 29, 1805, cols. 1024–33.

22. *Ibid.*, January 31, 1805, cols. 1064–80; Henry Adams, *History of the United States of America* (9 vols.; New York: Charles Scribner's Sons, 1889–91), II, 215.

23. Diary entry of February 1, 1805, *Memoirs of John Quincy Adams*, I, 343. Adams referred to Giles as one whose "tongue runs fast when once a going" and who is "very free in his animadversions both on men and things." *Ibid.*, p. 344.

24. The Randolph and Lyon speeches appear in the *Annals*, 8th Cong., January 31, 1805, cols. 1102–8, and February 1, 1805, cols. 1121–26. There is no way of knowing if there was any truth to Randolph's charge, though Lyon did change his position on the Yazoo claims. In 1800, as a House member from Vermont, he voted against the pro-Yazooist Gunn amendment. *Annals*, 6th Cong., April 25, 1800, col. 686. But after 1805, as a Kentucky representative, he sided with the Yazooists. Lyons, like many of the persons involved in the Yazoo drama, was a flamboyant figure. See Appendix F.

25. *Annals*, 8th Cong., January 29, 1805, col. 1032.

26. *Ibid.*, March 12, 1804, col. 1170.

27. *Annals,* 9th Cong., March 28, 1806, col. 208. Plumer's estrangement from the Federalists had already become serious by 1805; in 1808 the New Hampshire politician officially joined the Republican party. Lynn W. Turner, *William Plumer of New Hampshire, 1759–1850* (Chapel Hill: University of North Carolina Press, 1962), pp. 159–62, 183.

28. *Annals,* 9th Cong., March 29, 1806, cols. 920–21.

29. *Ibid.,* April 16, 1800, cols. 161–62.

30. *Ibid.,* April 25, 1800, col. 686.

31. The lone New England defector was Plumer, who commented that his vote against the Yazoo claims made him "detested by every man from New England and every Federalist in the Senate." Plumer, Jr., *Plumer,* p. 343.

32. A point that is thoroughly documented in a recent study by Paul Goodman, *The Democratic-Republicans of Massachusetts: Politics in a Young Republic* (Cambridge: Harvard University Press, 1964).

33. Bruce, *Randolph,* I, chap. v.

34. *Annals,* 9th Cong., March 28, 1806, col. 912. And see generally Bruce, *Randolph,* I, 233 ff., and Raymond Walters, *Albert Gallatin: Jeffersonian Financier and Diplomat* (New York: Macmillan Co., 1957), chap. xv.

35. Bruce, *Randolph,* I, 325–43; Noble E. Cunningham, Jr., *The Jeffersonian Republicans in Power: Party Operations, 1801–1809* (Chapel Hill: University of North Carolina Press, 1963), pp. 84–86.

36. Wilfred E. Binkley, *President and Congress,* 3rd rev. ed. (New York: Random House, 1962), chap. iii; Leonard D. White, *The Jeffersonians: A Study in Administrative History, 1801–1829* (New York: Macmillan Co., 1951), chaps. iii and iv. Randolph, it should be noted, was prominently identified with the Republicans' unsuccessful attempt to convict Supreme Court Justice Samuel Chase in impeachment proceedings before the Senate in 1805. Randolph was the principal manager of the House prosecutors; the loss of his case signified a decline in Randolph's influence among congressional Republicans and a consequent decline in his usefulness to the administration. Albert J. Beveridge, *The Life of John Marshall* (4 vols.; Boston: Houghton Mifflin Co., 1916–19), III, 221; Cunningham, *The Jeffersonian Republicans,* p. 81.

37. Although historians have commonly referred to Randolph's band as "Quids," organized as a small third party, the recent research of Noble E. Cunningham, Jr., has shown that both the name and the description are misapplied. See his "Who Were the Quids?" *Mississippi Valley Historical Review,* L (1963), 252–63.

38. Edward J. Harden, *The Life of George M. Troup* (Savannah: E. J. Purse, 1859), pp. 52–53.

CHAPTER IV

1. *Annals of the Congress of the United States,* 5th Cong., March 20, 1798, col. 1277.

2. Memorial of November 30, 1804, *American State Papers, Public Lands* (8 vols.; Washington: Gales and Seaton, 1832–61), I, 210.

3. The Supreme Court's appellate power under Article III of the Constitution extends to "cases" and "controversies," and it passes on questions of law only as a consequence of adversary proceedings. Throughout its history the Court has refused to give legal opinions in response to requests from the other branches of the federal government. The justices made their position clear within the first few years of the new government: in 1793 they politely but firmly refused to give President Washington legal advice on twenty-nine controversial questions of international law which he submitted to them; and in 1794 the justices sitting in the circuit courts ruled that Congress was without authority to require them to act as commissioners for the purpose of awarding pensions owed to veterans of the Revolutionary War. Charles Warren, *The Supreme Court in United States History*, rev. ed. (2 vols.; Boston: Little, Brown and Co., 1923), I, 69–82, 107–11.

4. See above, pp. 20–22.

5. Essay No. 78, *The Federalist* (New York: Modern Library, 1937), p. 509.

6. *Annals*, 8th Cong., March 10, 1804, col. 1151.

7. Albert J. Beveridge, *The Life of John Marshall* (4 vols.; Boston: Houghton Mifflin Co., 1916–19), III, 157.

8. *Ibid.*, chap. iv. The narrow failure of the effort to convict Chase in the Senate repudiated once and for all the Jeffersonian idea that judges could be ousted for political heresy.

9. The decision in *Derby* v. *Blake* was published in the Boston *Columbian Centinel* on October 9, 1799; it apparently became a forgotten case until rediscovered in the twentieth century by the legal historian Charles Warren. *Derby* v. *Blake* has been republished in the reports of the Massachusetts Supreme Judicial Court, 226 Mass. Reports 618 (1917).

10. *Beers* v. *Miller and Nightingale; Bishop and Bishop* v. *Nightingale and Miller; Miller and Nightingale* v. *Beers; Miller and Nightingale* v. *Bishop and Bishop*. These cases, which were commenced in 1797 and dismissed in 1805, grew out of the sale of 550,000 acres of Yazoo lands to nine Connecticut residents. Records of the United States Circuit Court for Connecticut, in the Federal Record Center of the General Services Administration, Boston.

11. *American State Papers, Public Lands*, I, 219–46, 253; Lynn W. Turner, *William Plumer of New Hampshire, 1759–1850* (Chapel Hill: University of North Carolina Press, 1962), p. 162. I have been unable to uncover any biographical information on Robert Fletcher.

12. Story to Robert Goodloe Harper, June 9, 1810, in Howell J. Heaney (ed.), "The Letters of Joseph Story (1779–1845) in the Hampton L. Carson Collection in the Free Library of Philadelphia," *American Journal of Legal History*, II (1958), 69.

13. *American State Papers, Public Lands,* I, 227. William Sullivan was a Federalist; his better-known brother, James, a Republican who became Massachusetts' governor in 1807 and 1808, was also a heavy speculator in Yazoo lands. See above, p. 38.

14. *Fletcher* v. *Peck,* Massachusetts Circuit Court Records, II, June, 1806, to October, 1811. The records in this case are presently stored in the Federal Record Center of the General Services Administration, Boston.

15. *Ibid.* The decision was not officially reported, and there is no formal opinion by Cushing and Davis in the records of the case. A check of five Boston newspapers for the months of October–November, 1807, has failed to uncover any circuit court opinion. *Boston Gazette; Columbian Centinel; Independent Chronicle; New-England Palladium; Repertory.* The only reference to the Yazoo issue in these Boston newspapers during this period was a long letter in the *New-England Palladium,* November 24, 1807, by an anonymous correspondent who, while taking the pro-Yazooist position, denied that he owned "a foot of Georgia land." He did not specifically refer to the federal circuit court decision but argued that the reaction of the federal courts was a foregone conclusion: "No *New-England* man will imagine that a Legislature can *repeal* a former *grant*—that they can *sell* and then at pleasure *take away* from the purchasers what they have sold. Nor is there the least doubt that any court of justice out of *Georgia* would confirm the right of the purchasers under GUNN and his associates. It is because *Georgia* and Mr. J. Randolph as much as any man alive perfectly well knows, that the title is good to those purchasers, and that a court would establish it, that such violent opposition in Congress has been made to the equitable proposal of submitting their claim to a court of the *United States.*"

16. Warren, *Supreme Court,* I, 193.

17. Kathryn Turner, "Federalist Policy and the Judiciary Act of 1801," *The William and Mary Quarterly,* 3rd Ser., XXII (1965), 3–32.

18. Governor of Delaware. The nominations are listed in *Journal of the Executive Proceedings of the Senate of the United States of America* (Washington: Duff Green, 1828), III, 381–86.

19. United States attorney in Massachusetts.

20. Attorney general of Pennsylvania; Ingersoll declined the nomination.

21. Former Federalist leader in the Maryland House of Delegates.

22. Attorney General of the United States; Lee declined the nomination.

23. United States senator from South Carolina.

24. Federal district judge in North Carolina.

25. Former Federalist congressman and United States attorney for the New Hampshire district.

26. Federalist lawyer and representative in the Pennsylvania legislature.

27. United States Secretary of the Treasury.

28. Today the case of *Marbury* v. *Madison,* 1 Cranch 137 (1803), is

remembered as the first decision in which the entire Supreme Court unequivocally stated that it had the power to declare acts of Congress unconstitutional. In 1803, however, the *Marbury* case attracted wide attention as
a bold attempt by a Federalist Court to control a Republican administration. John A. Garraty, "The Case of the Missing Commissions," in Garraty
(ed.), *Quarrels That Have Shaped the Constitution* (New York: Harper
& Row, 1964), pp. 1–14; Warren, *Supreme Court,* I, 245–55.

29. Beveridge, *Marshall,* III, 178; 176–79, 192–96, *passim.*

30. 2 United States Statutes at Large 445–46; *Annals,* 9th Cong., March
2, 1807, cols. 664–72.

31. Warren, *Supreme Court,* I, 170–71.

32. *Ibid.,* p. 173.

33. Story to Samuel P. Fay, February 25, 1808, in William W. Story
(ed.), *Life and Letters of Joseph Story* (2 vols.; Boston: Little, Brown
and Co., 1851), I, 167. This description of Marshall's personality is drawn
from Beveridge, *Marshall,* II, chaps. v and xi; IV, chap. ii.

34. The high point of Marshall's influence on the Court, in terms of
making his judicial views the law of the land, was in the decade 1810–
20. On this and on his willingness to compromise in order to represent
officially the Court's position, see Beveridge, *Marshall,* IV, 509–14, 582–
84; Donald G. Morgan, "Marshall, the Marshall Court, and the Constitution," in William Melville Jones (ed.), *Chief Justice John Marshall: A
Reappraisal* (Ithaca: Cornell University Press, 1956), pp. 168 85; Morgan,
*Justice William Johnson, the First Dissenter: The Career and Constitutional
Philosophy of a Jeffersonian Judge* (Columbia: University of South Carolina Press, 1954), p. 176n., pp. 215–17; Warren, *Supreme Court,* I, 789–90.
William W. Crosskey of the University of Chicago Law School, whose
interpretations of American constitutional history are extremely controversial, has argued that Marshall never succeeded in imposing his
nationalistic judicial philosophy on the Court. "Mr. Chief Justice Marshall,"
in Allison Dunham and Philip B. Kurland (eds.), *Mr. Justice,* 2nd ed.
(Chicago: University of Chicago Press, 1964), pp. 3–32.

35. Jefferson to Thomas Ritchie, December 25, 1820, in Paul Leicester
Ford (ed.), *The Works of Thomas Jefferson* (12 vols.; New York and
London: G. P. Putnam's Sons, 1904–1905), XII, 177–78. Similar comments
appear in his letters to William Johnson, October 27, 1822, March 4 and
June 12, 1823; and to James Madison, June 13, 1823. *Ibid.,* pp. 247–50, 259,
279–80, 295–96.

36. Charles Grove Haines, *The Role of the Supreme Court in American
Government and Politics, 1789–1835* (Berkeley: University of California
Press, 1944), pp. 649–50.

37. Morgan, *Johnson,* chaps. ix and x.

38. In the great case of *Gibbons* v. *Ogden,* 9 Wheat. 1 (1824), which
voided a New York law establishing a steamboat monopoly because it
conflicted with a congressional law regulating commerce, Johnson wrote

a concurring opinion that gave an interpretation of the federal commerce clause far more expansive than Marshall's.

39. Rodney to Jefferson, October 31, 1808, in Warren, *Supreme Court,* I, 336; chap. vii, *passim.*

40. *Dictionary of American Biography* (22 vols.; New York: Charles Scribner's Sons, 1928–58), XI, 313.

41. *Ibid.,* XVIII, 575.

42. Morgan, *Johnson,* p. 182.

43. Warren, *Supreme Court,* I, 400.

44. *Dictionary of American Biography,* XII, 343–45; Henry P. Goddard, *Luther Martin: The "Federal Bull-Dog,"* (Baltimore: Maryland Historical Society Fund-Publications, 1887), No. 24, Part I, pp. 9–42.

45. Charles Francis Adams (ed.), *Memoirs of John Quincy Adams* (12 vols.; Philadelphia: J. B. Lippincott Co., 1874–77), I, 546.

46. *Fletcher* v. *Peck,* 6 Cranch 87, 126 (1809).

47. *Memoirs of John Quincy Adams,* I, 547.

48. *Ibid.*

49. *Ibid.*

50. The relationship of Marshall's values to the issues raised by *Fletcher* v. *Peck* are discussed in the next chapter, pp. 70–74. Although Marshall very probably was reluctant to decide the case without a full Court, he finally decided the case in 1810 with only five justices. By then he had little choice: Chase and Cushing were still absent because of illness, and assuming Marshall was anxious to decide the case, it would have been awkward to delay a decision again.

51. John Quincy Adams and Luther Martin, "Agreement of Counsel," *Fletcher* v. *Peck,* March 15, 1809, in Correspondence on Appellate Cases, in the National Archives (Justice and Executive Branch), Washington.

52. Gerald T. Dunne, "Joseph Story: The Germinal Years," *Harvard Law Review,* LXXV (1962), 745. Wetmore overspeculated in Yazoo lands and fell into debt.

53. Joseph Story to Samuel P. Fay, February 16, 1808, in *Story,* I, 162.

54. Dunne, "Story," pp. 735–36.

55. *Fletcher* v. *Peck,* 6 Cranch 115–22 (1810).

56. Goddard, *Martin,* p. 35. Martin was a notoriously heavy drinker, but this did not normally affect the caliber of his legal work.

CHAPTER V

1. Albert J. Beveridge, *The Life of John Marshall* (4 vols.; Boston: Houghton Mifflin Co., 1916–19), III, 582.

2. *Ibid.,* I, 231; 222–31, *passim.*

3. The aims and effects of the paper money movement during the 1780's are an extremely complicated matter. According to the revisionist scholarship of Forrest McDonald, in many states the paper money move-

ment was motivated as much by a desire to erase *public* debts incurred in the Revolutionary War as it was by a concern with the problems of private debtors. Moreover, the debtor-creditor relationship does not lend itself to a class conflict interpretation that pits poor and radical debtors against rich and conservative creditors. "Ordinarily," McDonald writes, "the largest debtors were also the largest creditors." *We The People: The Economic Origins of the Constitution* (Chicago: University of Chicago Press, 1958), p. 392. McDonald, who follows Merrill Jensen, *The New Nation* (New York: Alfred A. Knopf, 1950), in rejecting the "critical period" thesis that portrays the Confederation years as a period of economic collapse and confusion, has also argued that the framers of the Constitution were not particularly interested in correcting the evils of paper money and debtor-relief laws. See generally his *We The People,* especially pp. 349–55, 384–93, and *E Pluribus Unum: The Formation of the American Republic, 1776–1790* (Boston: Houghton Mifflin Co., 1965), especially pp. 199–202. Although persuaded that sweeping generalizations are not possible, I have chosen in this book to follow the more conventional interpretation that views the contract clause as a deliberate brake on state laws interfering with the relationship between private debtors and creditors. McDonald himself observes that during the contest over ratification the expectation was that "adoption of the Constitution would alter existing relations between debtors and creditors," and that "most states had, in practice, passed at least some temporary legislation designed in behalf of private debtors, most commonly laws postponing the collection of debts." *E Pluribus Unum,* p. 199.

4. John Marshall, *Life of George Washington* (5 vols.; Philadelphia: C. P. Wayne, 1805–1807), V, 85–86, 111–12.

5. It is, in a sense, a conservative caricature of the once fashionable views of the progressive historian Charles A. Beard, whose *An Economic Interpretation of the Constitution of the United States* (New York: Macmillan Co., 1913) developed the thesis that the Confederation was marked by a sharp division between conservatives and radicals and that the framing and adoption of the Constitution of 1787 was an antidemocratic reaction led by financial speculators. For a thoroughly documented refutation of Beard's interpretation and an insight into the complexities of the period, see Forrest McDonald's two books, *We the People* and *E Pluribus Unum.*

6. Marshall, *Washington,* V, 178. In a eulogy of John Marshall that he delivered in 1835, his friend and colleague Justice Joseph Story quoted the following passage from a letter in which the Chief Justice described his feelings in 1787 and emphasized the importance he attached to Article I, section 10, of the newly proposed Constitution: "The questions, which were perpetually recurring in the state legislatures; and which brought annually into doubt principles, which I thought most sacred; which proved that every thing was afloat, and that we had no anchorage ground; gave

a high value in my estimation to that article of the Constitution, which imposes restrictions on the States." Joseph Story, "Life, Character, and Services of Chief Justice Marshall," in William W. Story (ed.), *The Miscellaneous Writings of Joseph Story* (Boston: Little, Brown and Co., 1852), p. 658.

7. Beveridge, *Marshall,* I, 224–40; II, 202–9; IV, 145–57.

8. William Blackstone, *Commentaries on the Laws of England* (2 vols.; Philadelphia: J. B. Lippincott Co., 1893), I, 138. Marshall's legal education is discussed in Beveridge, *Marshall,* I, 56.

9. *Fletcher* v. *Peck,* 6 Cranch 87, 128 (1810). All quotations from the Marshall opinion in this chapter are taken from the report of the case which begins on p. 87 of the sixth volume of Cranch's reports. Marshall's majority opinion and Justice Johnson's concurring opinion are reproduced in Appendix G.

10. This is particularly true of social and economic legislation, which the Court today rarely overturns. The continuing influence of Marshall's dictum on legislative motives is best summarized in a statement made by Justice Harlan Fiske Stone in a 1936 case sustaining a federal law: "Inquiry into the hidden motives which may move Congress to exercise a power constitutionally conferred upon it is beyond the competency of courts." *Sonzinsky* v. *United States,* 300 U.S. 506, 513–14.

11. Interestingly enough, Marshall's statement that legislation should be voided only in the clearest of cases has been quoted by generations of judges as a prelude to declaring laws unconstitutional.

12. The evidence of the framers' intent is set out in Benjamin F. Wright, Jr., *The Contract Clause of the Constitution* (Cambridge: Harvard University Press, 1938), pp. 3–16. On Wilson's concern with public contracts, see below, p. 102, n.5.

13. As early as 1798 a Supreme Court decision explicitly limited the application of the *ex post facto* clause solely to criminal legislation. *Calder* v. *Bull,* 3 Dallas 386.

14. Wright, *Contract Clause,* pp. 33–34.

15. In technical terms, Marshall was saying that the title purchased by Fletcher (the plaintiff) from Peck was unimpaired by the repeal act; on this count, therefore, Fletcher had no grounds for charging that Peck had sold him a defective title.

16. Johnson's opinion appears on pp. 143–48 of the report of the case in 6 Cranch 87.

17. Johnson joined Marshall in rejecting as "absurd" and presenting "insuperable difficulties" the contention that courts could invalidate laws because the lawmakers had been corrupted.

18. These attorneys, however, probably had little sense that their behavior violated legal ethics. Arranged cases of one kind or another, intended to elicit a constitutional ruling from the Supreme Court, were not uncommon in those days. Beveridge, *Marshall,* IV, 282–83, 343–45;

Charles Grove Haines, *The Role of the Supreme Court in American Government and Politics, 1789-1835* (Berkeley: University of California Press, 1944), p. 147.

19. His biographer, Donald G. Morgan, *Justice William Johnson, the First Dissenter: The Career and Constitutional Philosophy of a Jeffersonian Judge* (Columbia: University of South Carolina Press, 1954), pp. 213-14n., defends him against the charge that political considerations influenced the opinion. Yet Morgan's own account of Johnson's career shows that on other occasions the Justice allowed political pressures to influence his judicial behavior. Thus, Johnson's much-heralded role as the Court's first great dissenter began only after the man who had appointed him, Thomas Jefferson, persuaded him that dissent from the Federalist doctrines of John Marshall was a Republican duty. Morgan, *Johnson,* chaps. ix and x.

20. See below, chap. vii.

21. Strictly speaking, the first Supreme Court decision invalidating a state law was *United States* v. *Peters,* 6 Cranch 115 (1809). In *Peters* the Court nullified a Pennsylvania law that declared a federal court order invalid. Earlier, the justices participating in the work of the circuit courts had already asserted the power to pass on the constitutionality of state legislation. Charles Warren, *The Supreme Court in United States History,* rev. ed. (2 vols.; Boston: Little, Brown and Co., 1923), pp. 65-69.

22. Two other leading Marshall opinions, the decision in *Marbury* v. *Madison,* 1 Cranch 137 (1803), declaring the Court's power to nullify unconstitutional legislation, and *McCulloch* v. *Maryland,* 4 Wheat. 316 (1819), upholding the constitutionality of the Bank of the United States, drew heavily on earlier statements prepared by Hamilton. Recently, Samuel J. Konefsky has attacked the "myth" that Marshall derived his ideas from Hamilton: "However much the two men may have shared a common outlook on the problems of their time, Marshall's intellectual history demonstrates that he did not so much borrow from Hamilton as agree with him. Philosophic affinity is not necessarily the result of imitation." *John Marshall and Alexander Hamilton* (New York: Macmillan Co., 1964), p. 255. While philosophic affinity does not prove imitation, Marshall's constitutional views reveal an unmistakable indebtedness to the philosopher of Federalism, not merely a coincidence of ideas. See Clinton Rossiter, *Alexander Hamilton and the Constitution* (New York: Harcourt, Brace & World, 1964), pp. 240-43.

23. 2 Dallas 304, 320 (1795). The first federal case striking down a state law under the contract clause in which the records have been preserved is *Champion and Dickason* v. *Casey* (1792). A circuit court invalidated a Rhode Island law which gave debtors three years to settle their overdue accounts and made them exempt from imprisonment during this period. Warren, *Supreme Court,* I, 67.

24. *Huidekoper's Lessee* v. *Douglass,* 3 Cranch 70 (1805).

CHAPTER VI

1. Story to Harper, June 9, 1810, April 8 and September 19, 1811, and November 3, 1812, in Howell J. Heaney (ed.), "The Letters of Joseph Story (1779–1845) in the Hampton L. Carson Collection in the Free Library of Philadelphia," *American Journal of Legal History*, II (1958), 69–71. According to Gerald T. Dunne, who has written a useful account of the early career of Joseph Story, Peck's failure to pay his bill "scarcely suggests the existence of an agreement in which every detail has been prearranged." Dunne believes it will never be known if *Fletcher* v. *Peck* was a collusive case. "Joseph Story: The Germinal Years," *Harvard Law Review*, LXXV (1962), 749. Yet the evidence, both internal and circumstantial, that the case was collusive is overwhelming. See above, chaps. iv and v. Story's own communication to Harper speaks of the case as "a concern of the whole company." The Story letters in no way contradict the view that *Fletcher* v. *Peck* was a collusive case engineered by the New England Mississippi Land Company. They show only that John Peck was slow to pay a legal bill.

2. From a technical point of view the case decided only that John Peck had not defrauded Robert Fletcher in selling him 15,000 acres of Yazoo land.

3. New York *Evening Post*, March 21, 1810.

4. Boston *Columbian Centinel*, March 24, 1810; Boston *Independent Chronicle*, April 23, 1810.

5. The *Aurora's* anti-Yazooism reached its peak in 1804 and 1805. Sanford W. Higginbotham, *The Keystone in the Democratic Arch: Pennsylvania Politics, 1801–1816* (Harrisburg: Pennsylvania Historical and Museum Commission, 1952), pp. 110–11, 351, n.22. In a perusal of the Philadelphia *Aurora* from March 1 to June 1, 1810, I did not find even a passing reference to the Supreme Court's decision.

6. *Richmond Enquirer*, April 5 and 6, 1810; *Savannah Republican*, April 10, 12, and 14, 1810.

7. *Annals of the Congress of the United States*, 11th Cong., April 17, 1810, col. 1881.

8. Even the drive to impeach Justice Chase, which Randolph led and which threatened the independence of Marshall's Supreme Court, failed to separate them. Randolph, in fact, repeatedly praised the Chief Justice during the impeachment trial. Albert J. Beveridge, *The Life of John Marshall* (4 vols.; Boston: Houghton Mifflin Co., 1916–19), III, 187–88, 214–16; William C. Bruce, *John Randolph of Roanoke, 1773–1833* (2 vols.; New York and London: G. P. Putnam's Sons, 1922), I, 201; II, 617, 637.

9. *Annals*, 11th Cong., April 17, 1810, col. 1881.

10. By contrast, 15 of the 22 votes against postponement were supplied by New England representatives. *Ibid.*, February 11, 1811, col. 131; February 12, cols. 961–63.

11. Charles Warren, *The Supreme Court in United States History,* rev. ed. (2 vols.; Boston: Little, Brown and Co., 1923), I, 422.

12. Jefferson to Madison, May 25, 1810, in Paul Leicester Ford (ed.), *The Works of Thomas Jefferson* (12 vols.; New York and London: G. P. Putnam's Sons, 1904–1905), XI, 141. Jefferson applied his remarks to cover as well Marshall's handling of *Marbury* v. *Madison* and the Burr treason trial of 1807.

13. Thus, Beveridge describes the decision in *Fletcher* v. *Peck* as "highly unwelcome to the people." *Marshall,* III, 595; Warren claims it "aroused vivid and excited interest throughout the country." *Supreme Court,* I, 392. My examination of the *Annals of Congress* for 1810 and 1811 and of some dozen leading eastern newspapers in the period March–May, 1811—certainly rough barometers of public concern—uncovered little excitement over the Supreme Court's decision. *Boston Gazette;* Boston *Columbian Centinel;* Providence *Columbian Phenix;* Boston *Independent Chronicle;* Washington *National Intelligencer;* Boston *New-England Palladium;* New York *Evening Post;* Baltimore *Niles' Weekly Register;* Philadelphia *Aurora; Richmond Enquirer; Savannah Republican; Providence Gazette;* Boston *Repertory.*

14. *Annals,* 12th Cong., January 19, 1813, col. 55.

15. Randolph is not recorded as participating in any debate or vote on the Yazoo issue in the Twelfth Congress. By the time the compensation bill reached the House in January, 1813, he was a "lameduck" congressman who had lost his seat in the election of 1812. See below, p. 93.

16. *Dictionary of American Biography* (22 vols.; New York: Charles Scribner's Sons, 1928–58), XVIII, 650–51. An ante bellum politician of some prominence, Troup deserves a full-length biographical study. At present the major source on his political career is a eulogistic nineteenth-century biography, Edward J. Harden, *The Life of George M. Troup* (Savannah: E. J. Purse, 1859).

17. Troup's speech is reported in the *Annals,* 12th Cong., January 20, 1813, cols. 856–59.

18. Although some modern scholars have criticized Marshall for construing the sale act as a contract, the anti-Yazooists agreed with the Chief Justice to the extent that they accepted the sale as an attempted contract. But they argued that the corruption invalidated its legitimacy. For a critique of Marshall's conception of contracts see Charles Grove Haines, *The Role of the Supreme Court in American Government and Politics, 1789–1835* (Berkeley: University of California Press, 1944), pp. 317–20.

19. *Biographical Directory of the American Congress, 1774–1961,* rev. ed. (Washington: U.S. Government Printing Office, 1961), p. 1010.

20. All quotations from Harper's speech are taken from the *Annals,* February 15, 1813, cols. 1066–73. His comments were not wholly accurate. Although the Court relied heavily on the innocence of the later pur-

chasers, the full faith and credit clause (Article IV, section 1, of the Constitution) did not figure in its decision. The clause, moreover, is a request, not to private citizens, but to the states, asking them to extend full faith and credit "to the public Acts, Records, and judicial Proceedings of every other State." The Yazoo claimants, whatever their guilt or innocence in the fraud, did not purchase their titles out of respect for the state of Georgia.

21. See above, p. 58.

22. *Annals*, 12th Cong., January 20, 1813, col. 860. I have not attempted to tabulate the party breakdown in the Yazoo votes of 1813 and 1814, for it would be a meaningless exercise. By this time the Republicans, or Democrats as they were increasingly called, totally dominated the national political scene, so much so that they soon disintegrated into a number of competing factions and could no longer be considered an organized political party. The Federalists, while still active in the northern states, were strong only in New England, and virtually all congressmen from that region, regardless of party affiliation, supported the Yazoo claimants. On the breakup of the Federalist-Republican party system see William Nisbet Chambers, *Political Parties in a New Nation: The American Experience, 1776–1809* (New York: Oxford University Press, 1963), pp. 191–201.

23. *Annals*, 12th Cong., February 15, 1813, col. 1073. The vote on this motion was not by roll call, and therefore the sectional voting alignments cannot be tabulated.

24. *American State Papers, Public Lands* (8 vols.; Washington: Gales and Seaton, 1832–61), II, 877–80.

25. Bruce, *Randolph*, I, 386; Henry Adams, *History of the United States of America* (9 vols.; New York: Charles Scribner's Sons, 1889–91), VII, 51.

26. *Annals*, 13th Cong., February 28, 1814, col. 643; Charles Francis Adams (ed.), *Memoirs of John Quincy Adams* (12 vols.; Philadelphia: J. B. Lippincott Co., 1874–77), I, 343.

27. *Annals*, 13th Cong., March 15, 1814, cols. 1873–75.

28. Reprinted in the Philadelphia *Aurora*, March 16, 1814. Wright, who asserted that he had previously opposed compensation, set out his position in debates reported in the *Annals*, 12th Cong., January 20, 1813, col. 859; 13th Cong., March 9, 1814, col. 1854; March 21, cols. 1883–89.

29. Boston *Columbian Centinel*, March 30, 1814.

30. Boston *Repertory*, March 10, 1814, reprinted from the Philadelphia *United States Gazette*.

31. Philadelphia *Aurora*, March 15, 1814. The editorial further commented that passage of the bill was probably inevitable, because "we find of late so much principle sacrificed to expediency, and so much inconsistency in popular humors and tergiversation in popular leaders . . ." This was a slap at Madison's administration, with which Duane, a

temperamental oppositionist like John Randolph, had fallen out. See Higginbotham, *Keystone in the Democratic Arch,* pp. 257–58, 309–10.

32. Washington *National Intelligencer,* March 1 and 10, 1814.

33. *Annals,* 13th Cong., March 8, 1814, cols. 1838–48.

34. This assertion was of course an extreme statement of the view that constitutions ought to be strictly interpreted. Even though Troup, as a states' rights Southerner, took the position that the state governments, unlike the federal government, possessed a reservoir of inherent powers, he contended that "extraordinary powers not essential to the general power of legislation" were reserved to the people—as, for instance, the power to sell the western lands.

35. Quoted in the Boston *Repertory,* March 31, 1814, reporting a House debate on March 23. The *Annals,* 13th Cong., March 23, 1814, col. 1901, noted that Eppes gave "an animated and decided speech of nearly an hour" in opposition to the Yazoo bill, but the text was not published.

36. *Annals,* 13th Cong., March 8, 1814, cols. 1848–59; March 21, col. 1894; March 25, col. 1918.

37. *Ibid.,* March 21, cols. 1889–90.

38. *Ibid.,* March 8, cols. 1851–52; March 24, cols. 1903–11.

39. *Ibid.,* March 8, col. 1846.

40. *Ibid.,* March 26, col. 1925, incorrectly gives the final vote as 84 to 76 and lists the "Nays" as "Yeas" and vice versa. The Washington *National Intelligencer,* March 29, 1814, gives a correct listing, but it too errs in counting 84 votes in favor of the bill.

41. See, for example, the following congressional votes on the Yazoo issue: *Annals,* 6th Cong., April 25, 1800, col. 686 (2 Pennsylvania votes in favor of Gunn's pro-Yazooist amendment, 9 against); 8th Cong., March 12, 1804, col. 1170 (no Pennsylvania votes against postponement of Yazoo compensation bill, 14 in favor of postponement); 9th Cong., March 28, 1806, col. 208 (2 Pennsylvania votes against compensation bill passed by the Senate); 9th Cong., March 29, 1806, cols. 920–21 (2 Pennsylvania votes in favor of Senate compensation bill, 15 opposed).

42. See generally Sanford Higginbotham's excellent study of Pennsylvania politics in this period, *Keystone in the Democratic Arch.* I am indebted to Professor Higginbotham for a helpful communication on the subject of Pennsylvania's attitude toward the Yazoo speculation. Letter to author, August 24, 1965.

43. Boston *Columbian Centinel,* April 9, 1814.

44. *Annals,* 9th Cong., March 28, 1806, col. 909.

45. Adams, *History,* VII, 402.

46. 3 United States Statutes at Large 116–20.

47. On every $100 worth of land they were required to pay $95 in certificates and $5 in cash.

48. *American State Papers, Finance* (5 vols.; Washington: Gales and Seaton, 1832–34), III, 281–83. Because certain members of the New Eng-

land Mississippi Land Company had not paid the full purchase price when they bought their shares, the commissioners ruled that they were not entitled to full compensation. Despite their numerous appeals, Congress refused to pass legislation ordering full compensation for these claimants. The matter finally ended in 1864 when the United States Court of Claims decided against them. *New England Mississippi Land Company* v. *United States,* 1 Court of Claims 135 (1864); Charles H. Haskins, "The Yazoo Land Companies," *Papers of the American Historical Association* (5 vols.; New York and London: G. P. Putnam's Sons, 1891), V, Part 4, 102n.

CHAPTER VII

1. Leonard W. Levy, *The Law of the Commonwealth and Chief Justice Shaw* (Cambridge: Harvard University Press, 1957), p. 280.

2. A really large volume of federal regulatory legislation was first enacted in the Progressive Era, although one could date the beginning of significant regulation on a national scale from the passage of the Interstate Commerce Act in 1887.

3. Benjamin F. Wright, Jr., *The Contract Clause of the Constitution* (Cambridge: Harvard University Press, 1938), p. 95. If one adds to this figure the cases in which the post-Civil War Court required towns and cities to meet the obligation assumed in their municipal bonds (such decisions did not necessarily lead to a voiding of state laws), the role of the contract clause becomes even more prominent. Charles Warren, *The Supreme Court in United States History,* rev. ed. (2 vols.; Boston: Little, Brown and Co., 1923), II, 678, estimates that during the Waite period alone (1874–88) the Court decided nearly 200 municipal bond cases; in almost all of them the contract clause was held to prohibit a municipality from repudiating its debt.

4. Wright, *Contract Clause,* chap. i.

5. On August 28, 1787, the Constitutional Convention rejected a proposal by Rufus King that the states be forbidden to "interfere in private contracts"; however, a contract clause was subsequently inserted into Article I, section 10, by the Committee of Style. Although this action exceeded the committee's mandate, which was simply "to revise the style of and arrange the articles agreed to by the House," the Convention on September 14 accepted without complaint the revised Article I, section 10. (A motion by Elbridge Gerry that the contract clause also limit Congress failed for want of a second.) Max Farrand (ed.), *The Records of the Federal Convention,* rev. ed. (4 vols.; New Haven: Yale University Press, 1937), II, 439–40, 547, 619. According to Forrest McDonald, *E Pluribus Unum: The Formation of the American Republic, 1776–1790* (Boston: Houghton Mifflin Co., 1965), pp. 186–87, 187n., Gouverneur Morris was responsible for this surreptitious insertion of the clause into the Consti-

tution. Professor McDonald suggests that Morris was acting on behalf of James Wilson, who, as a lawyer and lobbyist for the Bank of North America, wanted to safeguard the bank's legislative charter of incorporation in Pennsylvania against revocation. It nevertheless seems most probable that the primary expectation about the clause was that it would prohibit state laws freeing private debtors from their obligations. Perhaps the clearest statement of this view appears in an uncompleted essay on the Constitutional Convention written by James Madison near the end of his life: "In the internal administration of the States a violation of Contracts had become familiar in the form of depreciated paper made a legal tender, of property substituted for money, of Instalment laws, and of the occlusions of the Courts of Justice; although evident that all such interferences affected the rights of other States, relatively Creditor, as well as Citizen Creditors within the State." *Records of the Convention,* III, 548.

6. *Fletcher* v. *Peck,* 6 Cranch 87, 137–38 (1810).

7. *Ibid.,* p. 138.

8. *Ibid.,* p. 143.

9. Edward S. Corwin, "The Basic Doctrine of American Constitutional Law," *Michigan Law Review,* XII (February, 1914), 255.

10. *New Jersey* v. *Wilson,* 7 Cranch 164 (1812). Any reader who hopefully wonders whether any tax-free haven still exists in America is in for a disappointment, however. Soon after the decision taxes began to be collected on the land without protest. In 1886, when an owner protested the constitutionality of the taxation, the Supreme Court ruled that the long acquiescence amounted to a surrender of the exemption. Wright, *Contract Clause,* pp. 36–37.

11. *Dartmouth College* v. *Woodward,* 4 Wheat. 518 (1819).

12. *Sturges* v. *Crowinshield,* 4 Wheat. 122 (1819).

13. *Green* v. *Biddle,* 8 Wheat. 1 (1823); Paul W. Gates, "Tenants of the Log Cabin," *Mississippi Valley Historical Review,* XLIX (1962), 3–31.

14. *Ibid.,* pp. 24–26; *Hawkins* v. *Barney's Lessee,* 5 Peters 457 (1831).

15. 12 Wheat. 213 (1827).

16. *Ibid.,* pp. 272–73.

17. 4 Peters 514, 560–63 (1830). It is very possible that Marshall disagreed with this decision but voted with the majority in order to state its decision as moderately as possible. Since Marshall was Chief Justice, he enjoyed the prerogative of assigning the opinion in all cases where he voted with the majority. We have the testimony of one of his associates that Marshall spoke for the Court "even in some instances when contrary to his own judgment and vote." Donald G. Morgan, *Justice William Johnson, the First Dissenter: The Career and Constitutional Philosophy of a Jeffersonian Judge* (Columbia: University of South Carolina Press, 1954), pp. 181–82. See also Walter F. Murphy, *Elements of Judicial Strategy* (Chicago: University of Chicago Press, 1964), p. 85.

18. *Charles River Bridge* v. *Warren Bridge*, 11 Peters 420, 549, 552. The case had been considered by the Marshall Court in 1831 and 1834, but it was too divided to reach a decision. Not surprisingly, Marshall believed that Massachusetts had violated the contract clause. Warren, *Supreme Court*, I, 773 and n., 790.

19. Wright, *Contract Clause*, p. 63.

20. *Ibid.*, pp. 61–82, *passim*, and, specifically, p. 62.

21. Warren, *Supreme Court*, II, 678. The best discussion of the municipal bond cases, a neglected area of American constitutional and political history, appears in Charles Fairman, *Mr. Justice Miller and the Supreme Court, 1862–1890* (Cambridge: Harvard University Press, 1939), chap. ix.

22. In the first legal tender case the Court ruled that Congress lacked the power to make paper currency legal tender for the payment of debts previously contracted in gold, in part because this "impairs the obligation of contracts, [and] is inconsistent with the spirit of the Constitution." *Hepburn* v. *Griswold*, 8 Wallace 603 (1870). But the next year in *Knox* v. *Lee*, 12 Wallace 457 (1871), the Court reversed this position and in 1879 rejected a strong plea by attorneys for the Union Pacific Railroad and the Central Pacific Railroad that the "spirit" and "principles" of the Constitution made the contract clause applicable to the federal government as well as to state governments. Samuel Shellabarger and Jeremiah Wilson, Brief for the Union Pacific Railroad Company, pp. 32–42; Benjamin H. Hill, Oral Argument for the Central Pacific Railroad Company, pp. 11–26, *Sinking Fund Cases*, United States Supreme Court Records and Briefs, in the Library of Congress, Washington.

23. State bond cases: *Louisiana* v. *Jumel*, 107 U.S. 711 (1883); *Antoni* v. *Greenhow*, 107 U.S. 769 (1883); *In re Ayres*, 123 U.S. 443 (1887). Regulation cases: *Peik* v. *Chicago & N.W. Ry. Co.*, 94 U.S. 164, and the other *Granger Railroad Cases* decided in 1877; *Spring Valley Water Works* v. *Schottler*, 110 U.S. 347 (1884); *Railroad Commission Cases*, 116 U.S. 307 (1886). See C. Peter Magrath, *Morrison R. Waite: The Triumph of Character* (New York: Macmillan Co., 1963), chaps. x and xi.

24. 101 U.S. 814 (1880). It should also be noted that the states themselves had become cautious when they granted charters of incorporation. The charters frequently contained "reservation" clauses, which reserved to the state the power to amend the charter in the future if required for the public good.

25. Felix Frankfurter, *Mr. Justice Holmes and the Supreme Court* (Cambridge: Harvard University Press, 1938), Appendix 1; Walton H. Hamilton, "The Path of Due Process of Law," in Conyers Read (ed.), *The Constitution Reconsidered* (New York: Columbia University Press, 1938), pp. 167–90; Alfred H. Kelly and Winfred A. Harbison, *The American Constitution*, 3rd ed. (New York: W. W. Norton & Co., 1963), chap. xx; Robert G. McCloskey, *The American Supreme Court* (Chicago: University of Chicago Press, 1960), chap. v.

26. Wright, *Contract Clause*, pp. 95–97.

27. *Illinois Central Railroad Company* v. *Illinois*, 146 U.S. 387, 460 (1892). This case was called to my attention by Wallace Mendelson's article, "New Light on Fletcher v. Peck and Gibbons v. Ogden," *Yale Law Journal*, LVIII (1949), 573n. Ironically, the decision in the *Illinois Central* case (which divided the Court 4 to 3) was given by Justice Stephen J. Field, one of the most procorporation judges ever to sit on the United States Supreme Court.

28. 290 U.S. 398 (1934).

29. Dissenting opinion of Justice Sutherland, 290 U.S. 398, 482.

30. 290 U.S. 398, 444. The italics are mine.

31. Among a large and growing literature the following works are especially noteworthy: Robert A. Horn, *Groups and the Constitution* (Stanford: Stanford University Press, 1956); Samuel Krislov, "The Amicus Curiae Brief: From Friendship to Advocacy," *Yale Law Journal*, LXXII (1963), 694–721; Walter F. Murphy and C. Herman Pritchett (eds.), *Courts, Judges, and Politics: An Introduction to the Judicial Process* (New York: Random House, 1961), chap. viii; C. Herman Pritchett and Alan F. Westin (eds.), *The Third Branch of Government: 8 Cases in Constitutional Politics* (New York: Harcourt, Brace & World, 1963); Benjamin F. Twiss, *Lawyers and the Constitution: How Laissez Faire Came to the Supreme Court* (Princeton: Princeton University Press, 1942); Clement Vose, *Caucasians Only: The Supreme Court, the NAACP, and the Restrictive Covenant Cases* (Berkeley: University of California Press, 1959), and Vose, "Litigation as a Form of Pressure Group Activity," *The Annals of the American Academy of Political and Social Science,* CCCXIX (September, 1958), 20–31.

32. Arthur F. Bentley, *The Process of Government: A Study of Social Purposes* (Bloomington, Ind.: Principia Press, 1949), chaps. xi and xvi.

33. *The Governmental Process: Political Interests and Public Opinion* (New York: Alfred A. Knopf, 1951). Although the interest group theory is a major contribution to our understanding of how the American political system works, it is hardly a total explanation of political phenomena. Moreover, Truman's and particularly Bentley's rigid insistence that judicial decisions are purely and simply a response to the pressure of interest groups does violence to the many complexities of the judicial process. See, for example, Benjamin N. Cardozo, *The Nature of the Judicial Process* (New Haven: Yale University Press, 1960); Paul A. Freund, *The Supreme Court of the United States: Its Business, Purposes and Performance* (Cleveland: World Publishing Co., 1961); Edward H. Levi, *An Introduction to Legal Reasoning* (Chicago: University of Chicago Press, 1949); Murphy, *Elements of Judicial Strategy;* John P. Roche, *Courts & Rights: The American Judiciary in Action* (New York: Random House, 1961).

34. On the activities of the short-lived Liberty League, see Twiss, *Law-*

yers and the Constitution, pp. 241–53; Vose, "Litigation as a Form of Pressure Group Activity," pp. 24–25; George Wolfskill, *The Revolt of the Conservative: A History of the American Liberty League, 1934–1940* (Boston: Houghton Mifflin Co., 1962), especially pp. 70–78. The best accounts of the NAACP in the courts are Jack Greenberg, *Race Relations and American Law* (New York: Columbia University Press, 1959); Alfred H. Kelly, "An Inside View of Brown v. Board," paper delivered to the American Historical Association, December, 1961 (mimeographed copy); Vose, *Caucasians Only.*

35. It would appear, for example, that such major nineteenth-century cases as *McCulloch* v. *Maryland* (1819), the *Granger Railroad Cases* (1877), and the *Income Tax Cases* (1895) were brought to the Supreme Court as a consequence of planned interest group activity. On *McCulloch* see Bray Hammond, *Banks and Politics in America from the Revolution to the Civil War* (Princeton: Princeton University Press, 1957), chap. x; Warren, *Supreme Court,* I, chap. xii. On the *Granger Railroad Cases* see Magrath, *Waite,* pp. 176–77, and my article on *Munn* v. *Illinois,* "The Case of the Unscrupulous Warehouseman," in John A. Garraty (ed.), *Quarrels That Have Shaped the Constitution* (New York: Harper & Row, 1964), chap. viii; in this instance, however, the railroad corporations gravely miscalculated the Court's response. On the *Income Tax Cases* see Gerald G. Eggert, "Richard Olney and the Income Tax Cases," *Mississippi Valley Historical Review,* XLVIII (1961), 25–26; Sidney Ratner, *American Taxation: Its History as a Social Force in Democracy* (New York: W. W. Norton & Co., 1942), chaps. ix and x.

36. In the debates of 1813 and 1814 I have counted at least sixteen separate references to *Fletcher* v. *Peck,* many of them extensive. *Annals of the Congress of the United States,* 12th Cong., January 20, 1813, cols. 857–59 (two speeches); February 15, 1813, cols. 1068–71; 13th Cong., March 8, 1814, cols. 1848, 1849–50, 1851; March 21, cols. 1888–89; March 23, cols. 1895, 1896–97; March 24, cols. 1902, 1903, 1909, 1911; March 25, cols. 1918 (two speeches), 1922.

37. Wallace Mendelson, *Capitalism, Democracy, and the Supreme Court* (New York: Appleton-Century-Crofts, 1960), p. 28.

38. One minor qualification should be added. Precisely because the most controversial Marshall Court decisions applied to specific state and local interests, which tended to be inherently parochial, they found it difficult to mobilize *national* resistance to those decisions. Some of the chapter headings in Charles Warren's history of the Supreme Court suggest the problem: "Pennsylvania and Georgia against the Court," "Virginia against the Court," "Kentucky against the Court." *Supreme Court,* I. A good illustration of this tendency is the Court's decision in *Green* v. *Biddle,* which voided Kentucky's occupying claimants laws. Henry Clay was embittered by the "selfishness" of Virginia in failing to join her sister state in an attack on the Court. Only a few years earlier Virginia had been loud in its

denunciations of judicial usurpations because then the decisions had gone against her interests. But *Green* v. *Biddle* was different; it favored Virginians with land claims in Kentucky. "Not a Virginia voice," Clay lamented, "is heard against this decision." *Ibid.*, p. 642. In this case, however, Kentucky successfully ignored the decision, which was endorsed by only three of the seven justices, and the Court later upheld the occupying claimants laws. Gates, "Tenants of the Log Cabin," pp. 24–26.

39. The data, as well as the interpretations, in this paragraph are taken from Wright, *Contract Clause,* pp. 60–61, 86–88.

40. John P. Roche, *The Quest for the Dream: The Development of Civil Rights and Human Relations in Modern America* (New York: Macmillan Co., 1963), gives a provocative description and interpretation of these developments.

41. Anyone who doubts this assertion should read the decisions of the Warren Court beginning in volume 346 (1953) of the United States Supreme Court Reports.

42. Since they had to wait nearly twenty years for compensation and had lobbying and legal expenses, the New England Yazooists probably made no profit on their investment. Only a guess is possible, but it seems most likely that they did no worse than break even.

APPENDIX A

1. The sketch is reprinted here with the permission of the Georgia Historical Society; except for the omission of two footnotes, it follows the version published by Lilla M. Hawes (ed.), "Miscellaneous Papers of James Jackson, 1781–1798," *Georgia Historical Quarterly,* XXXVII (1953), 152–56.

2. I am unable to decipher the meaning of this reference.

3. This assertion by Jackson is the only evidence that he publicly attacked the Yazoo sale prior to May, 1795. Since Senate debates were not reported in those early days, there is no way of checking whether or not Jackson openly clashed with Gunn. The record of proceedings in the Senate for February and March, 1795, does not indicate any conflict between Jackson and Gunn over the Georgia sale act. On February 27 Jackson laid the act before the Senate and moved that it pass a resolution endorsing a treaty between the United States and the Creek Nation which would extinguish the Indian claims to the Yazoo tract. On March 3 he successfully objected to the third reading of a bill (unanimous consent was required in this particular circumstance) authorizing the President to purchase the western lands claimed by or under the state of Georgia. If anything, Jackson's maneuver that day must have been pleasing to the Yazooists; the state had not yet repudiated its sale, and the land purchasers had nothing to gain by having the land come under federal control. *Annals of the Congress of the United States,* 3rd Cong., February–March, 1795, cols. 818–54.

APPENDIX B

1. Reprinted from *American State Papers, Public Lands* (8 vols.; Washington: Gales and Seaton, 1832–61), I, 156–58.

APPENDIX C

1. There is an excellent sketch of Harper's political career and creed in David Hackett Fischer, *The Revolution of American Conservatism: The Federalist Party in the Era of Jeffersonian Democracy* (New York: Harper & Row, 1965), especially pp. 36–38.

2. Harper's *The Case of the Georgia Sales on the Mississippi Considered* was first published in 1796. It was republished under the title, *The Yazoo Question,* in *The American Law Journal,* V (1814), 354–457, from which it is reprinted here. The following notes to this appendix are Harper's own unless otherwise indicated.

3. It is satisfactory to find this opinion corroborated by that of a very eminent lawyer in New-York who was sometime ago consulted on this point—See Col. Hamilton's opinion. *Ed.:* See Appendix D.

4. See affidavits of Flourney & Clayton. *Ed.:* The affidavits are published in *American State Papers, Public Lands* (8 vols.; Washington: Gales and Seaton, 1832–61), I, 144–49.

5: Affidavits of James Tyrol and Russel Jones.

6. Do. and Philip Clayton and John Thomas.

7. See affidavits throughout.

8. See affidavits of Van Allen, Rains and Lucas.

9. Do. of James M. Neil.

10. A leading member of the Senate, who was the governor's son-in-law, and lived in his house, was one of the most strenuous in opposition.

11. *Ed.:* Harper's assertion was incorrect. The repeal act, although not *guaranteeing* purchasers a refund, provided that refunds should be made if funds were available in the state treasury. Some of the individual shareholders sought and received refunds.

APPENDIX D

1. First published in 1796 as an appendix to Harper's *The Case of the Georgia Sales on the Mississippi Considered,* it was republished in the same year along with the pamphlet, in *The American Law Journal,* V, 454–56, from which it is reprinted here.

2. The year given here is incorrect. The repeal act was passed in 1796, and Harper's pamphlet and Hamilton's opinion were published later that year.

APPENDIX E

1. The sketch in this and the next paragraph is based on the brief bio-

graphy of Abraham Bishop in the *Dictionary of American Biography* (22 vols.; New York: Charles Scribner's Sons, 1928–58), II, 294–95.

2. Abraham Bishop, *Georgia Speculation Unveiled* (Hartford, 1797), reprinted from a copy in the John Carter Brown Library, Brown University, through the courtesy of the Library.

3. In the case of *Derby* v. *Blake* (1799), discussed in chap. iv, the Supreme Judicial Court of Massachusetts ruled that promissory notes given to sellers of Yazoo lands were legally enforceable.

4. *Bishop and Bishop* v. *Nightingale and Miller; Miller and Nightingale* v. *Bishop and Bishop,* United States Circuit Court for Connecticut. Apparently, in 1805 Abraham Bishop and John Nightingale (by then John Bishop and Phinehas Miller were dead) compromised their claims against each other, but the surviving legal papers are not precisely clear. The records of these, as well as of other Connecticut Yazoo cases, are contained in the Records of the Circuit Court of the United States of America for the District of Connecticut, Orders and Decrees in Chancery, 1790–1812, and in the Docket Books for the Circuit Court, 1797–1805. They are stored in the Federal Record Center of the General Services Administration, Boston.

5. *American State Papers, Finance* (5 vols.; Washington: Gales and Seaton, 1832–34), III, 282.

6. *Dictionary of American Biography,* II, 295.

APPENDIX F

1. Randolph's speech is reprinted from the *Annals of the Congress of the United States,* 8th Cong., January 29, 1805, cols. 1102–8; Lyon's reply is from the *Annals,* February 1, 1805, cols. 1121–26.

2. Much of this paragraph is drawn from the portrait of Lyon in the *Dictionary of American Biography* (22 vols.; New York: Charles Scribner's Sons, 1928–58), XI, 532–34.

3. Page Smith, *John Adams, 1735–1826* (2 vols.; New York: Doubleday and Co., 1962), II, 950.

4. James Gunn.

5. Joseph B. Varnum, of Massachusetts.

6. Postmaster General Gideon Granger.

APPENDIX G

1. The majority and concurring decisions are reprinted from the sixth volume of Cranch's Supreme Court reports, 6 Cranch 87, 128–48 (1810).

INDEX

Numbers in parentheses refer to the Notes

INDEX

INDEX

INDEX

INDEX